THE NEW WORLD
ORDER
OPPOSING VIEWPOINTS®

Other Books of Related Interest in the Opposing
Viewpoints Series:

American Foreign Policy
American Government
American Values
America's Future
Central America
China
Eastern Europe
Economics in America
Global Resources
Immigration
Israel
Japan
Latin America and U.S. Foreign Policy
The Middle East
Nuclear War
The Soviet Union
The Superpowers: A New Detente
‎rorism
‎Third World

‎Human Nature

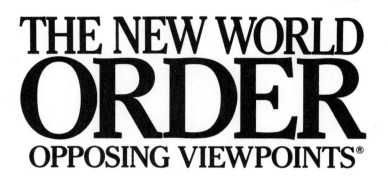

THE NEW WORLD ORDER

OPPOSING VIEWPOINTS®

David L. Bender & Bruno Leone, *Series Editors*

Matthew Polesetsky, *Book Editor*
William Dudley, *Assistant Editor*

OPPOSING VIEWPOINTS SERIES ®

Greenhaven Press, Inc.   PO Box 289009   San Diego, CA 92198-0009

Library of Congress Cataloging-in-Publication Data

The New world order : opposing viewpoints / Matthew Polesetsky, book editor; William Dudley, assistant editor.
     p.   cm. — (Opposing viewpoints series)
Includes bibliographical references and index.
Summary: Debates topics relating to today's changing world order such as the role of the U.S. in the world, the role of economics, military power, government forms which will predominate, and the roles of the UN and NATO.
   ISBN 0-89908-158-4 (pbk.) — ISBN 0-89908-183-5 (lib. bd.)
   1. World politics—1985-1995. 2. United States—Foreign relations—1989- [1. World politics. 2. United States—Foreign relations—1989-] I. Polesetsky, Matthew, 1968-   .
II. Dudley, William, 1964-   . III. Series: Opposing viewpoints series (Unnumbered)
D849.N522 1991
327'.09'049—dc20   91-12374

"Congress shall make no law . . .
abridging the freedom of speech,
or of the press."

First Amendment to the U.S. Constitution

The basic foundation of our democracy is the first amendment
guarantee of freedom of expression. The Opposing Viewpoints
Series is dedicated to the concept of this basic freedom and the
idea that it is more important to practice it than to enshrine it.

Contents

                                            Page

Why Consider Opposing Viewpoints?   9

Introduction   12

Chapter 1: What Will the New World Order Be?

Chapter Preface   16

1. The U.S. Will Remain the Leading World Power   17
   Alfred Balk

2. The U.S. Will Not Be a Leading World Power   24
   Jacques Attali

3. Japan Will Be a Leading World Power   32
   Shintaro Ishihara

4. Japan's Power Will Be Limited   38
   Karl Zinsmeister

5. Europe Will Be a Leading World Power   46
   Séamus O'Cléireacáin

6. Europe May Not Be a Leading World Power   53
   William Drozdiak

A Critical Thinking Activity: 59
   Evaluating Sources of Information

Periodical Bibliography   61

Chapter 2: What Role Will the U.S. Play in the New World Order?

Chapter Preface   63

1. The U.S. Should Maintain Its Role in World Affairs   64
   Josef Joffe

2. The U.S. Should Reduce Its Role in World Affairs   71
   Patrick J. Buchanan

3. The U.S. Should Maintain an International   79
   Military Role
   William R. Hawkins

4. The U.S. Should Reduce Its Military Role   86
   Ted Galen Carpenter

5. The U.S. Will Remain an Economic Leader   92
   Joel Kotkin

6. U.S. Economic Leadership Is Threatened   98
   Abu K. Selimuddin

A Critical Thinking Activity: 106
   Ranking Priorities for a New World Order

Periodical Bibliography   108

Chapter 3: What Role Will Economics Play in the New World Order?

Chapter Preface 110

1. Economic Competition Will Replace Military Conflict 111
   Edward N. Luttwak

2. Economic Competition Will Not Replace Military Conflict 118
   Eliot A. Cohen

3. The World Economy Will Benefit Many Nations 125
   Edward Yardeni & David Moss

4. Only the Wealthy Will Benefit from the World Economy 131
   Ronald Kwan

5. The Economies of the World Are Unified 138
   Kenichi Ohmae

6. The Economies of the World Will Dissolve into Trading Blocs 143
   Walter Russell Mead

A Critical Thinking Activity: Distinguishing Between Fact and Opinion 148

Periodical Bibliography 150

Chapter 4: How Will the End of the Cold War Affect the World?

Chapter Preface 152

1. The End of the Cold War Will Bring a New Era of Democracy 153
   Joshua Muravchik

2. A New Era of Democracy Is Uncertain 161
   Doyle McManus & Robin Wright

3. The End of the Cold War Will Lessen Worldwide Conflict 169
   Bruce Russett

4. The End of the Cold War Will Not Lessen Worldwide Conflict 177
   John J. Mearsheimer

5. The End of the Cold War Will Harm the Third World 185
   Vanessa Baird

6. The End of the Cold War Will Not Harm the Third World 192
   Richard E. Bissell

A Critical Thinking Activity: 200
    Recognizing Statements That Are Provable
Periodical Bibliography   202

Chapter 5: What Role Will International
              Organizations Play in the New
              World Order?
Chapter Preface   204
1. The United Nations Can Solve International   205
   Problems
    Richard S. Williamson
2. The United Nations Cannot Solve International   212
   Problems
    Michael Lind
3. The United Nations Can Prevent War   218
    Robert C. Johansen
4. The United Nations Cannot Prevent War   225
    Mark A. Franz
5. NATO Is Obsolete   232
    Doug Bandow & Ted Galen Carpenter
6. NATO Is Not Obsolete   239
    William E. Odom
A Critical Thinking Activity: 246
    Understanding Words in Context
Periodical Bibliography   248

Organizations to Contact   249
Bibliography of Books   255
Index   258

Why Consider Opposing Viewpoints?

"It is better to debate a question without settling it than to settle a question without debating it."

Joseph Joubert (1754-1824)

The Importance of Examining Opposing Viewpoints

The purpose of the Opposing Viewpoints Series, and this book in particular, is to present balanced, and often difficult to find, opposing points of view on complex and sensitive issues.

Probably the best way to become informed is to analyze the positions of those who are regarded as experts and well studied on issues. It is important to consider every variety of opinion in an attempt to determine the truth. Opinions from the mainstream of society should be examined. But also important are opinions that are considered radical, reactionary, or minority as well as those stigmatized by some other uncomplimentary label. An important lesson of history is the eventual acceptance of many unpopular and even despised opinions. The ideas of Socrates, Jesus, and Galileo are good examples of this.

Readers will approach this book with their own opinions on the issues debated within it. However, to have a good grasp of one's own viewpoint, it is necessary to understand the arguments of those with whom one disagrees. It can be said that those who do not completely understand their adversary's point of view do not fully understand their own.

A persuasive case for considering opposing viewpoints has been presented by John Stuart Mill in his work *On Liberty*. When examining controversial issues it may be helpful to reflect on this suggestion:

The only way in which a human being can make some approach to knowing the whole of a subject, is by hearing what can be said about it by persons of every variety of opinion, and studying all modes in which it can be looked at by every character of mind. No wise man ever acquired his wisdom in any mode but this.

Analyzing Sources of Information

The Opposing Viewpoints Series includes diverse materials taken from magazines, journals, books, and newspapers, as well as statements and position papers from a wide range of individuals, organizations, and governments. This broad spectrum of sources helps to develop patterns of thinking which are open to the consideration of a variety of opinions.

Pitfalls to Avoid

A pitfall to avoid in considering opposing points of view is that of regarding one's own opinion as being common sense and the most rational stance, and the point of view of others as being only opinion and naturally wrong. It may be that another's opinion is correct and one's own is in error.

Another pitfall to avoid is that of closing one's mind to the opinions of those with whom one disagrees. The best way to approach a dialogue is to make one's primary purpose that of understanding the mind and arguments of the other person and not that of enlightening him or her with one's own solutions. More can be learned by listening than speaking.

It is my hope that after reading this book the reader will have a deeper understanding of the issues debated and will appreciate the complexity of even seemingly simple issues on which good and honest people disagree. This awareness is particularly important in a democratic society such as ours where people enter into public debate to determine the common good. Those with whom one disagrees should not necessarily be regarded as enemies, but perhaps simply as people who suggest different paths to a common goal.

Developing Basic Reading and Thinking Skills

In this book, carefully edited opposing viewpoints are purposely placed back to back to create a running debate; each viewpoint is preceded by a short quotation that best expresses the author's main argument. This format instantly plunges the reader into the midst of a controversial issue and greatly aids that reader in mastering the basic skill of recognizing an author's point of view.

A number of basic skills for critical thinking are practiced in the activities that appear throughout the books in the series. Some of the skills are:

Evaluating Sources of Information. The ability to choose from among alternative sources the most reliable and accurate source in relation to a given subject.

Separating Fact from Opinion. The ability to make the basic distinction between factual statements (those that can be demonstrated or verified empirically) and statements of opinion (those that are beliefs or attitudes that cannot be proved).

Identifying Stereotypes. The ability to identify oversimplified, exaggerated descriptions (favorable or unfavorable) about people and insulting statements about racial, religious, or national groups, based upon misinformation or lack of information.

Recognizing Ethnocentrism. The ability to recognize attitudes or opinions that express the view that one's own race, culture, or group is inherently superior, or those attitudes that judge another culture or group in terms of one's own.

It is important to consider opposing viewpoints and equally important to be able to critically analyze those viewpoints. The activities in this book are designed to help the reader master these thinking skills. Statements are taken from the book's viewpoints and the reader is asked to analyze them. This technique aids the reader in developing skills that not only can be applied to the viewpoints in this book, but also to situations where opinionated spokespersons comment on controversial issues. Although the activities are helpful to the solitary reader, they are most useful when the reader can benefit from the interaction of group discussion.

Using this book and others in the series should help readers develop basic reading and thinking skills. These skills should improve the reader's ability to understand what is read. Readers should be better able to separate fact from opinion, substance from rhetoric, and become better consumers of information in our media-centered culture.

This volume of the Opposing Viewpoints Series does not advocate a particular point of view. Quite the contrary! The very nature of the book leaves it to the reader to formulate the opinions he or she finds most suitable. My purpose as publisher is to see that this is made possible by offering a wide range of viewpoints that are fairly presented.

David L. Bender
Publisher

Introduction

"I believe that our Great Maker is preparing the world, in His own good time, to become one nation, speaking one language."

—Grover Cleveland, president of the
United States, March 4, 1893.

"Anybody who feels at ease in the world today is a fool."

Robert Maynard Hutchins, American educator,
January 21, 1959.

The dramatic events of the last decade, especially changes in the Soviet Union, have left the world in a state of flux. Almost overnight the Soviet Union went from crushing independence movements, sustaining a policy of complete internal secrecy, and holding up an aggressive opposition to the United States, to vocalizing a new era of openness. This in turn left the United States to marvel at what seemed to be the end of the Cold War. It no longer made sense to cry out against the "evil empire." Yet surprisingly, the United States seems not to know whether to rejoice in what seems to be a clear victory in the ideological war with the Soviet Union, or to feel a strange confusion and lack of importance as other countries now seem to compete with the United States for world recognition. This confusion and the idea that the Cold War may no longer dominate world affairs has led many experts, including President George Bush, to declare that a new world order is emerging.

But what is this new world order, and is it appropriate to welcome it? These questions dominate international news journals, press conferences, and, especially, the U.S. State Department. For all of the terrifying moments it created—the Cuban Missile Crisis, the Korean War, and the Berlin Wall to name a few—the Cold War defined an order to things. For the U.S. and the U.S.S.R., foreign policy was determined by their competition with one another. Other nations, too, defined themselves in relation to the policies of the U.S. and the U.S.S.R. It is easy to forget that prior to the Cold War, the world was not a more peaceful place.

Western Europe had long been in an almost perpetual state of war. In the 1870s, France and Germany fought the Franco-Prussian War. Bitter feelings over land concessions during this war would directly involve both countries in World War I. At the end of World War I, Germany's bitterness over concessions in the Treaty of Versailles would lead to World War II. Asia too, was fraught with tension. Japan and China, traditional enemies, were locked in battles as Japan continually attempted to gain territory and power from its enormous neighbor. Japan's success in these land wars would give it the confidence it needed to attack the U.S. at Pearl Harbor. After World War II, even though battles continued to rage in small countries around the world, the Cold War seemed to have ended worldwide conflict between major powers.

Does the end of the Cold War signal a return to more troubling battles? Instead of land, will nations use international trade to dominate world markets and hence the world? Many experts argue that they will. According to John J. Mearsheimer, a professor of political science at the University of Chicago, "We may . . . wake up one day lamenting the loss of the order that the Cold War gave to the anarchy of international relations." Without the unifying threat of the Soviet Union, Mearsheimer argues, the nations of Western Europe will resume patterns of conflict. In addition, some experts believe that worldwide trade wars are destined to become more prominent. In the opinion of economic analyst Doug Henwood, "economic rivalry . . . only seems likely to intensify in the 1990s." This rivalry, Henwood warns, may lead to a renewed era of political, and eventually, military conflict.

In addition, many political experts worry that the United States will not fare well if world conflict centers on economic strength. In a recent cover story, *Business Week* editors shouted, "Wake up America! . . . We have spent too much, borrowed too much, and imported too much. We have lived beyond our means, relying on foreigners to finance our massive budget and trade deficits. The bill is now coming due." Just as the Soviet Union's economy has crumbled from the effects of funneling too much of its money and resources into maintaining a massive military complex to fight the Cold War, experts believe the U.S. will suffer a similar fate. In the new world order, the United States may fall from first place to a place somewhere behind Japan and a unified Germany.

Other experts remain unconvinced that a new world order is even in the offing. These people believe the United States will keep its position of prominence in both world affairs and the international economy. Susan Strange, a professor of international relations at the European University in Italy, claims that what the U.S. lacks in economic strength it makes up for in military

13

strength. No other nation can boast strengths in both of these areas, she concludes. "The U.S. lead in the ability to make and deliver the means of nuclear destruction is the complement to its lead in influencing, through past investments overseas, the nature, modes and purposes of modern industrial production," she states.

These experts who believe the new world order will look much like the old (except for a less prominent Soviet Union) cite as an example the events in the Iraq war. The United States, in cooperation with the United Nations, played a lead role in eliminating Saddam Hussein's threat to Kuwait's sovereignty. In spite of critics who predicted nothing short of a nuclear holocaust in Israel and surrounding Arab nations, the war proceeded rather uneventfully. This is proof, United States leaders assert, that the U.S. remains not only willing, but entirely able to keep its world leadership role. Its combined military and economic strength will allow the U.S. to negotiate and stabilize other future world conflicts that might arise.

Whether the new world order will bring about major changes in international relations remains an unresolved issue. The viewpoints in *A New World Order: Opposing Viewpoints* reflect the discussion on how this question will be answered. The following issues are debated: What Will the New World Order Be? What Role Will the U.S. Play in the New World Order? What Role Will Economics Play in the New World Order? How Will the End of the Cold War Affect the World? What Role Will International Organizations Play in the New World Order? With two world wars and many other conflicts dominating humanity's memory of the twentieth century, it is unclear whether the world will be able to transcend this legacy in the twenty-first.

What Will the New World Order Be?

THE NEW WORLD
ORDER

Chapter Preface

With the exception of the United States, World War II devastated the economies of the industrialized nations. The U.S. emerged from the war with its factories, residences, and infrastructure intact. For the next twenty-five years, as other countries rebuilt, the U.S. dominated the world economy. For example, in 1950 the United States produced about one-third of the world's goods and services. At the same time the U.S. stationed its troops across the globe and was the undisputed leader of the countries allied against the Soviet Union.

By the 1970s, however, some politicians and experts began to question how long American supremacy would last. These critics saw the failure of American policy in Vietnam as a signal of America's declining ability to control world affairs. Critics also believed the growing competitiveness of Japanese products on the world market was a threat to American economic domination. By the beginning of the 1990s, according to Jacques Attali, a leading European policymaker, the United States had fallen behind Japan "from the most basic activity of economic life to the most advanced." Attali predicts that Europe, targeted for economic integration at the end of 1992, and Japan will contend for leadership of the world economy in the post-Cold War era.

Many experts, however, vehemently disagree with the notion of American decline. Alfred Balk, author of *The Myth of American Eclipse*, argues that the immense power enjoyed by the United States in the years immediately following World War II decreased naturally as the rest of the world recovered from the war. Moreover, Susan Strange, a professor at the London School of Economics, argues that neither Japan nor Europe can match America's military and economic power.

Which nations will be the leading powers in the new world order? The authors of the following viewpoints debate this question.

"Neither Europe nor Japan can equal the Americans' performance."

The U.S. Will Remain the Leading World Power

Alfred Balk

In his influential 1987 book *The Rise and Fall of the Great Powers*, Yale historian Paul Kennedy argued that the United States was declining in power. This book began a heated debate over whether the U.S. is falling behind economic powers such as Japan and Germany. In the following viewpoint, Alfred Balk refutes the notion of America's decline and contends that the United States will remain the world's leading power. According to Balk, the United States' combined economic, military, cultural, and technological strengths remain unmatched by any other nation. The author is an editor of *Saturday Review* magazine.

As you read, consider the following questions:

1. What period does the author refer to as "Camelot"? Why does he call it this?
2. According to the author, what share of world production has the United States contributed since the 1970s?
3. What weakness must the Japanese surmount to become a superpower, in Balk's opinion?

Published by permission of Transaction Publishers, from *The Myth of American Eclipse* by Alfred Balk. Copyright © 1990 by Transaction Publishers.

Americans are seen abroad as an insecure lot. We affect a posture of confidence, even bravado. The boastful booster, usually a Texan, is part of our image. Yet to the bemusement and occasional despair of less privileged peoples, we seem constantly to feel threatened.

So it has been for most of the past two decades. The Russians were coming, the Russians were coming. Then the OPEC [Organization of Petroleum Exporting Countries] oil sheiks. Now the Japanese, the 1992 European "single market," you name it. We seem persuaded that internationally we are in decline, if not eclipse—that "the American Century" is over and our future lies behind us. . . .

Historically the great powers all have had their autumns. Take the sobering examples of Great Britain, France, Spain, and other once-imperial hegemonists chronicled by Paul Kennedy in *The Rise and Fall of the Great Powers*. Or, from still earlier eras, Rome, Venice, the Ottomans, Austro-Hungary, and the like. Look at them. How all-powerful and intimidating they once were, and for so long. How humbled they now are. Why not us, too?. . .

Framing the Issue

Consider several realities of history. By its slow-drip timetable, conclusive evidence of decline must be cumulative over decades. Can we say it is in our case? Over how many decades is there conclusive evidence? This is our first caveat.

Then there is the term "decline" itself. It is comparative. The first question it invites is, "Decline compared to what?" Therein lies the next caveat.

Declinists customarily point to a grandiose baseline for power comparisons: not our international status over the past century, or even fifty years, but the early postwar years. It was then that we seemed unsurpassed as a superpower and our ears rang with Henry Luce's proclamation of "the American century." But can that be a definitive comparison? Logic suggests that this deceives.

The immediate postwar period was an atypical blip in history. World War II was the largest, most destructive conflagration ever. It laid waste all the other leading industrial nations. Thus at its end, by serendipity we towered over the world like a colossus.

As the "arsenal of democracy," using depression-idled capacity and a work force augmented by women and blacks, we nearly tripled our gross national product (GNP) in six years. When peace descended, we possessed more than half the shattered world's industrial capacity. Among the great powers, says historian Kennedy, we were the only one that "became richer—in fact, much richer—rather than poorer because of the war."

That snapshot in history is not a rational baseline for long-term comparisons. It might be if one logically could presume that a war-shattered world and colonialism, with its enforced underdevelopment, might have been perpetuated. They could not have been. Nor did we intend them to be. Our enduring pride was postwar statesmanship, unlike Europe's after World War I, that promoted global stability, freedom, and prosperity.

We were marvelously rewarded. Both we and the world attained prosperity on a scale never before seen: In 1953-73 global manufacturing output tripled. In 1960-80 gross world-product growth averaged double the historical norm—some 5 per cent annually. Our own growth set records, doubling our median family income in a quarter-century.

Farewell to Camelot

This was unprecedented—an economic Camelot. Yet like its namesake, destined to be a brief "shining moment" historically atypical and probably unique. It was the "flip" side of the devastation and suffering of World War II.

But that has become part of history's attic. The war ended nearly a half-century ago. . . . How long can we remain in the thrall of this Camelot?

First Among Equals

The United States in 1946 was richer and more powerful in relation to its allies and enemies than any nation in modern history, far more powerful than Britain had ever been. It is impossible to imagine the persistence of such an unequal distribution of wealth and power.

Over four decades later we are seeing the results of an evolution to a more natural, and, viewed globally, a more stable distribution of economic and military power. Of course the United States has become less powerful in relation to its allies and enemies. But its absolute power, based on an adaptable, evolutionary market economy spread over a uniquely large and strategically protected continent, is great enough to maintain its status as first among equals.

John H. Makin, *Sharing World Leadership?*, 1989.

The same caveat applies to U.S. geopolitical power. It, too, constituted a war-related Camelot, bestowing as "artificially high" a status—in Kennedy's term—as Great Britain's after the Napoleonic wars.

We do not, however, think of it as "artificial." Rather it has been transmogrified into our norm. If we recognize and accept it as atypical and by no defensible logic attainable for the long term, then descending from this "artificial high" need not bespeak decline. It could mean a return to long-term trends.

Such trends do not place us in eclipse. Again, look at history. Before World War II there were five great powers: Great Britain, France, Germany, Japan, and the United States, with the Soviet Union and China at the margins. Now there are two superpowers. Of the two, we are indisputably the leader. Other prewar powers march in second or third ranks. This is decline?

Leading the World Economy

We occupy the pinnacle of world leadership. Consider our economic power: We are the Mount Everest of nations, at a rarefied altitude shared by none, and still thrusting upward. Our wealth (GNP) is some twenty times its total at war's end—about $5 trillion, compared to $220 billion (in constant dollars).

This makes us the world's richest nation, with wealth (GNP) comparable to that of all of Western Europe, and double that of Japan or the Soviet Union. For a century, including the 1980s, our growth has forged steadily upward with only minor deviations. That is decline?

Beyond our borders our record is envied. In the "real world"— the planet of the possible, reflecting cyclical changes and the constraints of the human condition—we merit this envy.

The respected *Financial Times* of London points out: . . .

• We maintain a stunning job-creation record: "Unemployment [is] below 7 per cent, compared with 11 per cent in the European Community. . . ."

• We lead in research: "The U.S. . . . spends far more on research and development than any other Western country—almost $120 billion in 1986 . . . and has an unrivaled record of imaginative breakthroughs at the frontiers of science. . . ."

• We excel in high-technology competitiveness: "U.S. companies account for two-thirds of the world's commercial aircraft; . . . half of all computer sales; and in semiconductors are still the world leader."

A Return to Normalcy

Our economic bloodstream frequently is portrayed as anemic. But Samuel P. Huntington, director of the Center for International Affairs at Harvard, provides this evidence to the contrary:

• We have maintained a consistent global market share: The U.S. ratio of gross world product has remained at 20 to 25 per cent since the late 1960s, and "certainly has not declined more rapidly in the past two decades than it did during the previous two decades." In 1970-87 our share varied between 22 and 25 per cent.

• Our share of developed-world exports is little-changed: Our ratio of exports among the seven "economic summit" countries was about the same in 1987 as in 1970—23 versus 24 per cent.

• Our high-technology export share has remained consistent: Our ratio of world exports of technology-intensive products has varied only about two percentage points between 1965 and 1984—27.5 versus 25.2.

• We have accelerated economic growth, not declined: During the 1980s, our economic performance "improved markedly" compared to that of other leading nations: from number fifteen in economic growth among nineteen industrialized market economies in 1965-80 to number three in 1980-86.

• In the 1980s we surpassed Japan in the rate of economic growth: In 1980-86 our growth spurted to 110.7 per cent of 1965-80, while Japan's fell to 58.7. In 1983-87 we grew at about the same rate as Japan, and in three of those five years we led it.

"The argument can be made," he concludes, "that the GNP pattern that has emerged in the past two decades is in some sense a historically normal pattern, roughly approximating the distribution that existed before World War II."

A New Challenge

The United States at the end of the century retains more traditional resources of power than any other country has. It also has the ideological and institutional resources to retain its leadership in the new domains of transnational interdependence. . . . The problem for American power today is not new challengers for hegemony; it is the new challenge of transnational interdependence.

Joseph S. Nye Jr., *The Atlantic*, March 1990.

For the foreseeable future, aside from accelerated growth in some developing nations, this comparative pattern is forecast as unlikely to change. One Pentagon study, for example, put our share of fifteen major countries' gross national product at 31.6 per cent in 1980 and projects it for 2010 at 29.2 per cent—twice the projected GNPs of China, Japan, or the Soviet Union.

This is our trumpeted-from-the-ramparts decline?

Relational and Structural Power

Judged against the imperial nations discussed in Kennedy's *The Rise and Fall of the Great Powers*, of course we have declined. We do not possess the relative—or, as Professor Susan Strange of the London School of Economics and Political Science calls it, "relational" hegemonic power of the giants of history. That is, "the power of A to get B to do something it would not otherwise do."

We did possess that power in Camelot. But except with tiny nations in our own sphere of influence, did we ever consistently at any other time? Now times have changed for everyone. . . .

In this new, postimperial era we must calibrate our position by a different measure: what Professor Strange calls "structural power." That is, "the power to choose and to shape the structures of the global political economy within which other states, their political institutions, their economic enterprises, and (not least) their professional people have to operate."

Such structural power, she postulates, consists of four interrelated frameworks "like the four sides of a pyramid." Each is supported by the other three. The four are the ability to exercise control over the following: others' security from violence; the system of production; the structure of finance and credit, through which purchasing power is obtained "without having either to work or to trade for it"; and the acquisition, communication, and storage of knowledge and information.

By these criteria, she says, there is little question about our combined structural power. "Neither Europe nor Japan can equal the Americans' performance across all four structures. Since each of them interacts with the other three, and the Europeans and Japanese are so far behind militarily, it seems likely that America will enjoy the power to act as a hegemon for some time to come."

A Solid Tripod

In a variation, Huntington sees America's influence as resting on a tripod unmatched by any other nation:

1) "Peculiarly multidimensional" strength. Our chief global rival, the Soviet Union, is "a one-dimensional superpower," with influence based almost entirely on military might. Our main economic challenger, Japan, derives its power from manufacturing performance and control of financial resources. In contrast we rank "extraordinarily high" not only in these realms but in almost all other major sources of power. Thus reverses in one area are compensated by strengths in others—an advantage that no nation can challenge for the foreseeable future.

2) Influence based on our "structural position" in world politics. This position stems from five advantages, all of which he sees as creating "a demand for the American presence overseas" that draws us naturally to leadership. These are: our geographical distance from "most major areas of world conflict," a history "relatively free of overseas imperialism," an anti-statist philosophy that is "less likely to be threatening to other peoples," a "diversified network of alliances," and "identification with universal international institutions." Again, no other nation approaches us in these attributes.

3) No likely alternative hegemonic power in the next century. In the media and in back-fence conversation, Japan frequently is mentioned as a candidate to succeed us. On close examina-

tion that won't wash. Huntington summarizes why. Japan, he notes, "has neither the size, natural resources, military strength, diplomatic affiliates, nor, most important, the ideological appeal to be a twentieth-century superpower."

Only One Truly Great Power

Japan is seen abroad as the quintessential "me" nation, standing clearly and unabashedly for its own self-interest. Yet "an idea with appeal beyond its borders" is a prerequisite to superpower status. In recent years, only the United States and Soviet Union have possessed this. The Soviets' message now is defunct.

Helmut Schmidt, former chancellor of West Germany, puts it this way. In weight of raw power, he says, there are three capitals: Washington, Moscow, and Beijing. In the economic realm there are three: the United States, Western Europe, and Japan. Only the United States qualifies in both categories.

"The signs of America's relative decline are converging and unquestionable."

The U.S. Will Not Be a Leading World Power

Jacques Attali

Jacques Attali is a top aide to French president Francois Mitterand and a likely candidate to head the European Bank for Reconstruction and Development, the institution being created to help modernize Eastern Europe. In the following viewpoint, Attali argues that the United States is unable to compete in the new global economy. America's decline, the author contends, stems from a short-sighted outlook that leads to overconsumption and a lack of planning. Attali believes that America has already fallen behind Japan and that it cannot be long before this shift in power is widely recognized.

As you read, consider the following questions:

1. Which two powers does Attali believe will be the leading rivals for predominance in the new world order?
2. What kind of products will dominate the world consumer market, according to Attali?
3. In the author's opinion, why will Japan be the central power in the Pacific Rim region?

An abridged version of "Lines on the Horizon: A New Order in the Making," by Jacques Attali, *New Perspectives Quarterly*, Spring 1990. Reprinted with permission.

Like Luther and Muhammed before him, Mikhail Gorbachev is bending history. And he is doing it at such a speed that it is impossible to know the results. The world, it seems, will change more in the next 10 years than in any other period of history. What was beyond the grasp of imagination yesterday is already happening today.

Even so, the lines on the horizon are clear enough to compose a rough sketch of our world as we prepare to enter the next century.

The Order of Money

In the emergent order taking root on the eve of the millennium, the two military superpowers, the US and USSR, are slouching toward relative, if not absolute, decline. The Order of Force has been supplanted by the Order of Money, that is, the reign of the market. In place of two ideologically antagonistic blocs, the whole globe is becoming an ideologically homogeneous market where life will be organized around common consumer desires.

With ideological homogeneity, geography will re-exert its power over history. Having overcome their strategic subordination to the rule of military force, the two new powers, a unifying Europe and a Japan tied to the Pacific region, are entering an infinitely more dangerous economic rivalry for the core hegemonic position in the new order. The core region will be determined by who dominates production of the new goods that will satisfy the desires of the ubiquitous consumer in the first globe-spanning marketplace.

What kind of consumer desires, and what kind of consumer products will drive the new Order of Money? Throughout the history of capitalism, the answer to these questions has held the secret to the enormous creation and accumulation of wealth, and indicated the new forms of value that define power.

Serving the Individual

At the end of the 20th century, the unprecedented degree of prosperity, democracy and mass literacy in the privileged regions of the world have empowered the individual as never before. The empowered individual, always hungry for more freedom, will seek ever greater personal autonomy.

It is this cultural aspiration, which the triumphant market translates into consumer desire, that will drive economic dynamism in the future. New consumer products, like the car or the washing machine before them, will be developed to satisfy the rising demands, primarily in services, of hyper-individualism.

The economic order organized around supplying this demand, however, will not be postindustrial, where services replace industry, but hyper-industrial, where services are transformed into mass-produced consumer goods. Microchip-based technologies, such as the transistor and the computer, have opened the way for this industrialization of services.

The most vital economic growth is now taking place in areas where new products based on the microchip are replacing the costly, debt-incurring, time and labor-intensive delivery of services: communication, management, information processing, food preparation, health (which in the US has grown from eight percent to 11 percent of GNP [gross national product] in only the last decade) and education.

Nomadic Objects

The cellular telephone, the fax machine, the ready-teller machines at banks, the portable computer, the portable compact-disc player, answering machines, auto-diagnostic medical devices, VCRs, intelligent controls for cars, robots, the microwave oven for cooking food industrially prepared in advance—all vastly increase the productivity of services.

I call these new goods "nomadic objects." Inevitably, as they fortify our personal autonomy, they will subvert our links to family, culture and nationality; they will enable us both to transcend our own roots and transgress other contexts. As never before, the privileged inhabitants of the two core regions, and most of the rich regions of the periphery, will be transformed into nomads.

Man has always had "nomadic objects"—those instruments of most value to his survival: fire for errant tribes, amulets for the first inhabitants of villages when the Order of the Sacred prevailed, arms for the men of empire, the coin and the check of the market. Power within each social order has been determined by the possession and accumulation of these objects. Tomorrow also, the global hierarchy will be determined by those who possess the new instruments of value and those who don't. . . .

The Pacific Rim

In the Pacific Basin, we are witnessing the formation of an integrated economic core. This immense region—which by my definition excludes China but includes Japan, Korea, Malaysia, Indonesia, Singapore, Taiwan, the Philippines, Hong Kong and the West Coasts of both Americas—is partaking of one extensive economic boom. Population and production are growing strongly; transportation and communication networks are rapidly expanding; internal commerce is growing faster than the rest of the world.

Inside this Pacific region, the internal balance is shifting as overall power increases: the dominant locale of power is about to jump from its East Coast—the US—to its West Coast—Japan.

The signs of America's relative decline are converging and un-questionable. Japanese productivity is increasing at three times the US rate while European productivity increases at twice the US rate. Traditional consumer items once associated with American industrial strength, like television sets or cars, are no longer produced competitively for export. Periodic bouts of de-valuation to compensate for a weakening competitive position change nothing fundamentally.

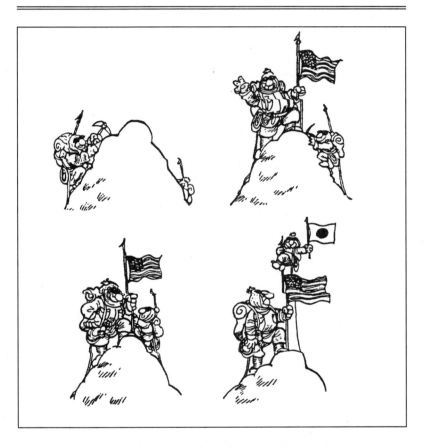

Palomo, © 1991 Cartoonists & Writers Syndicate. Reprinted with permission.

With the exception of two areas in which the US has had a long-standing position of quasi-monopoly—computers and aerospace—the trade deficit in high-technology exports has in-creased sixfold in the last decade.

The growing US commercial deficit accompanies the shrink-age of the American role in the global economy. Over the past

15 years, the US share of global product fell six percent while Japan's rose by 15 percent. For example, America's share of the worldwide machine tool market dropped from 25 percent to five percent in the last 30 years. Japan has increased its share from zero to 22 percent in the same period.

In the US, the state itself hasn't sufficient resources for the maintenance of the once admirable American education system, for health care or for control of the drug trade and other crime. Infrastructure, especially in the Eastern US, verges on the decrepit.

Even though the American savings rate remains persistently weak, US financial markets have still not adjusted. The large institutional investors of Wall Street still primarily channel capital toward large, traditional industry instead of to innovative ventures that are building blocks of the future. Investment continues to flow abroad looking for cheaper production costs rather than seeking cost-saving innovations at home. There is also a loss of the attitude that manufacturing matters and an absence of long-term vision of the global consumer market, neither of which helps the US improve its export position so that it can finance its debt.

The imbalance of trans-Pacific trade cruelly reveals the relative decline of the US, for merchandise moves across the Pacific mainly in one direction. The American trade deficit with Asia will soon comprise two-thirds of its total deficit. Japan alone will be owed $100 billion.

The Cult of the Immediate

Sadly for America, it has already fallen to a secondary position behind Japan—from the most basic activity of economic life to the most advanced. America has become Japan's granary, like Poland was for Flanders in the 17th century. More land in America is devoted to agricultural production destined for Japanese mouths than the entire land surface of Japan. Japanese savings already help pay the salaries of Washington's civil servants through financing the deficit. American universities are largely forming the scientific cadre of its principal economic rival.

While Japanese protectionism aggravates American decline, it is not the primary cause. The cause is slackening competitiveness. Economic history has demonstrated time and again that no protectionism can long endure the competitive production of consumer products.

It is improbable that these trends will be reversed because they are rooted in a fundamental cultural ethos which has come to dominate late 20th-century America: the cult of the immediate. America today seems to be a nostalgic nation, lacking foresight and turned sadly inward out of resentment over its diminishing weight in the world. This, more than any economic dissertation, explains the present American malady.

In the course of relative decline, economic power within the US will shift to the Pacific Southwest, following the gravitational pull of Japanese financial power and geographic proximity. America's famed strengths of immigration, technology, scientific skills, university research capabilities, and cultural openness are concentrated there, especially in California.

Japan, however, possesses the key attribute necessary for it to become the core of the Pacific—control of investment capital that will structure the industries of the future.

At present, the 10 largest banks in the world are Japanese. While the US share of the global value of equities has diminished from 40 percent to 20 percent during the 1980s, the value of Japanese stock assets has risen from 10 percent of the global share to 55 percent. Japan is wisely using its surplus to further establish a hegemonic position in world markets.

Japanese companies define very far in advance the consumer goods for which they believe there is a market, and derive the necessary technologies therefrom. Through a banking system intertwined with industry, the Japanese can offer low-priced products that enable them to conquer markets through undercutting competitors. In the all-important $500 billion world microchip market, for example, Japan produces 50 percent of microprocessors compared to 38 percent by the US (where they were invented) and 10 percent by Europe.

Japanese Culture

Much of Japan's success, like America's demise, finds its explanation in cultural factors. The scarcity of inhabitable land on an insular island has favored the mentalities of frugality and miniaturization; the fear of isolation has fostered development of communication technologies; a long and violent history has produced a method of consensus-based change that provides for a steady, steam-roller momentum once the direction is set. The word "change" in Japanese also means "transplant": this island nation has learned to successfully assimilate and improve everything from Buddhism to Henry Ford's assembly line.

More than any other nation, Japan's cultural characteristics propel it toward the future. It saves more than it consumes; it exports more than it imports; it has a long-term vision of its interests; it possesses the capacity to work and maintain quality; it has the aptitude to conceive and produce new consumer products *en masse*; it is aggressively expanding its external commercial networks.

The rising tide of the Japanese core is lifting the other economic boats of the Asian region. Rapidly approaching a European level of development, the countries and regional centers surrounding Japan—such as Hong Kong, Singapore, Taiwan and

South Korea—grow at the rate of about 10 percent a year. The population growth—and therefore the number of consumers—in these countries is also high.

In a Single Decade

The United States still has strong military forces. On every other point of comparison it has fallen behind, and shows few signs of reversing its decline. It has dropped to number five in GNP [gross national product] per capita. It is falling behind in productivity growth. It has lost the lead in many key technologies: semiconductors, silicon, semiconductor equipment, consumer electronics, and advanced materials. It is losing the lead in most others. There is not a single high technology area in which the relative American position was strengthened in the 1980s. Even in aerospace, the area of greatest American dominance, its position is being eroded.

In 1981 the United States was the world's largest creditor nation. At the end of the decade it was the world's largest debtor, and faces the prospect of paying three to five percent of national output to foreign lenders by the mid-1990s.

Clyde V. Prestowitz, *Powernomics*, 1991.

Already, the Asian countries of the Pacific Rim produce one-sixth of the global wealth. In only 10 years, their collective GNP will equal that of the European Community or the US.

Six of the eight most important seaports in the world are already situated on the Asian Pacific coast and more than half of all cargo transported by air on our planet crosses the Pacific. By the end of the century, the present level of air-cargo traffic is expected to multiply by six!

Conquering the Blue Distance

Despite this enormous dynamism, Japan's capacity to organize the Pacific Rim as a rival to Europe depends on its ability to conquer that blue distance across the Pacific.

Telephone, fax, cables and satellites now permit transmissions of plans, calculations, software and money at the speed of light. It is no accident that Japan ranks first in information transmitting technologies.

Plans for a Mach 3.5 and Mach 5 jet, which would bring any point in the Pacific to within two hours travel time from Tokyo, are already on the drawing board. To accommodate hypersonic transport, Japan is building an artificial island off its east coast replete with all the communication and meeting facilities necessary for rapidly expanding commerce.

Within 15 years, scientific progress in materials research and propulsion will put all Asian ports at less than a day at sea from

Japan, also reducing the trans-Pacific journey by three days.

Japan is also working on a revolutionary hydrogen-powered motor that promises, within the next 15 years, to place all cities in Japan within one hour of Tokyo. This development will transform the Japanese archipelago into a unified metropole of a scope that can anchor the vast Pacific prosperity.

Power to the Producer

Undoubtedly, the US will, initially, have difficulty swallowing its new subordination to Japan. The first seizures of Japanese-owned property in the US in the name of national security cannot be far off. Yet, the US cannot long resist because it hasn't the means to finance the Pacific Rim on its own. Sooner rather than later, the proud but fading superpower will discover that all paths lead to the source of provisions. Japan already supplies most of the key technologies for America's arsenal.

For the immediate future, the institutional organization of the Pacific Rim cannot but remain informal and fuzzy as a way of saving face over the reality of a momentous power shift. In time, with characteristic good humor and easiness, the US will surely adjust to a new identity in a century no longer American. Perhaps 10 years from now the reality can be codified in a new set of institutions.

"Japan is the nation most strongly positioned to play a major role in this new era."

Japan Will Be a Leading World Power

Shintaro Ishihara

Shintaro Ishihara is a popular Japanese politician who has been minister of transportation, director general of the Environmental Agency of Japan, and a nominee for prime minister. He is currently a member of the Standing Committee on Foreign Affairs of the Japanese legislature. In the following viewpoint, Ishihara argues that Japanese interests have been subordinated to American wishes for too long. Japan should contemplate using its economic and technological strengths to free itself from undue American control, the author contends, as well as to establish itself as a leading country in the community of nations.

As you read, consider the following questions:

1. Why does the author believe that Japan's interests are not served by its defense arrangements with the United States?
2. According to Ishihara, what will be the defining features of the "new era" in international affairs?
3. What role does Ishihara want Japan to play in the modernization of the Third World?

Shintaro Ishihara, "A Japan That Can Say No," *New Perspectives Quarterly*, Summer 1990. Reprinted with permission.

Thirty years have passed since the renewal of the US-Japan Security Treaty. Now it's time for a change.

The *raison d'etre* of the Treaty—that Japan would provide the front line of defense for the American-led postwar order in Asia against expanding communism—has collapsed.

Consequently, the US-Japan Security Treaty is gradually losing its significance and will eventually become totally obsolete.

Although it would be hasty, even careless, at this time to call for the abolition of the treaty, it should be dramatically changed from a one-sided arrangement that supports only the US strategic objectives to one that enables Japan to provide for its own defense and pursue its own interests.

Illusory Protection

Despite the illusory protection of Japan by the strategic US nuclear umbrella, Japan cannot tactically defend itself under the present terms of the treaty—as even Germany can do as a member of the NATO [North Atlantic Treaty Organization] Alliance.

As top ranking officials of the Japan Defense Agency continually point out, only one division of the US forces stationed in Japan is devoted to the defense of Japanese territory. The rest are assigned to a strategic mission that encompasses the defense of an area West of Hawaii all the way to Capetown, South Africa —in other words, half the world! Why is it in the interest of Japan to defend Australia or New Zealand and the whole Southern Hemisphere? I don't really think that the Japanese people are very interested in defending Africa.

Although we have spent much money revamping our maritime self-defense force, it comprises just a single division of the American Seventh Fleet under whose command it is integrated. It functions only to monitor submarines in the seas around Japan, not as a means of defending Japanese territory.

The situation is similar with respect to ground forces. The northern-most island of the Japanese archipelago, Hokkaido, is the first most likely place for an invasion of Japanese territory. Yet, there is not a single American soldier stationed on this island.

Serious Questions

From the Japanese standpoint, one is obliged to ask two questions about these ridiculous arrangements: Aside from the US strategic agenda, why are American forces stationed in Japan if not for the defense of Japan? And, if they are not defending Japan, why are we constantly being pressured by the US to pay more for them?

Answers to the first question can readily be found in Pentagon planning documents, where the Soviet Union is listed as enemy number one, China as enemy number two and Japan as enemy number three. Recently, a commander of the US Marine Corps, in testimony before the US Congress, frankly admitted that the reason US troops are in Japan is to ensure that we cannot enhance our military capabilities and once again become a major military power.

Yet, we are expected to foot the bill so America will, supposedly, save us from ourselves. Already, Japan is shouldering 40 percent of the necessary expenses of maintaining American forces stationed here. This amounts to about eight million yen per soldier, or the average annual pay of a typical *salaryman*, as the price we must pay for forces not directly defending Japan.

Foreign Aid: Japan's Growing International Role

In billions, U.S. dollars, 1982.

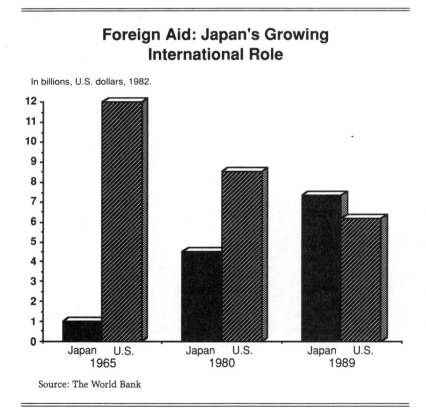

Source: The World Bank

Talk of Japan's enjoying a "free ride" of military protection at the expense of the US taxpayer is thus obviously unfounded. We in Japan are really fed up with such nonsense. As it is, the Japanese are prohibited from using either their brains or their hands to defend their homeland.

It is time for this to change. While staying well within the constraints of the Japanese Constitution—both its one percent of GNP [gross national product] cap on military spending and its restriction against offensive weapons—Japan can reorganize its forces under the terms of the Treaty so that we are tactically capable of defending our territory by ourselves.

First, we could defend our own coastline with high-speed cruisers that possess ship-to-air missiles: We must be able to close Japan's three most vital sea straits in the event of foreign attack. Secondly, we need our own jet fighter, the FSX. Thirdly, we can dispense with the ridiculously out-of-place tank defense of an island nation that is mainly mountainous and forested.

Additionally, we should seek the return of at least one of the three large US air bases on the outskirts of Tokyo. The Yakota Air Base, in particular, is not used to any great extent, while the air control situation around Tokyo is dangerous due to very heavy congestion at both Narita and Haneda airports. If I were prime minister of Japan, or governor of the Tokyo metropolitan government, I would demand the return of Yakota immediately. We need it desperately and the US hardly uses it.

I do not oppose cooperation with the US and even the maintenance of US forces on Japanese soil. To the extent they help defend Japan, our own forces must be capable of defending the US bases from attack. But, to the extent the strategic mission of US forces is beyond direct Japanese interests, they should not be based here rent free.

By reconfiguring our forces in this way, we can improve Japan's defense fourfold while remaining within the one percent of GNP constraint. It would not go unnoticed, of course, that because of the size of Japan's GNP our nation would then have the third largest expenditures for defense after the USSR and the US.

Economic Might

The importance of the size of Japanese military spending, however, should not be exaggerated. At the end of the 20th century, civilization is entering a new era where economic and technological might outweighs the importance of military power.

Japan is the nation most strongly positioned to play a major role in this new era, especially with our mass-production capabilities in semiconductors. Indeed, as the Pentagon's own Very High Speed Integrated Circuit Committee Report of 1986 made alarmingly clear, the weaponry upon which the US world strategy relies already depends fundamentally on Japanese mass production of high-quality semiconductors.

It is precisely this vital technological role that gives us the leverage that will allow us to chart an independent course in which Japan designs its own contribution to the world order.

For example, the US will not allow the sale of reconnaissance satellites to Japan. Yet, without reconnaissance satellites of our own, how can we obtain the information that will allow us to independently and accurately assess not only military threats, but also the ecological and development problems that we are called upon to help alleviate? Under present arrangements, if a developing country wants aid from Japan, they must first go to Washington for approval—then Washington calls on us. Japan is not willing to continue such stupid efforts. Our money just disappears down a hole with no measurable effect.

A Sense of Purpose

The time has come for Japan to develop a sense of purpose for contributing to a peaceful world on a scope commensurate with its enormous economic and technological strength. Japan needs a grand strategy consonant with its self-image as a humanistic, democratic and peaceful nation, and a strategy able to win broad support among the Japanese people. To this end, the geographic horizon of Japan's defense policy must expand beyond the region of the Japanese islands.

Tokyo has pursued global economic policies for years by participating in international financial organizations and economic assistance programs and by guiding the far-flung investments of large Japanese corporations. But the Japanese body politic may be inclined to resist commensurate expansion of the nation's security horizon. Japanese public sentiment reflects a reluctance to become engaged in issues of foreign policy and defense. Over time, however, the disparity between the global horizon of Japan's economic policies and the regional horizon of its security strategy cannot persist. A nation with the economic and technological strength of Japan is unlikely to remain a purely regional power in the 21st century.

Fred Charles Iklé and Terumasa Nakanishi, *Foreign Affairs*, Summer 1990.

I think it is time for Japan to consider the possibility of playing our microchip card in order to bring the US to its senses over arrogantly and arbitrarily constraining our capacity for initiative in the world.

Japan's technological prowess, however, is not only a negative lever, but also a positive asset. In fact, it is the basis for the global ideal of the "dynamics of Japanese aid," which I believe can be Japan's chief contribution to the new international order.

Providing Infrastructure

Information and resource-efficient technologies are central to modernizing the developing world. More than anything else, these countries need an information and renewable-energy infrastructure if they are not going to be left out of the 21st century.

In all these areas—from consumer electronics such as VCRs and TVs to the most sophisticated microchip, optical fibers and flat display, to solar batteries—Japan has the most advanced technologies. Since all of these technologies were developed commercially rather than for military purposes, they are both cost efficient and non-threatening. Other countries may be able to provide the infrastructure of the past, such as highways, railroads and huge power stations, but only Japan can mass produce the communications and energy infrastructure of the new age at a low cost.

The "dynamics of Japanese aid" could make an even more powerful contribution to countries with a higher level of skills and education, such as Hungary or Czechoslovakia. I am convinced that if a concerted multilateral effort supported this idea of Japanese-style aid, we could turn those two countries around within five years. And, no doubt, Great Britain and France would welcome our efforts, since they would provide a counterweight to German economic domination of Eastern Europe.

An Independent Course

Thirty years after the signing of US-Japan Security Treaty, which subordinated Japan to the strategic objectives of the US, Japan is capable of going its own way. We are capable of devising a global strategy and should do so.

A Japan that can say no to US orders is a Japan that has recovered its full sovereignty, just like any other nation.

"By the end of the 1990s it is quite likely that Japan's Superman mantle will have disappeared."

Japan's Power Will Be Limited

Karl Zinsmeister

Karl Zinsmeister is an adjunct scholar at the American Enterprise Institute, a public policy research center in Washington, D.C. In the following viewpoint, Zinsmeister argues that Japan will not surpass the United States as the world's leading economic power. Japan's economy, the author contends, suffers from weaknesses which limit the nation's international influence. In addition, Zinsmeister asserts, social trends within Japan, such as an aging population, increasing labor costs, and the development of consumerism will slow Japan's expansion.

As you read, consider the following questions:

1. How does Japanese economic productivity compare to that of the United States, according to Zinsmeister?
2. Why does the author believe that energy is a weak sector in Japan's economy?
3. Why does Zinsmeister think Japan's financial markets are unstable?

An abridged version of "Shadows on the Rising Sun," by Karl Zinsmeister, *The American Enterprise*, May/June 1990. Reprinted with the permission of the American Enterprise Institute for Public Policy Research, Washington, D.C.

Japan . . . is not an unerringly successful nation. The Japanese, too, have their societal weaknesses, their inefficient sectors, their economic failures. What follows is a survey of some of these frailties, with a brief consideration of their likely effect on Japan's overall competence in the 1990s.

Uneven Productivity

The first thing to be said about Japanese productive prowess is that an inventory of the consumer products in your house and garage is a misleading way to gauge it. Japanese successes are concentrated in manufacturing—which constitutes only about a fifth to a third of the economic activity in a modern nation—and further focused within a narrow band of export durables like home electronics and cars.

A broad comparison of productivity in Japan and the United States released in 1989 by economists from Harvard University and Keio University in Tokyo found that Japanese output lagged behind U.S. standards in 16 of 29 major industries (and that the United States was actually widening the gap in 12 of these). Japan had an edge in ten.

Using GNP [gross national product] per person—the broadest possible measure—overall Japanese productivity is still only about three-quarters of the American level. U.S. transportation and communications workers, for instance, are about twice as productive as those in Japan. In retailing and service industries, Americans are about half again as fruitful, and U.S. farmers are more than four times as efficient as their Japanese counterparts. Japan's poor performance in such areas is often masked by measures that shelter her weak industries from competition. These protective measures are a source of friction with her trading partners, and they also exact a stiff penalty on the Japanese standard of living. . . .

Services and Infrastructure

Now that Japanese are beginning to travel abroad and otherwise become more open to the world, they are at last recognizing the weakness of many of their public services and demanding improvements in everything from parks to sewers. This will require vast expenditures—the government expects to commit trillions of dollars in the 1990s to infrastructure spending. While improvements in the quality of Japanese life will certainly result, there will also undoubtedly be some damping effect on private investment as a result of so much cash being soaked up for other purposes.

This is particularly important in light of recent political and demographic trends. For all the hullabaloo over U.S. budget deficits, the truth is that Japan has been the deficit and debt champ among major countries since the mid-1970s. Japan's budget went deeply into the red after 1975, with government borrowing covering more than a quarter of all spending in some years during the 1980s. They ran deficits around 6 percent of GNP (as bad as the U.S. level at its recent worst). As a result, the Japanese have piled up an enormous government debt—equivalent to nearly 70 percent of the economy's total national output by the late 1980s. In the same years, Uncle Sam's accumulated debt, subject of so much concern, amounted to a little over 50 percent of GNP.

Japan's rising infrastructure bills and high debt are particularly relevant in light of its coming retirement (and social security and health expenditure) boom. Japan is rapidly on its way to becoming the world's oldest nation. The percentage of elderly in the population will pass U.S. levels in 1990, and between now and 2010, the ratio of working-age to above-working-age citizens will tumble rapidly.

As a result, demand on the national income stream for old-age support will increase sharply—from 12 percent of average pre-tax wages now to around 23 percent 20 years hence. Having had the advantage of a very light public-sector load for more than a generation, Japan's private producers are going to find their burden increasing dramatically from now on.

Weak Political Leadership

Its rising costs is only one of the problems of the Japanese government. A deeper one is weak political leadership. Japan is hardly democratic in the American sense of that word. While a political meritocracy sprang from the ashes of World War II, political leadership today is rarely rejuvenated by fresh talent. One-third of ruling politicians have inherited their seats from their fathers or business groups, and the office-holding clique is solidifying itself through intermarriage and nepotism. "It's like the Brezhnev system," says one Japanese critic.

Graft is also far more common in Japan than in most other representative systems. The Recruit influence-buying scandal directly implicated 45 ruling politicians. It was hard for party leaders to find a single qualified candidate for prime minister who had not been tainted. The ineptness of the ruling Liberal Democratic Party that has monopolized political power in Japan for 35 years is compounded by the fact that Japanese voters enjoy few responsible alternatives.

Part of the problem with Japanese political leadership stems from the fact that the nation's prime minister has the least power of any major government head. The country is run by backroom elders and bureaucrats. Of all the legislation passed by Japan's Diet in 1988, for instance, 86 percent was written by ministry functionaries instead of legislators.

Private industry, too, has its laggards in Japan. Telecommunications, for instance, are not particularly efficient. A domestic long-distance call costs more than three times as much in Japan as in the United States, and calling abroad from Japan is much more expensive than the reverse. Though the Japanese are significant exporters of telecom equipment, it is mostly low-end technology not in heavy demand in the United States and other competitive markets. Much the same situation applies to Japanese computers. Japanese attempts to build a leading biotechnology industry have also fizzled, as have efforts to manufacture civilian airliners.

Avoiding Leadership

As the world's second-largest economy, Japan is increasingly finding itself in the uncomfortable position of being asked to accept the mantle of global leadership, especially in economic affairs.

The new challenge facing Tokyo goes beyond the sorts of demands that have been presented in the past—for more open markets, for more altruistic Third World aid, for more responsible environmental behavior. Now Japan is expected to help set the new agendas in areas such as these rather than simply responding to *gaiatsu*—foreign pressure from abroad. Yet only the most optimistic observer would bet that Japan can—or will—pick up this mantle soon.

Paul Blustein, *The Washington Post National Weekly Edition*, February 4-10, 1991.

Energy is a critical sector in which Japan is particularly frail. The country is dependent upon imports for every bit of its petroleum; worse, the Ministry of International Trade and Industry [MITI] has badly damaged the nation's oil industry over recent decades with what has been called the worst national energy policy on the globe. . . .

Tighter oil supplies and higher prices in the years ahead will pinch the Japanese disproportionately, not only because of their complete reliance upon imports, but also because 35 percent of Japanese gross domestic product comes from manufacturing— the most oil-hungry of productive sectors. (By comparison, only 19 percent of U.S. output comes from manufacturing.)

A Shaky Financial Sector?

The Japanese are finally realizing that many of their financial assets have become grossly overpriced. In the years 1986 and 1987, the price of all equities listed on Tokyo's main stock exchange rose more than 40 percent. Over the same period, the total value of the nation's private residential land rose 65 percent (to roughly $8 trillion). In the greater Tokyo area, land-value inflation was even fiercer.

Japanese land prices are now 25 times higher, on average, than U.S. levels. Shares on the Tokyo stock market have recently traded at costs 60 times the companies' annual earnings, while in London and New York, 12 or 14 times earnings is normal. In a giddy speculative bubble, people have been buying because prices are going up, and prices go up because people buy. There is the potential for a dangerous Ponzi game to develop in this way.

After shrugging off the risks for some time, Japanese financial markets seem recently to have begun to notice. In the first three months of 1990, Tokyo's Nikkei stock average fell more than 20 percent, and the market as a whole lost $800 billion dollars in value. If this new sobriety holds up, the cost of capital for Japanese corporations—which until now has been very low, giving them a significant international advantage—will increase.

Other factors, too, will change the availability of capital. Japanese, as we will see, are becoming more spendthrift, and a large bulge of the population is reaching an older age when living off savings is more common than adding to them. Further, important tax incentives for stashing away money have recently been ended. The result is that Japan's savings relative to disposable income has fallen from 23 percent in 1976 to 15 percent in 1988. Further decline may be expected. Other trends discussed here will also work to shrink Japan's current enormous capital surplus. Given more government spending, more imports, more foreign travel, and the like, Japan's banks and other financial firms will not be swimming in currency forever. . . .

Buying and Selling

Japan is in the midst of an explosion of consumerism. Traditionally, the Japanese frowned on borrowing. Today, however, home equity loans have caught on, and the number of credit cards in Japan jumped from 40 million in 1983 to 110 million by 1987. A boom in expensive overseas travel is underway, with 10 million Japanese going abroad in 1989. Japan's saving rate, as mentioned, has fallen. . . .

On the whole, more consumption, pleasure seeking, and importing will probably be good for the Japanese, making their lives more comfortable and interesting as well as rounding out the functioning of their economy. For example, despite the rhetoric about Japanese exports "invading" America and Europe, the fact is that Japan exported only 17 percent of its GNP in 1987, compared with 21 percent for France, 32 percent for West Germany, 26 percent for Britain, and 57 percent for the Netherlands. What has made Japan so unpopular internationally is less its "flood" of exports than its inhospitableness to imports. (Manufactured imports equal only 3 percent of GNP in Japan.) If the Japanese are beginning to amend the disparity between what they buy and what they sell, benefits will accrue to them, even while the accelerator on their hotrod economy eases back a bit.

Pressures from beyond Japan's borders are driving much of its move away from parasitically structured commercial relationships. The proportion of Americans who told the *New York Times*-CBS News poll that they had "generally friendly" feelings toward Japan fell from 87 percent in 1985 to 74 percent in June of 1989 to 67 percent in January 1990. Recognizing the danger in this backlash, the Japanese have at last begun to undertake reforms. This will allow them to safeguard their long-term seat at the prosperous global trading table. At the same time, the changes they are necessarily undertaking make it less likely that their economy will be so inherently overpowering in the future. Though Japan remains a natural athlete, some of the springs are being taken out of her sneakers. . . .

Rising Competition

Another factor that is moderating some growth is the fact that Japan has lost its wage advantage. The country is in the midst of a serious worker shortage, and pay levels are rising sharply. In manufacturing, Japanese wage costs per worker are now higher than in the United States and about five times prevailing standards in South Korea and Singapore. In labor-intensive industries like textiles, the "Four Dragons" (Taiwan, Hong Kong, Singapore, and South Korea) had overtaken Japan in competitiveness by the early 1970s. For durable consumer goods, they passed the Japanese in the mid-1980s. Fifty-two percent of Japan's calculators were imported in 1987, versus 13 percent in 1980; 40 percent of its cameras, 60 percent of its portable radios, 56 percent of its electric fans, and growing numbers of its television sets and VCRs were imported that same year.

Even in famously successful Japanese industries like steelmaking and shipbuilding, offshore cost advantages have sometimes idled domestic production. In areas of current Japanese superiority like silicon chip production, competitive pressure from newly industrialized countries will also increasingly be felt. Already, South Korea holds more than 3 percent of the world market in mass-produced chips, a share that may triple within five years. Indonesia and others will follow.

Competition from the United States is also increasing. The fall in the value of the dollar from its artificial heights in the late 1980s returned a considerable number of American exports to comparative advantage. Some longer-term structural changes favor American competitiveness as well. For one, tax conditions in America and Japan have to a considerable extent reversed.

43

The Japanese virtually invented supply-side fiscal policy. To launch their comeback from economic ruin in the 1950s, they abolished levies on interest and capital gains and cut their income-tax rates by 30 percent in one year. Between 1954 and 1974, individual tax rates fell 11 times and rose once, while corporate tax rates fell six times and increased twice. In all but three years over that period, individual income-tax exemptions were increased. These actions gave Japan the lowest tax rates in the industrial world. From 1951 to 1970, combined national and local taxes in Japan fell from 22.4 percent of national income to 18.9 percent. Meanwhile, comparable U.S. taxes rose from 28.5 percent to 31.3.

The Japanese Government

Japan's government—read "political system"—is more a part of the problem than the solution. For behind its dynamic, high-technology facade, Japan is a nineteenth-century society akin to that of our own robber baron, Boss Tweed era. Its plodding, bureaucracy-ridden, corruption-prone young democracy fosters obstructionism and multi-billion-dollar boondoggles befitting our most notorious nineteenth-century political machines.

Alfred Balk, *The Myth of American Eclipse,* 1990.

That situation has now changed for both countries. In the United States, the overall tax bite has stopped growing, and lower marginal rates have been instituted. In Japan, meanwhile, capital gains are being taxed again, the popular *maruyu* postal savings accounts are no longer exempt, social security taxes are rising above American levels for the first time, and a nationwide 3 percent sales tax has just been instituted. Japan slipped past the United States in total tax burden as the decade turned.

The United States is beginning to solve other problems that have hampered it in matching Japanese performance. The ratio of engineers and scientists to the total labor force, for instance, has recently been rising faster here than in Japan. Many American corporations slimmed down and toughened up their operations during the 1980s. The federal budget deficit has been reduced from 26 percent of total spending in 1983 to 13 percent in 1989. Immigration continues to bring new talent and inspiration to the American labor force. And our defense burden is shrinking. Unsurpassed wealth, the world's most-educated populace, and nonpareil science give the United States three very strong cards for the long haul.

To say that the confluence of factors that produced Japan's remarkable successes in the 1980s will be difficult to sustain indefinitely is not to say Japan is going to crash in the decade ahead. It is impossible not to be impressed by the ability of the Japanese to conquer adversity. They overcame a tenfold rise in the price of their imported oil in the 1970s. They plowed through a doubling in the value of the yen over just three years in the later 1980s. They have initiated the necessary shift toward a domestic-consumption economy with remarkable speed and aplomb. Japan will almost certainly be a fast-growing, impressively prosperous nation for many years to come. Its people's attitudes and the soundness of its social institutions guarantee that.

An Abnormal Era

The point here is simply that the Japanese are not exempt from the laws of gravity or economics. Their present-day triumphs are aberrant in many ways, even by their own high standards, and by the end of the 1990s it is quite likely that Japan's Superman mantle will have disappeared. Japan will then have to content itself with being "merely" one of the world's most productive societies, the second-leading economic power for the foreseeable future.

It is a good wager that these times will someday be viewed as the peak of Japan's contemporary bloom, an abnormal era that whisked Japan into a rightful position among the top rank of nations, where she then settled in for a long period of shining, but not overwhelming, success.

"Through a combination of its own efforts and the pressure of external events, the [European] Community may be about to have greatness thrust upon it."

Europe Will Be a Leading World Power

Séamus O'Cléireacáin

The EC, or European Community, is a group of twelve Western European nations scheduled to unite economically by the end of 1992. In the following viewpoint, Séamus O'Cléireacáin argues that the EC could become a major international power. The creation of a single European economy and changes in Eastern Europe and Germany will allow Europe to reach unprecedented levels of wealth and influence, according to O'Cléireacáin. The author is a professor of economics at the State University of New York at Purchase, and a research associate at the Institute on Western Europe, Columbia University.

As you read, consider the following questions:

1. According to the author, how has Europe performed in the world economy?
2. What issues prompted European unification, in O'Cléireacáin's opinion?
3. How does the author believe America will respond to growing European influence?

Just as the European Community's (EC) eight-year effort passed the halfway stage on the way to 1992, the collapse of the last great European imperial power, the Soviet empire, cast the Community's efforts at its own construction in a new light. German unification and the resurgence of democracy in Eastern and Central Europe have not only introduced the need to create new political and security architectures for intra-European and Atlantic relations, but they have altered as well the role of the EC in the international system, placing it on the brink of transformation from a regional to an economic superpower. In the words of EC president Jacques Delors to the European Parliament on 17 January 1990, "As the superpowers map out their vision of our continent the question is this: Is Europe to be a mere spectator or is it to play an active role in shaping tomorrow's world?"

As member states fashion a more assertive EC, superpower status is made more likely by the emergence of new security arrangements in Europe which place greater emphasis on the economic and political, rather than military, dimensions of this security. At the same time, the Community is involved in five important areas of policy development, all of which contribute to its leadership role: (1) completion of the EC's internal market; (2) the EC-European Free Trade Agreement (EFTA) creation of a European Economic Space (EES); (3) new ties with Eastern and Central Europe; (4) German unification; and (5) Economic and Monetary Union (EMU). As political and economic relations are reshaped, the Community may be expected to be drawn inexorably into security issues. The arrival of a European economic superpower with an eventual security dimension has major implications for both the United States and the Mediterranean.

The Future Ascent of Europe

The years since the publication of the 1985 White Paper on Completion of the Internal Market have coincided with a burst of dynamism in European economies. After languishing through six consecutive years of double-digit unemployment, the EC rate finally fell below 10 percent in 1989. Down the road, the potential economic power of 470 million people encompassed by the EC with a unified Germany, EFTA, Poland, Hungary, Czechoslovakia, Romania, and Bulgaria is considerable. At $6 trillion, the gross domestic product (GDP) of this group of nations exceeds the 1989 U.S. gross national product (GNP) of $5.4 trillion.

Despite such progress, the global presence of the EC to date has been stunted. A number of indicators on this score . . . suggest that, until now, the ability of the Community to project itself into the global economy has been limited. While the EC share of world production has remained constant, the Community was not until recently where new jobs were being created. It is also clear that the EC share of world trade has been declining.

Europhoria

My projections show an average five percent growth rate in Europe during the 1990s—twice that of the projected US rate of 2.5 percent. The combined GNP of the 18 countries of Western Europe, with their 400 million people, could be as high as six trillion dollars by the mid-nineties—that is 1.5 times larger than the US economy and two to three times higher than the Japanese economy.

Gianni De Michelis, *New Perspectives Quarterly*, Spring 1990.

Of the five indicators of economic power [gross domestic product, civilian employment, world merchandise trade shares, world international reserves, and share of national currency in world foreign exchange], in all but one, civilian employment, the American share has fallen, while Japan's share, except in civilian employment, has risen. For the EC, only one indicator, currency composition of foreign exchange holdings, gives a clear signal of increased economic influence, and this may result from greater intra-Community holdings of member state currencies rather than from an international preference for EC currencies. Such a record is not that of an emerging economic superpower. Yet, through a combination of its own efforts and the pressure of external events, the Community may be about to have greatness thrust upon it.

It may be argued that the roots of future greatness lie in the five current enterprises in which the EC is now engaged, and in the importance that a changed external environment gives to these efforts. Three of these areas of development—the 1992 program, German unification, and EMU—will strengthen the economic union if they prove successful. The other two—EES and new ties with Eastern and Central Europe—could provide the economic union leverage in advancing its already considerable economic influence even further in the international system. One may add to these enterprises the emergence of a common EC foreign policy as a precursor to a Community security dimension.

The program to complete the EC's internal market was conceived during an era of "Eurosclerosis" characterized by double-digit unemployment and the evident failure of Community industry to compete with the United States and Japan in any areas

48

save limited, niche markets. As a defensive reaction to its slipping global competitiveness, the EC was not considered a likely candidate for the status of an economic superpower. The promise of the 1992 program was one of greater Community competitiveness, faster economic growth, and more jobs. Original estimates of the effects of completing the internal market are now considered underestimates. If the 1992 program raises the EC growth rate permanently by a full percentage point, living standards will triple over the life expectancy of the Community's citizens rather than doubling as at present.

In addition to these internal effects, the 1992 program promises to increase the bargaining power of the EC in the international economic system by providing Brussels with the ability to project a more sharply articulated image. Completion of the internal market offers the prospect of "free circulation" of goods and services. Goods imported into the EC from the rest of the world could be transshipped without hindrance anywhere in the Community. "Free circulation" will present the rest of the world trading system with a common EC commercial policy. As the dwindling policy gaps in the unified commerce are closed, the 1992 program will provide EC trading partners with a more coherent, unified commercial policy that will be projected outward onto the global trading system. . . .

The 1992 program has acted as a magnet for world savings, attracting considerable new flows of direct private investment from the United States, Japan, and EFTA. Further, the recent mergers and acquisitions wave ratifies the original 1992 premise that European industry can take advantage of the economies of scale and scope offered by a less segmented market. The large role played by non-EC-headquartered firms in this merger activity threatens to further discredit the national champion policies pursued by member states in the past. Irrespective of the ultimate ownership of the economic activity occurring with a completed internal market, the 1992 program and member state acquiescence in strengthening the antitrust powers of the commission place it in a much better position to shape the industrial organization of the EC economy. Applicable to a major part of the global economy, this will alter the behavior not only of EC-headquartered multinationals but of U.S. and Japanese ones as well. . . .

New Ties with Eastern Europe

The sudden appearance of a large untapped market on its doorstep is further propelling the EC into a major leadership role in managing the international economic system. This role is being thrust on it by the potential size of trade and investment flows, by the active participation of EC political parties in elections in Eastern and Central Europe, and by the Community's coordination of the Group of 24 (G-24) aid program. The movement of Eastern and Central Europe inside the EC's concentric circles of foreign relationships in global economic flows, which had previously been arm's length East-West flows, will be a further boost to EC standing.

Currently, trade with Eastern and Central Europe accounts for less than 4 percent of extra-EC trade. Some forecasts suggest that this trade will, over the next fifteen years, replace the United States as the Community's second most important export market. Trade may be expected to grow rapidly with the advent of market economies, infrastructure investments, direct private foreign investment, aid from the new European Bank for Reconstruction and Development (EBRD), and the second wave of bilateral trade agreements between the EC and individual countries in the area. While these markets have not been important for the Community in the past, the EC has been an important trading partner, particularly for Poland and Hungary. . . .

Considerable Responsibility

The European Community, which grew up in the shadow of the United States and the Soviet Union, has exercised a growing influence of its own on world affairs, especially since its first enlargement in 1973. The Community assumed many of the worldwide commercial and political links that its member states had developed over the years and has built further ties. The Community has diplomatic relations with some 130 countries. It is today the world's greatest trading power, accounting for nearly 20% of international trade. It therefore shares with the United States and Japan considerable responsibility for the maintenance of a liberal world trading system.

The European Communications Group Brussels, *The Politics of the European Community*, 1988.

In the next wave of trade relations with Eastern and Central Europe, two distinct processes are now in motion. First, limited partnerships with Bulgaria, Czechoslovakia, and Romania may be upgraded to full trade and economic cooperation agreements. Upgrading depends on progress toward democracy and a recent removal of an impediment created by Bulgarian human rights violations, the forced migration of people of Turkish origin.

Second, trade and economic cooperation agreements may pave the way for a new class of associated membership agreements announced by the EC in August 1990. While these do not necessarily carry a presumption of eventual full membership and are conditional on political and economic reform, they offer aid, eventual free trade, and entry into the EES. Likely candidates for early associated member status are Czechoslovakia, Hungary, and Poland. Associated membership for the USSR would present problems because of the potential size of economic flows.

These new economic relationships will produce few transitional difficulties for the 1992 program. In particular, new export-oriented investments in Eastern and Central Europe will not be allowed to disrupt EC markets. Industries facing structural damage induced by the 1992 program may even find that openings into Eastern and Central Europe promise to make this transition easier for them. For example, while the EC is already the world's largest automobile market, the Pan-European market promises to be even more dynamic. . . .

Finally, the choice of currency in which to express capitalization of the EBRD represents a further indicator of the growing international status of the EC. The choice between capitalization in dollars and in the European Currency Unit (ECU) pitted the United States against the Community. The choice of the ECU signifies an important break from an earlier era of postwar, multilateral lending agencies. The EBRD is the first, within this family of institutions, where the United States does not have a veto. While the United States, with 10 percent, is the largest single shareholder in the EBRD, the block of EC shares amounts to 51 percent. Symbolically, the currency capitalization choice, rather than the distribution of voting privileges, may be a more important indicator of where the EC is headed. . . .

Implications for the U.S.

The emergence of an EC-centered European economic superpower has major implications for both the United States and the Mediterranean. Some of these implications are still well in the future. External assertiveness by the Community first requires internal union. In synchronizing progress toward internal economic and political union with a redefinition of its external role, the EC faces considerable but surmountable difficulties. The ability to make the transformation from a regional power depends not only on progress toward internal union and the Community's international competitiveness, but also on the place of nonmilitary dimensions, such as economics and the environment, in redefining national security, as well as on whether a military dimension is eventually added to the EC.

For the United States, the transformation underway in the EC's role presents a challenge. While the role of the EC as a regional power is central to American efforts at encouraging political and economic liberalization in Eastern and Central Europe, the U.S. may not yet have fully come to terms with the prospect of a more assertive EC in the global economic system. On the latter front, American policymakers face a more competitive EC likely to pose new challenges to the U.S. not only in bilateral trade but also in third-country markets. On the global political front, Community positions on the Middle East—Iraq's invasion of Kuwait is an exception—and on Central America have not always been completely consonant with American positions. There is a need to ensure coherence in U.S. policy in dealing with the EC on these two fronts. Contradictions may be expected to emerge within the American policy-making establishment between the Europe-oriented wing accustomed to viewing the Community as its main ally in fostering change in Eastern and Central Europe, and those charged with dealing with the EC as a potential economic superpower on the wider stage of world economic and political affairs. Although the American ability to influence the policies of this European superpower may be expected to decline, global system management would be made easier by the presence of a coherent EC-centered European perspective, provided the U.S. is prepared to accept further sharing of its leadership position.

"Troubling developments . . . threaten to derail Europe's pretensions of becoming a dominant political and economic power."

Europe May Not Be a Leading World Power

William Drozdiak

In the following viewpoint, William Drozdiak contends that Europe is far from becoming a world power. Despite the claims of some Europeans that unification will bring unprecedented power and prosperity, numerous obstacles, such as the enormous task of modernizing Eastern Europe, will keep Europe from playing a more international role for some time, according to Drozdiak. In addition, European companies have not demonstrated that they can compete without government assistance, raising doubts, the author contends, about their future success in the world economy. William Drozdiak writes for the *Washington Post* newspaper.

As you read, consider the following questions:

1. Why does Drozdiak believe that European prosperity depends on stability in the Persian Gulf, North Africa, and the Soviet Union?
2. What role will immigration play in Europe's future, in Drozdiak's opinion?
3. Why does the author believe that Europe may turn to protectionist trade policies?

The European Community [EC] will [soon] enter a brave new world that many of its movers and shakers believe will create an era of unparalleled prosperity and breathtaking historical change.

On Jan. 1, 1993, all national borders will tumble between the 12 member states (Belgium, Britain, Denmark, France, Germany, Greece, Ireland, Italy, Luxembourg, the Netherlands, Portugal and Spain), creating a single market that will allow their 340 million citizens to travel and change jobs, invest their money and sell their products as freely as Americans can within their own country.

Even more ambitious plans will follow. By the end of the decade the German mark, English pound, French franc and Italian lira may become as obsolete as the Edsel. A single currency, known as the "ecu" and managed by a European federal reserve, would replace all those assorted currencies.

That, in turn, is expected to build irresistible momentum toward a single European economic policy that would inevitably require full political union. National governments would pool their sovereignty and elected leaders would make all important decisions at a single, European level.

Those remarkable goals, coupled with the democratic revolution that swept Eastern Europe, have infused Western European countries with a sense of dynamism and ambition that they have lacked since World War II. With the collapse of the Soviet empire and troubled economic conditions confronting America after the profligacy of the Reagan era, Europe has suddenly emerged as the darling of think tankers and moneymen alike, the land of golden opportunity in the 1990s.

But is it, really?

A Political Dwarf and Military Worm

Since the Persian Gulf crisis erupted in August 1990, a more sober assessment of Europe's potential has been taking place. Iraq's seizure of Kuwait again demonstrated how both Western and Eastern Europe have become precariously dependent on oil and gas sources in politically unstable regions, notably the Persian Gulf, North Africa and the Soviet Union. Sustained turmoil in any of those areas—coming on the heels of worldwide economic slowdown—would certainly slash growth projections and transform a limitless horizon of affluence into a gloomy scenario of high inflation and high unemployment.

Such fears are not merely hypothetical; in Europe, it has happened before. In 1972, after a period of steady economic expansion and Britain's entry into the European Community, the EC's leaders agreed to a timetable for an economic and monetary union that was supposed to be achieved by the end of that decade. But a year later, war broke out in the Middle East and an oil embargo sent European governments scrambling to salvage their economies and electoral prospects. The meticulous agenda for European unity in 1980 became a shambles and was not resurrected until recently. Indeed, the history of European integration has shown that the member states make important progress during good times but experience trouble reconciling their myriad national interests during periods of economic downturn, which seems the most likely condition for the coming years.

An Inability to Agree

It is overlooked that Europeans have found it extraordinarily difficult to agree on anything. Until very recently, the Continent was divided along ideological lines. In Western Europe, only some states are members of NATO [North Atlantic Treaty Organization], only some members of NATO are full members, and many European states still prefer neutrality. Even on an issue such as terrorism it has proved enormously difficult to achieve any common policy. There are wide differences of opinion on economic and social policy and on the fate of different parts of the world, such as the Middle East, South Africa, and Latin America. What then does Europe really have to offer in terms of world leadership?

Alan Sked, *The National Interest*, Winter 1990/1991.

Europe dithered while the United States mobilized the troops and firepower to stop Iraqi President Saddam Hussein after he kidnapped Kuwait and turned his gaze toward Saudi Arabia. It was another painful reminder that despite its clout as a leading commercial power, Europe is still not prepared to act decisively and quickly to protect its own security and economic interests. The gulf crisis has shown, says Belgium's Foreign Minister Mark Eyskens, that Europe "is an economic giant, a political dwarf and a military worm.". . .

There are other troubling developments that threaten to derail Europe's pretensions of becoming a dominant political and economic power around the world.

The Costs of Integration

The tremendous difficulties facing Eastern European countries and the Soviet Union in transforming state-run systems into market economies and altering the work habits and consumer instincts of their populations will require massive and sustained assistance from their Western neighbors.

Investing enough hard cash to rebuild those economies is a big part of the problem, but only part. Increasingly, Western business and political leaders stress that incorporating the economies of the East bloc and Soviet Union will require an infusion of technological, financial and management talent that is likely to be focused on the integration of Western European economies for most of the decade.

Still, the EC countries know that they have no other choice but to make this massive investment of money, talent and attention to help the East. For if they allowed those economies to collapse, the material deprivations would drive much of the population toward the West in search of food, work and shelter.

A study by the EC's executive commission concluded that even if there is no breakdown, up to 8 million people from Eastern and Central Europe are likely to move west in the next five years. That huge influx could exacerbate a persistent shortage of jobs and housing, especially in Germany, and worsen social tensions in Western Europe.

Although the immigrants might provide a new source of cheap labor—and, indeed, high labor costs are a central problem for European countries trying to compete with the United States and Japan on world markets—they would also be a serious drain on the generous social welfare benefits, such as six-week paid vacations and subsidized medical care, that are considered sacrosanct in Europe.

Economic Reforms Needed

Besides the problem of the East and its preoccupation with the process of integration, Western Europe will also need to undergo important economic reforms.

For too long, many European firms enjoyed the cozy protection of national governments that were willing to subsidize losses and build barriers to competition because they could not tolerate the political costs of plant shutdowns and job losses. A key question now, as global economic challenges grow more intense, is whether European companies can learn to survive on their own in an open continental market—and world markets—without such aids.

In key industries such as computers and automobiles, the United States and Japan have already consolidated big leads over their European competitors and are poised to take greater advantage of the huge internal market that will open up in the EC.

In the computer industry, for example, International Business Machines Corp.'s overwhelming dominance has forced European computer firms such as Philips NV, Olivetti Group and Honeywell Bull to eliminate thousands of jobs in a desperate attempt to rebuild their firms and make them more efficient, and in the end only state subsidies may keep them alive.

Subsidized automakers such as Peugeot, Fiat, Volvo and Jaguar, looking at declining market share, have already been forced to lay off workers and seek international partners.

Airbus Industrie, the European commercial aircraft manufacturing consortium, has yet to operate on anything like a break-even basis, despite more than a decade of government subsidies.

Even the pharmaceutical industry, which thrived during a decade of mergers and profits in the 1980s, is anticipating rough times as governments increase pressure to slash prices and patents expire on some of the best-selling drugs produced by companies such as Bayer A.G. and Ciba-Geigy A.G., inviting a rush of competition from lower-cost generic drug manufacturers.

Optimists and Pessimists

Despite such daunting hurdles to the creation of a dynamic and united economy, the optimists believe that Europeans realize they can surmount these challenges only by further pooling their sovereignty and their resources. The EC executive commission is touting a study claiming that the introduction of a single currency by itself will create efficiencies worth $130 billion to European companies each year, an amount equal to the entire gross national product of the Netherlands. With the help of such efficiencies, and a big, prosperous market at home, the EC looks to a day when its products and services compete successfully with the best from Japan and the United States.

Unification Is Not Enough

The much-discussed plans for European economic unification in 1992 cannot obscure the harbingers of continental decline: a decade of flat levels of industrial investment, rising unemployment, slow growth rates and fading technological leadership. Yet many residents in and admirers of Europe—the world's most brilliant economic force for nearly half a millenium—have only slowly perceived its eclipse. "Europeans do not often see their own decline," observes Jean Rimboud, chairman of French-based Schlumberger. "They do not believe in it, just as a traveler does not sense that the boat is moving down the river because the current is too regular."

Joel Kotkin and Yoriko Kishimoto, *The Third Century*, 1988.

"Even if the gulf crisis has been a cold shower for those who believed in rapid progress toward political and military union, Europe still retains great potential to emerge as this decade's economic superpower," says Dominique Moisi, associate director of the French Institute for International Relations. "While differing political interests may cause friction from time to time, [European] Community members increasingly see that their long-term national economic interests are best served by moving toward greater integration."

The pessimists, however, can point to the collapse of worldwide trade talks in Brussels as fresh evidence that Western Europe is not yet ready to exchange the security of relatively closed economic borders for the efficiencies of consolidation and the possibilities of competing more successfully for business around the world.

Those talks failed largely because France and Germany would not abandon agricultural subsidies that allow their farmers to sell surplus cereals around the world below the cost of production. And should that stalemate continue, Europe—like the rest of the world—is likely to drift toward protectionism, shunning trade with Asia and North America and increasingly turning its attentions inward.

The Decade of Economics

"I believe the 1990s will still be known as the decade of economics, and to that extent, the European Community will be a major geopolitical factor," says Robert Hunter, vice president of the Center for Strategic and International Studies.

"But the difficulties of coping with the crisis in Eastern Europe, rebuilding the eastern part of Germany, fending off immigration pressures and sustaining prosperous democracies will be so great that Europe's attention will be focused almost exclusively on its own continent."

a critical thinking activity

Evaluating Sources of Information

When historians study and interpret past events, they use two kinds of sources: primary and secondary. Primary sources are eyewitness accounts. For example, the diary of a Soviet citizen describing the changes occurring in his country would be a primary source. A newspaper article that paraphrases the citizen's diary entries would be a secondary source. Primary and secondary sources may be decades or even hundreds of years old, and often historians find that the sources offer conflicting and contradictory information. To fully evaluate documents and assess their accuracy, historians analyze the credibility of the documents' authors and, in the case of secondary sources, analyze the credibility of the information the authors used.

Historians are not the only people who encounter conflicting information, however. Anyone who reads a daily newspaper, watches television, or just talks to different people will encounter many different views. Writers and speakers use sources of information to support their own statements. Thus, critical thinkers, just like historians, must question the writer's or speaker's sources of information as well as the writer or speaker.

While there are many criteria that can be applied to assess the accuracy of a primary or secondary source, for this activity you will be asked to apply three. For each source listed on the following page, ask yourself the following questions: First, did the person actually see or participate in the event he or she is reporting? This will help you determine the credibility of the information—an eyewitness to an event is an extremely valuable source. Second, does the person have a vested interest in the report? Assessing the person's social status, professional affiliations, nationality, and religious or political beliefs will be helpful in considering this question. By evaluating this you will be able to determine how objective the person's report may be. Third, how qualified is the author to be making the statements he or she is making? Consider what the person's profession is and how he or she might know about the event. Someone who has spent years being involved with or studying the issue may be able to offer more information than someone who simply is offering an uneducated opinion; for example, a politician or layperson.

Keeping the above criteria in mind, imagine you are writing a book on how Japan's economic and political decisions might affect the new world order. You decide to cite an equal number of primary and secondary sources. Listed below are several sources that may be useful for your research. *Place a P next to those descriptions you believe are primary sources. Place an S next to those descriptions you believe are secondary sources.* Next, based on the above criteria, *rank the primary sources, assigning the number (1) to what appears to be the most valuable, (2) to the source likely to be the second-most valuable, and so on, until all the primary sources are ranked. Then rank the secondary sources, again using the above criteria.*

		Rank in
P or S		Importance
	1. A 1991 article by a German economist discussing the U.S. in the world economy from 1945 to 1965.	
	2. A *Time* magazine article paraphrasing comments made by the U.S. ambassador to the United Nations.	
	3. A commentary on Japanese management techniques by a leading Japanese executive.	
	4. An article from a Japanese magazine that reports on Europe's steps toward integration.	
	5. A report by the U.S. Army that argues for a strong national defense.	
	6. A French historian's 1990 book that analyzes the rise of Nazism during the 1920s in Germany.	
	7. An editorial from a Colombian magazine that criticizes the United States' aid program to Latin America.	
	8. A press release from the embassy of a Middle Eastern nation, criticizing U.S. aid to Israel.	
	9. An interview with Fidel Castro, in which Castro argues that the Soviets must take a guarded approach toward improved relations with the United States.	
	10. An article by a Dutch social scientist describing West German foreign policy during the 1980s.	

Periodical Bibliography

The following articles have been selected to supplement the diverse views presented in this chapter.

Peter Brimelow   "The Dark Side of 1992," *Forbes*, January 22, 1990.

Jacques Delors   "Europe's Ambitions," *Foreign Policy*, Fall 1990.

James Fallows   "Getting Along with Japan," *The Atlantic*, December 1989.

Niall Ferguson   "Über the Hill," *The New Republic*, February 4, 1991.

Jeffrey E. Garten   "Japan and Germany: American Concerns," *Foreign Affairs*, Winter 1989/1990.

Jim Impoco   "When in Doubt, Dodge and Delay," *U.S. News & World Report*, October 15, 1990.

Herve Jannic   "No Peace Dividend Is Yet in Sight," *World Press Review*, December 1990.

Toshiki Kaifu   "Japan's Vision," *Foreign Policy*, Fall 1990.

Paul Kennedy   "Fin-de-Siècle America," *The New York Review of Books*, June 28, 1990.

Paul Krugman   "Japan Is Not Our Nemesis," *New Perspectives Quarterly*, Summer 1990.

Richard McKenzie   "The Decline of America: Myth or Fate?" *Society*, November/December 1989.

Gianni De Michelis   "From Eurosclerosis to Europhoria," *New Perspectives Quarterly*, Spring 1990.

Joseph S. Nye Jr.   "The Misleading Metaphor of Decline," *The Atlantic*, March 1990.

Robert J. Samuelson   "Superpower Swan Song?" *Newsweek*, December 24, 1990.

Murray Sayle   "Axis, Ltd.," *The New Republic*, June 5, 1989.

Karel van Wolferen   "The Japan Problem Revisited," *Foreign Affairs*, Fall 1990.

What Role Will the U.S. Play in the New World Order?

THE NEW WORLD ORDER

Chapter Preface

From the end of World War II through the 1980s, United States foreign policy was dominated by its rivalry with the Soviet Union. As part of this rivalry, the U.S. developed a nuclear arsenal and deployed American troops in Western Europe to deter Soviet bloc aggression. In addition, the United States fought the Korean and Vietnam wars to limit Soviet influence in these areas. It also directed economic and military aid to allies who claimed to side with the U.S. against the Soviet Union, such as the Central American nations of El Salvador and Guatemala and the rebels in Afghanistan.

With the easing of Cold War tensions between the Soviet Union and the U.S. and the end of Soviet domination of Eastern Europe, many experts argue that it is time for America to reduce its role in world affairs. For example, Cato Institute scholar Ted Galen Carpenter maintains that since the communist threat no longer exists, the U.S. should withdraw from the financial and political burden of its many international commitments, especially military alliances such as the North Atlantic Treaty Organization (NATO). Jeane Kirkpatrick, former U.S. ambassador to the United Nations, contends, "Most of the international military obligations that we assumed were once important are now outdated." Experts on this side of the issue argue that the U.S. should not waste its resources on international commitments that are no longer relevant.

Other experts believe that the United States should maintain a leading military and political role in international affairs. Harvard professor Joseph S. Nye Jr. believes that only the United States has the economic, ideological, and military strength required of a leading world power. Nye and others worry that without the United States at the helm of world affairs, the resulting vacuum of power could lead to political and economic turmoil. Furthermore, foreign policy analysts such as Josef Joffe argue that the United States would benefit from being the leading world power because it could then shape developments, such as trade agreements, in its favor.

The viewpoints in the following chapter debate the future international role of the United States.

"With the decline of the Soviet Union, there is only one truly great power left."

The U.S. Should Maintain Its Role in World Affairs

Josef Joffe

In the following viewpoint, Josef Joffe argues that the decline in Cold War tensions does not mean America should lessen its role in world affairs. While the ideological conflict with the Soviet Union has subsided, Joffe contends, the military power of the USSR still poses a threat to the United States. Furthermore, the author asserts, the United States is the only nation capable of managing global problems such as Third World conflicts or instability in the world economy. The author is foreign editor of the German newspaper *Suddeutsche Zeitung.*

As you read, consider the following questions:

1. Why does Joffe believe that conflict will continue to play an important role in international affairs?
2. According to the author, what is the future of Soviet-American relations?
3. How would the United States benefit from continuing to be a world leader, in the author's opinion?

Josef Joffe, "Entangled Forever," *The National Interest,* Fall 1990, no. 21, © 1990 *The National Interest,* Washington, D.C. Reprinted by permission.

"If communism is dead," Irving Kristol pointed out to the 1990 gathering of the Committee for the Free World, "then anticommunism is dead, too.". . . Alas, there is more than a vacuous truism to this proposition. For it puts the axe to the roots of almost half a century of American foreign policy.

Or does it?

Realpolitikers would fiercely deny such a . . . pronouncement. They would insist that anticommunism was but the icing on the cake, rich as it was. American foreign policy since 1945 has followed interest rather than ideology, and so the former will outlive the latter. Cut through the anticommunist clamor, they would contend, and you discern the classic behavior of a normal great power. . . .

If the *realpolitikers* are right, then all is not lost now that "communism is dead" and Mikhail Gorbachev is dragging his country into democracy and the free market. If Russian power rather than Soviet ideology is the problem, then America's purpose must still address itself to the great existential threat embodied by Moscow. Communism might disappear, but thermonuclear weapons and vast conventional forces will not. (Precisely for this reason, even a disintegrating Muscovite empire will pose the single most important danger for world stability and American security.) Russian democracy would change hardball into softball, but not the rules themselves (which, at any rate, must always take into account a reversion to yesterday's pitching and slugging). Alas, in spinning this tale, the *realpolitiker* has left out a critical part. Democracies do not like *realpolitik*, and none has disliked it more than America, the oldest democracy which was founded in revulsion against the "corrupt game of princes" that was Europe's bloody lot. . . .

Isolationists and Internationalists

Yet if the Cold War . . . is over, then we have a problem. Neoisolationists could point to the collapse of Soviet power, declare victory, and go home. Internationalists could point to the collapse of communism, declare the "end of history," and also join the homeward trek. Both sides would unite in the conviction that America no longer needs to sustain the struggle—indeed, remain chained to the world—because the threat had vanished. Isolationists would feel safe in physical insulation; internationalists would conclude that the vision of the Enlightenment had at last come true. Since only despots make war, while democracies are inherently pacific, international politics henceforth will be reduced to global domestic policy. Welfare, not warfare, will shape its rules; global threats like ozone holes and pollution will dictate the agenda—and cooperation, to boot.

Realpolitikers ignore the domestic side of democratic foreign policy and pooh-pooh change. *Idealpolitikers* fall for the opposite temptation. Believing, as had Jefferson, that there is "but one system of ethics for men and for nations," they are always quick to spot a new "paradigm" in the making while ignoring that states, no matter what their constitution, remain chained to the self-help system. . . . In the self-help system, great conflicts like the Cold War may abate, even vanish—but not so the necessity to worry about security, status, and position. Old conflicts might return, new conflicts might supersede them. Even in peace, nations cannot take tranquility for granted as long as they live in a "state of nature" lacking both an arbiter of conflict and enforcer of peace.

The Potential for Conflict Remains

The existence of *states* defines the essence of the game. Whence it follows that only their disappearance could usher in a new paradigm of global politics. Yet despite the onslaught of trans-, sub-, and supranational forces, the nation-state is alive and well. And so, the old rules of the self-help system will survive, too. Nor do the retraction of Soviet power and the collapse of Soviet ideology change the fundamentals. Even without its far-flung empire, Russia will still be the largest country on earth. Even with a democratic political culture, nuclear-armed Russia will still be the only country that can annihilate the United States.

Third World Conflict

Instead of a new age of peace in the Third World, the post-cold war era may well witness the pursuit of expansionist policies by several regional powers. As Iraqi aggression has shown, the hegemonic ambitions of even relatively small states can have extremely serious repercussions throughout the world as well as in a particular region. No one regional power's expansionism poses the same worldwide threat as Soviet expansionism did in the past. But because regional hegemonism does pose serious threats to U.S. security interests, and because there are numerous potential hegemons in the developing world, the task of deterring and countering regional expansionism will require a more flexible and sophisticated U.S. foreign policy in the post-cold war era than did countering Soviet expansionism in the past.

Mark N. Katz, *The Washington Quarterly*, Winter 1991.

Has nothing changed then? This is not the real issue. If completed, the democratization of the Soviet Union certainly would remove the peculiar intensity that attended the conflict in decades past. If continued, the retraction of Soviet power will remove many sources of the struggle—above all in Europe, the original and foremost arena of the Cold War. . . . Yet waning stridency and diminishing stakes do not signify the end of conflict, let alone the end of the self-help system. And so, there is no exit for the United States.

First, take the Soviet Union. Though lily-white democrats they might yet become, the heirs of Lenin and Stalin will still preside over the greatest military power apart from the United States. Though the competition will be muted and encased by cooperation, one thing will and cannot change: Unless the USSR self-destructs or another superpower arises, only America and Russia can extinguish one another. That is an existential fact with consequences. It limits both trust and cooperation, and it will keep the game of containment and counter-containment going. Each must still keep a wary eye on the other, and each must take care that his competitor-partner does not accumulate too many assets that might yet be turned to malign uses. And so, American policy must still harken the commands of the self-help system, cooperating where it can and competing where it must.

Second, take the international system. Twenty years after the first wave of "multipolarism," whose proponents declared the death of bipolarity and the birth of a tri- or quintapolar world, there is now the sequel with the subtitle "The Decline of American Power." The obvious need not be gainsaid. The U. S. is good merely for a quarter of the gross global product, and no longer for one-half. Germany (plus the European Community) and Japan are serious, though still much smaller, commercial competitors, and there are at least five nuclear powers. As force has become less fungible, other "currencies" of influence have moved to the fore; power in general has become more diffused. Yet in a critical respect, the world is more "unipolar" than ever.

The Dominant Player

As was true twenty years ago, the U.S. is the only nation present at each gaming table—the strategic, the conventional-military, the diplomatic, economic, and ideological-cultural one. And at each table, it is the dominant player to boot. The Soviet Union was always a developing country with thermonuclear weapons; today, it is an economic basket case which has lost even its ideological trump card. To make this case is not to crow but to stress the special responsibility that has devolved upon America as its existential rival is deflating.

Nor are the new centers of power—Germany, Japan, China— ready to assume the burden of global management. China is a societal earthquake waiting to happen. Germany has its hands full with reunification and thereafter will be busy with its many conflicting obligations. . . . Japan will have to come to grips with the sharpening tensions between consumerism and mega-mercantilism before even beginning to contemplate an autonomous strategic role in East Asia. The mighty yen and deutschemark can always bring down the American dollar, beholden as it is to the German interest rate and to Japanese bond hoarders. But neither MITI [Ministry of International Trade and Industry] nor the Bundesbank can deal with Soviet SS-24 missiles, Lithuanian separatists, or Iraqi poison gas.

Which brings us to the third reason why there is no exit for the United States. As the previous dominant conflict (Cold War) is declining, many lesser ones (with a heavy growth potential) are jostling to take the Cold War's place. Here is an abbreviated checklist: the disintegration of the Soviet Union, Iraqi ambitions, Libyan mischief, economic catastrophe in Eastern Europe, Yugoslavia's explosion, Arab-Israeli war, nuclear and poison gas proliferation, Islamic fundamentalism, the collapse of the marvelous Western economy that stretches from Frankfurt via New York to Tokyo. Take your pick and try to imagine any crisis management minus the United States.

To all of this, a neo-isolationist might rightfully reply: "You have made the *world's* case for America's entanglement. But what's in it for the *United States?*" The point is well taken. To shoulder the burden would require a sense of responsibility that is (a) costly and (b) not self-evident . . . in the absence of an overweening ideological threat. Moreover, many items on the checklist of conflict do not undermine the isolationist creed because such crises do not necessarily affect American physical security. Let the Europeans take care of Libya's Qaddafi. Yugoslavia '90 is not Sarajevo '14; today, no great power will start World War III because of Serbian nationalism.

The American Role

The counter-reply is an old one. If you don't believe that power is destiny, then how about: "What is good for the world, is good for America?" While it is true that a nucleararmed United States can assure its own security (as it always could), great powers have interests which transcend their national space, requiring order beyond borders. Conflict in Yugoslavia may not spill over; conflict in the Middle East, a strategic locale harboring a strategic resource (oil), has a nasty habit of attracting outsiders. Europe may be on the road to pacification, but it is not foreordained that the Continent can take care of itself.

The underlying problem has hardly vanished. There is Russia, larger and militarily more potent than anybody else, and there is Germany, the biggest economic player at the fulcrum of the European balance which is now being liberated from the fetters of dependence the Cold War has wrought. On the other hand, there is an abiding American interest in European order for reasons both strategic and economic. . . . If the past 120 years are a guide, Germany and Russia are not the ideal co-managers. When they have not been at each other's throat, they have conspired against the rest while simultaneously trying to weaken each other. By contrast, Europe has flourished, as after 1945, when a power stronger than both was ensconced in the system. That power was, and remains, America.

The World's Leading Nation

The first thing to note about the decades immediately ahead is that the United States will be the world's leading nation—militarily and politically, and to a large extent economically as well. It may be that it will consent to leadership only reluctantly: will have "greatness thrust upon it." But it cannot, it seems to me, escape its destiny.

William A. Rusher, *Conservative Chronicle*, January 1, 1991.

The U.S. need not be there with 300,000 troops once force levels come down everywhere. But given America's stake in a prosperous and peaceful Europe, the U.S. ought to play the same role tomorrow as it did yesterday: as protector and pacifier from within. America on the inside would hold the balance against a diminished, but still potent Soviet Union. And in so doing, the U.S. would pull the sting of German power, thus allowing the entire continent to acquire the cooperative habits that came to bless Western Europe in the past forty years. . . .

Ambition, Fear, and Violence

But what if there is a "new paradigm" in the making—with welfare shouldering aside warfare? That would add, rather than subtract, reasons for America living up to its Number One role. Twenty years ago, exports came to 4 percent of American GNP [gross national product]; today, that proportion has more than doubled. At the same time, America's vulnerability to global economic forces (interest rates, capital movements, protectionism) has soared. While the U.S. can no longer dominate the world economy, its two closest competitors (Germany-EC and Japan) are neither willing nor able to assume the burden of global management that underlies the marvelous resilience of the Western economy. By virtue of size and position, the U.S. remains the hub. That role and new vulnerabilities hardly counsel self-sufficiency because the United States will suffer more than most if free trade and monetary stability collapse. But there is more: Precisely because the U.S. has accumulated new economic handicaps in the 1970s and 1980s, it must not abandon its politico-strategic assets. Being present in Europe, for instance, gives the U.S. a more audible say in economic decision-making than from a solitary perch across the Atlantic.

Granted, but why should Washington bomb Qaddafi, stop Iraqi nuclear ambitions, fiddle with Messrs. Yitzhak Shamir and Yassir Arafat, "resocialize" Iran, democratize Nicaragua, and seek a settlement in Cambodia? The answer is twofold. First, while peace and the "new paradigm" might yet rule over the "northern" world that stretches eastward from San Francisco to Vladivostok, the "old paradigm"—ambition, fear, and violence—is alive and well everywhere else. Second, these conflicts have a way of impinging on the United States. Iraqi nuclear weapons may pose threats at one step removed, but when Pan Am 103 explodes over Lockerbie, the challenge is direct, brutal, and bloody.

Wherever the "old paradigm" persists, American interests will be affected. Nor could American interests be scaled down like those, say, of Canada, in order to get out of harm's way. The United States is too big, too visible, and too much of a weight in the balance to revert to the role Tocqueville had described thus: . . . "the foreign policy of the United States . . . consists more in abstaining than in acting." Yet today, even abstention will have consequences for the world and then for America itself, and so there is no exit.

The Purpose and the Profit

Finally, there is also *pleasure* in being Number One. To exert power is better than suffering it; to be at the helm is better than hunkering down in the hold. With the Soviet Union (temporarily) receding from the world scene, the U.S. need not respond to each and every change by treating it as harbinger of bigger and worse things to come. There will be some safety in indifference, and not every crisis need be approached as if it were a wholly-owned subsidiary of American diplomacy. But the death of communism spells neither the birth of a new order nor the end of conflict. It is the great powers that build and maintain international order, and those who shape it most also gain most. With the decline of the Soviet Union, there is only one truly great power left in the system. Therein lies the purpose and the profit of American power at the threshold of the twenty-first century.

70

"With pacific neighbors, north and south, and vast oceans, east and west, to protect us, why seek permanent entanglement in other people's quarrels?"

The U.S. Should Reduce Its Role in World Affairs

Patrick J. Buchanan

In the following viewpoint, Patrick J. Buchanan argues that the United States should withdraw from its leadership role in international affairs. According to Buchanan, military and foreign aid commitments around the globe sap the strength of the United States. America, the author asserts, should concern itself with protecting only its vital interests. Buchanan is a syndicated columnist and a former presidential assistant to Richard Nixon and Ronald Reagan.

As you read, consider the following questions:

1. What is America's "national purpose," according to Buchanan?
2. What effect will the decline of the Soviet Union have on its allies, in the author's opinion?
3. What does the author believe should be the cornerstone of U.S. foreign policy?

Patrick J. Buchanan, "A New Nationalism," *The Wanderer*, March 15, 1990. Reprinted by permission: Tribune Media Services.

On the birthday of Thomas Jefferson, dead half a decade, the President of the United States raised his glass, and gave us, in a six-word toast, our national purpose: "The Union," Old Hickory said, "it must be preserved."

It was to "create a more perfect Union" that the great men came to Philadelphia; it was to permit the Republic to grow to its natural size that James K. Polk seized Texas and California; it was to preserve the Union—not end slavery—that Lincoln invaded and subjugated the Confederate states.

"A republic if you can keep it," Franklin told the lady in Philadelphia. Surely, preservation of the Republic, defense of its Constitution, living up to its ideals, that is our national purpose.

"America does not go abroad in search of monsters to destroy," John Quincy Adams said. "She is the well-wisher of the freedom and independence of all. She is the champion and vindicator only of her own."

Yet, when the question is posed, "What is America's national purpose?," answers vary as widely as those who take it. To Randall Robinson of TransAfrica, it is overthrow of South Africa; to Jesse Jackson, it is to advance "justice" by restoring the wealth the white race has robbed from the colored peoples of the earth; to AIPAC [American Israel Public Affairs Committee], it is to keep Israel secure and inviolate; to Ben Wattenberg, America's "mission" is a crusade to "wage democracy" around the world.

Each substitutes an extra-national ideal for the national interest; each sees our national purpose in another continent or country; each treats our Republic as a means to some larger end.

"National purpose" has become a vessel, emptied of original content, into which ideologues of all shades and hues are invited to pour their own causes, their own visions.

Is It Worth Fighting for?

In Charles Krauthammer's "vision," the "wish and work" of our nation should be to "integrate" with Europe and Japan inside a "super-sovereign" entity that is "economically, culturally, and politically hegemonic in the world." This "new universalism," he writes, "would require the conscious depreciation not only of American sovereignty but of the notion of sovereignty in general. This is not as outrageous as it sounds."

While Krauthammer's superstate may set off onanistic rejoicing inside the Trilateral Commission, it should set off alarm bells in more precincts than Belmont, Mass. As national purpose, or national interest, like all of the above, it fails the fundamental test: Americans will not fight for it.

Long ago, Lord McCauley wrote:

And how can man die better

72

Than facing fearful odds
For the ashes of his fathers,
And the temples of his Gods.

A nation's purpose is discovered not by consulting ideologies, but by reviewing its history, by searching the hearts of its people. What is it for which Americans have always been willing to fight?

Ed Gamble. Reprinted with permission.

Well, let us go back to a time when the Establishment wanted war, but the American people did not want to fight.

In the fall of 1941, Europe from the Pyrenees to Moscow, from the Arctic to North Africa, was ruled by Hitler's Third Reich; east of Moscow, Stalin's Gulag extended across Asia to Manchuria, where it met the belligerent Empire of the Rising Sun, whose domain ran to mid-Pacific. England was in her darkest hour. Yet, still, America wanted to stay out; we saw, in the world's bloody conflict, no cause why our soldiers should be sent overseas to spill a single drop of American blood. Pearl Harbor, not FDR [Franklin Delano Roosevelt], convinced America to go to war.

The isolationism of our fathers is today condemned, and FDR is adjudged a great visionary, because he sought early involvement in Britain's war with Hitler. But, even the interventionists' arguments were, and are, couched in terms of American national interest.

73

Perhaps we did not see it, we are told, but our freedom, our security, our homes, our way of life, our Republic were at risk. Thus do even the acolytes of interventionism pay tribute to the true national interests of the United States, which are not to be found in some hegemonic and utopian world order.

When Adams spoke, he was echoing Washington's farewell address that warned his fickle countrymen against "inveterate antipathies against particular nations, and passionate attachments for others. . . . The nation which indulges toward another a habitual hatred, or a habitual fondness, is in some degree a slave. It is a slave to its animosities or to its affections, either of which is sufficient to lead it astray from its duty and its interest.". . .

After V-E [Victory in Europe] Day and V-J [Victory in Japan] Day, all America wanted to "bring the boys home," and we did. Then, they were sent back, back to Europe, back to Asia, because Americans were persuaded—by Joseph Stalin—that the Cold War must be waged, because Lenin's Party had made the United States the "main enemy" in its war against the West. As the old saw goes, you can refuse almost any invitation, but when the man wants to fight, you've got to oblige him.

Troop Withdrawals

If the Cold War is ending, what are the terms of honorable peace that will permit us to go home? Are they not withdrawal of the Red Army back within its own frontiers, liberation of Central Europe and the Baltic republics, reunification of Germany, and de-Leninization of Moscow, i.e., overthrow of the imperialist party that has prosecuted the 70 Years' War against the West?

Once Russia is rescued from Leninism, its distant colonies, Cuba and Nicaragua, must eventually fall, just as the outposts of Japan's empire, cut off from the home islands, fell like ripe apples into the lap of General MacArthur. Withdrawal of the Red Army from Europe would remove from the hand of Mikhail Gorbachev's successor the military instrument of Marxist restoration.

The compensating concession we should offer: total withdrawal of U.S. troops from Europe. If Moscow will get out, we will get out. Once the Red Army goes home, the reason for keeping a U.S. army in Europe vanishes. Forty years after the Marshall Plan, it is time Europe conscripted the soldiers for its own defense.

As the Austrian peace treaty demonstrates, troop withdrawals are the most enduring and easily verifiable form of arms control. If we negotiate the 600,000 troops of the Red Army out of Central Europe, they cannot return, short of launching a new European war.

There is another argument for disengagement. When the cheering stops, there is going to be a calling to account for the crimes of Teheran, Yalta, and Potsdam, where the Great Men acceded to Stalin's demand that he be made cartographer of Europe. In the coming conflicts, over Poland's frontiers east and west, over Transylvania, Karelia, Moldavia, the breakup of Yugoslavia, our role is diplomatic and moral, not military.

In 1956, at the high-water mark of American power, the U.S. stood aside as Soviet tanks crushed the Hungarian revolution. With that decision, Dwight Eisenhower and John Foster Dulles told the world that, while we support freedom in Central Europe, America will not go to war with Russia over it. The year of revolution, 1989, revealed the logical corollary: from Berlin to Bucharest to Beijing, as Lord Byron observed, "Who would be free, themselves must strike the blow."

Would America be leaving our NATO [North Atlantic Treaty Organization] allies in the lurch? Hardly. NATO Europe contains 14 states, which, together, are more populous and three times as wealthy as a Soviet Union deep in an economic, social, and political crisis. Moreover, NATO would have a new buffer zone of free, neutral, anti-Communist nations between the Soviet and German frontiers. Our job will have been done.

To conquer Germany, the Red Army would have to cross a free Poland of 500 miles and 40 million, before reaching the frontier of a united Reich of 80 million, whose tradition is not wholly pacifist. In the first hours of invasion, Moscow would see her economic ties to the West severed, and a global coalition forming up against her, including Germany, France, Britain, China, Japan, and the United States. As the Red Army advanced, it would risk atomic attack. To what end? So the Kremlin can recapture what the Kremlin is giving up as an unwanted and unmanageable empire?

The day of the *realpoliticians*, with their Metternichian "new architectures," and balance-of-power stratagems, and hidden fear of a world where their op-ed articles and televised advice are about as relevant as white papers from Her Majesty's colonial office, is over. . . .

The Monroe Doctrine

But disengagement does not mean disarmament.

Still the greatest trading nation on earth, the U.S. depends on freedom of the seas for its prosperity. The strength of the U.S. Navy should be nonnegotiable; and when the President is invited to enter naval arms control negotiations, the answer should be no, even if it means Moscow walks out.

With the acquisition of ballistic missiles by China, Iran, Iraq, Syria, and Libya, with atomic weapons work being done in half a dozen countries of the Third World, the United States needs nay, requires, a crash research and development program for missile defense, to protect our homeland, our warships, our bases. No arms control agreement is worth trading away SDI

75

[Strategic Defense Initiative].

An island continent, America should use her economic and technological superiority to keep herself permanent mistress of the seas, first in air power, first in space. Nor is the cost beyond our capacity. For, it is not warships and weapons that consume half our defense budget; it is manpower and benefits. When defense cuts are made, they should come in army bases, no longer needed for homeland defense, and ground troops no longer needed on foreign soil.

A Normal Country

The United States performed heroically in a time when heroism was required; altruistically during the long years when freedom was endangered.

The time when Americans should bear such unusual burdens is past. With a return to "normal" times, we can again become a normal nation—and take care of pressing problems of education, family, industry, and technology. We can be an independent nation in a world of independent nations.

Jeane J. Kirkpatrick, *The National Interest*, Fall 1990.

As U.S. bases close down in Europe, we should inform Moscow we want all Soviet bases closed in the Caribbean and Central America, all Soviet troops out of the Western hemisphere. They have no business here. This is our hemisphere; and the Monroe Doctrine should be made again the cornerstone of U.S. foreign policy.

As the U.S. moves off the mainland of Europe, we should move our troops as well off the mainland of Asia. South Korea has twice the population, five times the economic might of North Korea. She can be sold the planes, guns, missiles, and ships to give her decisive superiority; then, U.S. troops should be taken out of the front line.

We are not going to fight another land war in Asia; no vital interest justifies it; our people will not permit it. Why, then, keep 30,000 ground troops on the DMZ [demilitarized zone]? If Kim Il Sung attacks, why should Americans be first to die? If we must intervene, we can do so with air and sea power, without thousands of Army and Marine dead. It is time we began uprooting the global network of "trip wires," planted on foreign soil, to ensnare the United States in the wars of other nations, to back commitments made and treaties signed before this generation of American soldiers was even born.

The late Barbara Tuchman wrote of the Kaiser that he could not stand it if, somewhere in the world, a quarrel was going on and he was not a party to it. Blessed by Providence with pacific neighbors, north and south, and vast oceans, east and west, to protect us, why seek permanent entanglement in other people's quarrels?. . .

The American Century

As we ascend the staircase to the 21st century, America is uniquely situated to lead the world.

Japan has a population older and not half so large as ours; her land and resources cannot match California's. Even united, the two Germanies have but a third of our population, a fifth of our gross national product, and a land area smaller than Oregon and Washington. Neither Japan nor Germany is a nuclear power; neither has a Navy or Air Force to rival ours; even their combined GNP is dwarfed by ours. While the Soviet Union has the size, resources, and population to challenge us as a world power, she is a prison house of nations whose ethnic hatreds and unworkable system mean a decade of turmoil. Who is left? The corrupt, bankrupt China of Deng Xaio-ping? It will not survive the decade. [Yasuhiro] Nakasone was right: The 20th century was the American Century. The 21st century will be the American Century as well.

But America can lead the world into the 21st century only if she is not saddled down by all the baggage piled up in the 20th.

For 50 years, the United States has been drained of wealth and power by wars, cold and hot. Much of that expenditure of blood and treasure was a necessary investment. Much was not.

We cannot forever defend wealthy nations that refuse to defend themselves; we cannot permit endless transfusions of the lifeblood of American capitalism into the mendicant countries and economic corpses of socialism, without bleeding ourselves to death. Foreign aid is an idea whose time has passed. The Communist and socialist world now owe the West a thousand billion dollars and more, exclusive of hundreds of billions we simply gave away. Our going-away gift to the globalist ideologues should be to tell the Third World we are not sending the gunboats to collect our debts, neither are we sending more money. The children are on their own. . . .

With the Cold War ending, we should look, too, with a cold eye on the internationalist set, never at a loss for new ideas to divert U.S. wealth and power into crusades and causes having little or nothing to do with the true national interest of the United States.

High among these is the democratist temptation, the worship of democracy as a form of government and the concomitant ambition to see all mankind embrace it, or explain why not. Like all idolatries, democratism substitutes a false god for the real, a love of process for a love of country.

When we call a country "democratic," we say nothing about

77

whether its rulers are wise or good, or friendly or hostile; we only describe how they were chosen, a process that produced Olaf Palme, Lopez Portillo, Pierre Trudeau, Sam Nujoma, Kurt Waldheim, and the Papandreous [father and sons], as well as Ronald Reagan.

Raul Alfonsin, elected president, led Argentina to ruin; while General Augusto Pinochet, who seized power in a coup, rescued Chile from Castroism, and leaves her secure, prosperous, and on the road to freedom. Why, then, celebrate Alfonsin, and subvert Pinochet?

As cultural traditions leave many countries unsuited to U.S.-style democracy, any globalist crusade to bring its blessings to the natives everywhere must end in frustration, and surely will be marked by hypocrisy. While the National Endowment for Democracy (NED) meddles in the affairs of South Africa, the State Department props up General Mobutu. Where is the consistency?. . .

How other people rule themselves is their own business. To call it a vital interest of the United States is to contradict history and common sense. And for the Republic to seek to dictate to 160 nations, what kind of regime each should have, is a formula for interminable meddling and endless conflict; it is a textbook example of that "messianic globaloney" against which Dean Acheson warned; it is, in scholar Clyde Wilson's phrase, a globalization of that degenerate form of Protestantism known as the Social Gospel.

Castles in the Air

"We must consider first and last," Walter Lippmann wrote in 1943, "the American national interest. If we do not, if we construct our foreign policy on some kind of abstract theory of rights and duties, we shall build castles in the air. We shall formulate policies which in fact the nation will not support with its blood, its sweat, and its tears." Exactly.

What do Tibetans, Mujahedeen, UNITA [National Union for the Total Independence of Angola] rebels, and contras have in common? Not belief in a bicameral legislature, or in separation of church and state, but love of liberty and a hatred of Communism. Is it not that spirit of patriotism that brought down the vassal regimes of Central Europe, that today threatens to tear apart the Soviet Empire?

"Enlightened nationalism," was Lippmann's idea of a foreign policy to protect America's true national interest. What we need is a new nationalism, a new patriotism, a new foreign policy that puts America first, and not only first, but second and third as well.

78

"Interdependence . . . makes it vital for governments to project their power to distant lands, or to mold the international system in their interests."

The U.S. Should Maintain an International Military Role

William R. Hawkins

William R. Hawkins is the director of the Hamilton Center for National Strategy, a Knoxville, Tennessee think tank concerned with foreign affairs and international economics. In the following viewpoint, Hawkins argues that, despite the collapse of communism, the United States requires a strong military to defend its interests. The greatest threat to the United States, the author contends, remains the Soviet Union, which has a powerful military. If the U.S. reduced its military, Hawkins concludes, it would lessen its ability to deter other countries from starting a war.

As you read, consider the following questions:

1. Why does the author believe that military conflict will not end with the collapse of communism?
2. In Hawkins' opinion, why does the Soviet Union remain a threat?
3. What does the author mean by the term "relative capabilities"?

William R. Hawkins, "New Enemies for Old," *National Review*, September 17, 1990, © 1990 by National Review, Inc., 150 E. 35th St., New York, NY 10016. Reprinted by permission.

A 1984 study by the Norwegian Academy of Sciences determined that since 3600 B.C. there had been 14,531 wars with only 292 years of peace over the entire span of 5,584 years studied. At that, the Academy undoubtedly missed some wars whose documentation has been lost in the mists of time. Historians James Dunnigan and William Martel, in their book *How to Stop a War*, describe some four hundred wars fought over the last two hundred years. The Lenz Peace Research Laboratory in St. Louis reports that there were 17 wars in progress during 1989. Conflict is inevitable in a world system divided into scores of culturally diverse and sovereign states competing to increase their share of wealth and power.

The Importance of Force

Those who claim that this will change with the advent of a global economy fail to realize that we have had some form of global economy for five hundred years. The effect of globalization has been to widen the scope and increase the scale of conflict. It is the very fact of interdependence that makes it vital for governments to project their power to distant lands, or to mold the international system in their interest. Only isolated states can afford to ignore each other.

During this century Communism generated a great deal of bloodshed through war and revolution. Yet there have been other wars in this century, including the two world wars, that were rooted in other ideologies, in religion, or in plain old power politics. In the 1980s, during which the U.S. liberated Grenada and supported the Contras' war in Nicaragua, it also used military force against foes not primarily (or at all) motivated by Communism in Libya, the Persian Gulf, Lebanon, and Panama. The breakup of the Communist world will not mean the end of war.

Military forces are the product of years of effort. Once degraded through neglect, they cannot be instantly regenerated in a crisis. The U.S. has a volunteer military with a small pool of reserves. Its standing forces must be strong enough to fight and win a limited war or hold the line in a larger conflict until the country can mobilize. As the Iraq crisis demonstrates, only conventional forces are capable of power projection to support American interests. The Navy, with its carriers and amphibious forces, is the basis of America's global reach. It has been called upon more often than any other service to respond in a crisis or to play a role in coercive diplomacy. The "reformers" and economy-minded critics of the aircraft carrier were left floundering in the wakes of the powerful battlegroups that were once again first on the scene.

Iraq also provides an example of why the U.S. must maintain

a strong army to practice "politics by other means." Against the 5,500 tanks and massed artillery of Iraq, it is clear that the "light" divisions of Marines and paratroopers favored by many post-cold-war commentators would not be enough. Heavy units (armor and mechanized infantry) are not just for Europe. Their mobility and firepower have proven indispensable from the jungle to the desert.

A World of Weapons

The resurgence of a militant Islam continues, and new waves of nationalism are sweeping across both ancient and modern states. Heavy tanks, high-performance aircraft, submarines, and missile systems of all types fill the arsenals of governments around the world. Forty-one Third World states possess a total of over 250 submarines. A dozen countries have one thousand or more heavy tanks. Forty have domestic armament industries. Many states in Latin America and the Middle East are developing ballistic missiles of intermediate range. . . . Nuclear-, chemical-, and even biological-weapon technologies have also proliferated. The countries most involved in acquiring these new systems (Argentina, India, Iran, Iraq, North Korea, and Syria) would require a substantial military effort to subdue. In such a world, U.S. forces must be both mobile and potent in firepower, with large munition stockpiles to sustain the high tempo of modern combat.

Regional Threats

With respect to regional conflicts, the centrality of military strength continues unabated. The proliferation of nuclear weapons, chemical weapons and ballistic missiles is simultaneously placing enormous military capabilities at the disposal of national leaders, some of whom have not shown a great capacity for moderation.

Michael Nacht, *The Washington Post National Weekly Edition,* April 23-29, 1990.

Though there is little political support in the abstract for U.S. intervention in another "land war in Asia" (or the Middle East, or Latin America), wars are not fought in the abstract. At some point a concrete situation arises that requires large-scale military action. The armed forces must be ready if such action is to be a viable option. In the words of General Colin Powell, chairman of the Joint Chiefs of Staff, "If we're going to have a superpower sign outside our door, we've got to be ready to back it up. . . . We've always got to be ready for the contingency nobody has planned for and the crisis nobody knew was coming until it arrived."

But even though maintaining world order against the threats of Third World dictators like Saddam Hussein will be an increasing responsibility for the U.S. Government, our principal defense task will remain deterrence of the Soviet military threat. For, whatever its changing political intentions—which may, of course, change back again—and whatever the current divisions and lack of morale in the Red Army—and these could, of course, be remedied by a vigorous new military leadership—the Soviet Union remains a superpower with the world's most powerful military machine. Even if a START [Strategic Arms Reduction Talks] agreement reduces heavy ICBMs [intercontinental ballistic missiles] by 50 per cent, the Soviets will still be able to improve, in relative terms, their capabilities against hard targets. Continued deployment of new mobile missiles like the SS-24 and SS-25, a new modification of the SS-18, and improved submarine-launched missiles (SS-N-20 and SS-N-23) will result in a more accurate, survivable, and dangerous Soviet nuclear force.

Soviets Still a Threat

Even during the Reagan buildup of the early 1980s, the USSR expanded its conventional forces faster than the U.S. did. Recently, of course, the 2.5 to 1 edge that the Warsaw Pact held over NATO's [North Atlantic Treaty Organization] Central Front has been reduced by the withdrawal of the armies belonging to the non-Soviet members of the Pact. In addition, Mikhail Gorbachev has announced some unilateral cuts. Yet even so the Red Army alone, without its former Warsaw Pact partners, is still stronger than NATO. Indeed, if the entire military might of the Central European states were added to NATO, the USSR would still be numerically stronger in a campaign for Central Europe.

The Soviet navy continues to grow, with more tonnage delivered in 1989 than in any other year in the decade thanks to the commissioning of its first full-deck fleet aircraft carrier, the *Tbilisi*. At 75,000 tons, it will deploy naval versions of first-line combat aircraft (MiG-23 and MiG-19). A second carrier of the same class, the *Riga*, is being fitted out, and a larger carrier, perhaps nuclear powered, is under construction. The Soviets are also increasing their amphibious-landing capabilities. Meanwhile, Moscow's large and expanding airborne/air-transport capacity will continue to give it a substantial capability for power projection outside Europe.

The current enthusiasm for military cuts in Washington is based on the assumption that the risk of war in Europe has diminished. But even if the USSR renounces Communism and becomes again merely Russia, a "normal" great power, the potential for conflict will remain. After all, Russia conquered the largest land area in the world before Lenin was born. And it should be kept in mind that the purpose behind Gorbachev's reforms is to make the USSR/Russia a more capable and effective competitor in the world arena. As Donald M. Snow, a professor at the Army War College, recently stated, "The Stalinist system has become a millstone around the neck of Soviet national aspirations." Gorbachev wants to remove the millstone, and we cannot forecast his aspirations with certainty.

Formidable Force

Until Kuwait, the "disarms race" going on between the White House and Congress had rekindled the Soviets' belief that their position would be enhanced by American withdrawal from Europe. If (as seems likely) the Soviets do eventually withdraw their own troops from Central Europe, would the Administration be able to persuade Congress to maintain the troop level (195,000) set by President George Bush?

The Red Army

We must understand what is really happening to Soviet military capabilities. We know that right now their armed forces appear to be the instrument of a much more benign foreign policy. But we also know that while reductions and restructuring are in fact ongoing, the Soviets are not demobilizing or disarming. . . . Yes, the Soviet army is going home. But it is not disbanding. When this is all over, the Red Army will still be modern and capable and several million strong. Still the major Eurasian military power. Others may wish to ignore that or say it doesn't matter. . . . It does matter.

And as far as their nuclear capacity is concerned, the Soviets are not giving up any capabilities that will be allowed under a new strategic arms agreement. The Soviet nuclear arsenal that threatens our very homeland, is still intact and it is being modernized to the state-of-the-art.

Colin L. Powell, speech to the California Town Hall, Los Angeles, March 23, 1990.

Of course, even after a withdrawal, Soviet troops would remain only a train ride away, whereas American forces would have to recross the Atlantic with limited air- and sea-lift capacity. The risk of a Soviet "bolt from the blue" attack against NATO would be reduced. However, this has never been the most likely way for a European war to start. Most scenarios assume a period of crisis that escalates, a time during which both sides reinforce the front line. Soviet commanders have been practicing methods for rapid mobilization based on higher peacetime readiness. Jeffrey W. Legro, a Fellow at the Rand/ UCLA [University of California, Los Angeles] Center for Soviet Studies, has recently written that Soviet officials "continue to recognize the offensive as the dominant form of operations. . . .

It may be that the forward-based, standing-start threat has decreased, yet the USSR will continue to maintain a powerful force potential on its territory." Pre-emptive strikes also remain a key element in Soviet thinking. Albert L. Weeks of New York University has recently cautioned that "it is necessary, at all times, to temper one's convictions that wholesale change is in the air with respect to the deep-rooted Soviet principles of war-fighting."

It is also wise to study the impact of reform on Red Army strength. In the November 1989 *International Defense Review,* Edward Ezell of the Institute for Research on Small Arms in International Security argued that Soviet ground forces were being transformed into a "technologically based and more efficient force."

Another noted observer of Soviet military affairs, Stephen Zaloga, reported in the May 1990 *Armed Forces Journal* that the Red Army is close to deploying battlefield beam weapons, such as lasers to blind electro-optical sights and air crews, and radio-frequency weapons and particle-beam projectors to burn out electronics.

In the air, the Soviets are hard at work on follow-on designs for the MiG-29 and SU-27 all-weather multirole fighters, both of which only entered service in the 1980s. Meanwhile, the U.S. is cutting back funds for its own Advanced Tactical Fighter (many in Congress want the program canceled) and the various European programs for a new fighter are experiencing technical and financial problems.

Relativity Theory

Above all, however, what counts in conflict is not absolute force levels, but relative capabilities. If virtually all U.S. combat units are withdrawn from Europe, the army of a unified Germany is reduced to half its current size, and substantial cuts are made by other NATO members, the Soviets' position could actually improve even as their forces decrease in numbers. A smaller, but harder-hitting and more mobile, Red Army might be able to blitz its way through a NATO army that was only a shadow of its former self. As Lieutenant General Horst Jungkurth, Chief of Staff of the Luftwaffe, points out, the Soviet Union's "geostrategic advantage of interior lines allows a rapid concentration of forces." Further, massive numerical superiority is not necessary across the entire front, only at the decisive points. In short, a combination of Western disarmament and Soviet military modernization may make a numerically smaller Red Army a greater strategic threat.

Advocates of a "peace dividend" claim that $30 billion could be saved annually if half the U.S. troops deployed in Europe were brought home. Yet this would be true only if these units were not only withdrawn but also disbanded. The additional cost of keeping troops in Germany rather than Texas is small next to the total cost of personnel, fuel, weapons, and supplies that these units need simply to exist wherever they are located.

Many Americans—including some conservatives—see defense cuts as a way to balance the federal budget without raising taxes. The nation has given in to this kind of penny-wise, pound-foolish thinking before. After the 1930 London Naval Treaty, President Hoover initiated major cuts in warships in order to balance the budget, a decision that weakened deterrence later in the decade, with dire consequences. As Selig Adler said of this period in his classic book *The Isolationist Impulse*, "The treaties they made relied for enforcement only on the good will and the continued power of the Japanese liberals. Today we know this was a vain hope." The United States dares not risk providing a future historian with the material for making the same comment about our current policy.

"It no longer is necessary or desirable for the U.S. to play the role of Atlas, carrying the security burdens of the planet on its shoulders."

The U.S. Should Reduce Its Military Role

Ted Galen Carpenter

During the Cold War, the United States stationed troops around the world in its struggle against communism. In the following viewpoint, Ted Galen Carpenter argues that the Cold War is over, and the United States should drastically reduce its military. Not only is the maintenance of Cold War military strength unnecessary, Carpenter says, but it is also extremely expensive. Carpenter is director of foreign policy studies at the Cato Institute, a public policy research foundation.

As you read, consider the following questions:

1. Why does the author believe that the U.S. should not use its military to prevent instability?
2. Why does Carpenter dislike military alliances?
3. According to the author, what foreign policy should the United States adopt?

Ted Galen Carpenter, "Uncle Sam as the World's Policeman: Time for a Change?" Reprinted from *USA Today* magazine, January 1991. Copyright © 1991 by the Society for the Advancement of Education.

The Bush Administration apparently intends to preserve the principal features of America's activist Cold War strategy in a post-Cold War world and to maintain unnecessarily high levels of military spending. Its proposed $306,000,000,000 1991 defense authorization bill is 16% higher in real terms than was the 1981 budget adopted immediately after the Soviet invasion of Afghanistan and the collapse of detente. Even the original projections for the 1995 budget were nearly eight percent higher. The Bush Administration gradually has been retreating from that position, with the President announcing plans for a 25% reduction in military personnel. That action is a belated step in the right direction, but we can and should make far deeper cuts, both in personnel and weapon systems.

Blueprint for Disaster

More disturbing than the grudging nature of the Administration's budget cuts has been the pervasive attitude that the fundamentals of America's Cold War strategy of global interventionism should remain intact despite vastly altered international conditions. Typical of the reasoning is the comment in Secretary of Defense Richard B. Cheney's 1990 report to the President and Congress that the U.S. must strive to "attain the same basic strategic objectives with a somewhat smaller defense budget." The President himself has sought to preserve venerable Cold War institutions such as NATO [North Atlantic Treaty Organization] by formulating vague alternative missions. NATO and the U.S. military presence in Europe, he affirms, will be needed for decades, not to deter a Warsaw Pact invasion (which even he concedes is now utterly improbable), but to prevent "instability and unpredictability."

That approach is a blueprint for the indefinite prolongation of expensive and risky U.S. military commitments around the globe. The international system always has been quite unstable and unpredictable, and there is little evidence that the future will be significantly different. However, instability *per se* does not threaten America's security. Indeed, in a post-Cold War world, there may be many local or regional disputes that are (or at least should be) irrelevant to the security interests of the U.S. . . .

U.S. leaders must learn to distinguish between vital and peripheral—much less nonexistent—security interests. During the Cold War, American policymakers tended to regard even the most trivial geopolitical assets as essential. However, to be considered a threat to a vital interest, a development should have a direct, immediate, and substantial, connection with America's physical survival, its political independence, or the preservation of its domestic freedoms. Threats to truly vital interests are relatively rare, and they may be even rarer in a post-Cold War setting where no potential adversary is capable of making a bid for global domination.

Irrelevant Commitments

In that context, the preservation of America's Cold War system of alliances is ill-advised. Not only are such commitments expensive, they are profoundly dangerous. As Cato Institute senior fellow Earl C. Ravenal has noted, alliances are "lethal transmission belts for war," converting what should be minor, localized conflicts into wider confrontations between great powers.

The World's Changing.
I WANT FEWER OF YOU FOR THE U.S. ARMY.

Reprinted by permission of Mike Luckovich and Creators Syndicate.

There are various flash points around the world where Cold War-era commitments to clients could entangle the U.S. In addition to the volatile Persian Gulf, the tense situations involving Pakistan and India, Syria and Israel, and the two Koreas are the most visible examples. The Balkans and other portions of Eastern Europe also could become caldrons of ethnic strife.

There has been much discussion of a "peace dividend" emerging from the end of the Cold War, but without an entirely new defense strategy, there will be no such dividend for Americans to enjoy. Instead, Washington will perpetuate a vast array of increasingly irrelevant commitments and the military forces to defend them. The statements of Secretary of State James A. Baker III and other Administration officials that the U.S. will need a long-term military presence in the Persian Gulf . . . exemplify both the logic and the consequences of global interventionism.

The pursuit of stability is a chimera. Even when a problem is "solved" and stability in a particular region is restored, it is rarely more than a temporary achievement. New revisionist powers invariably arise, revolutions can replace pliant regimes with hostile ones, and the maneuvering for advantage on the part of rival states continues unabated. That is especially true of the volatile Middle East, but it also applies to most regions. If the U.S. insists on linking its security interests to the achievement of global stability, and thereby injects itself into a host of regional quarrels, it will need military forces that are larger, more diverse, and more expensive than those maintained to wage the Cold War.

Expensive Mistakes

The connection between force levels and commitments is crucial. Military units do not exist for their own sake, but to fulfill specific missions, and creating and maintaining those forces is inherently costly. For example, 11 of the Army's 18 divisions exist to help defend Western Europe from a Warsaw Pact invasion. Similarly, the Navy's alleged need for 14 aircraft carrier battle groups is predicated on the continuation of U.S. commitments to allies and clients in Europe, the Far East, and the Persian Gulf. Even the size of the U.S. strategic arsenal is largely the result of embracing the doctrine of extended deterrence—shielding other nations with our nuclear umbrella.

The pertinent question is whether such commitments serve America's security interests, especially now that the Cold War is over. With the decline of the Soviet threat and no other would-be hegemonic power on the horizon, a global network of U.S.-dominated alliances appears to make little sense—particularly given its enormous expense. NATO alone costs American taxpayers more than $130,000,000,000 each year. Washington's commitments to Japan, South Korea, and other nations in the Far East run $40,000,000,000, and our Persian Gulf commitments add another $40,000,000,000.

It was one thing to undertake such expensive and risky obligations to prevent Soviet global domination, as improbable as that danger may seem in retrospect. It is quite another to perpetuate those obligations merely to prevent vaguely defined instability or discourage the outbreak of local quarrels that have little or no relevance to America's security interests.

Washington fails to recognize that other democratic powers are now important actors in the global arena—the Bush Administration proceeds on the assumption that only the U.S. can deter aggression. That may have had some validity in the years following World War II when Europe lay in ruins, Germany and Japan were occupied and disarmed, and the geostrategic environment was starkly bipolar, but today the situation is changed radically. It no longer is necessary or desirable for the U.S. to play the role of Atlas, carrying the security burdens of the planet on its shoulders. The time has come—indeed, it is long overdue—to transfer the entire responsibility for their own defense to prosperous and capable world powers. . . .

Outdated Policies

The fact is that communism is now almost everywhere in disintegration, and that the part of it which truly represented a military threat—the Soviet Union—is unraveling, preoccupied with its own internal problems, and has lost as allies its subjected satellites in Eastern Europe. There is no longer a meaningful Warsaw Pact. One must ask why there is need any longer for a military alliance called NATO? One concludes that the only reason we seem committed is inertia. And so we continue to think of new nuclear missiles, and we remain committed to maintaining armies in Europe and Japan, bases around the world, and a huge military establishment proportionately twice the size of those of our allies.

Nathan Glazer, *The National Interest*, Fall 1990.

Instead of attempting to preserve expensive and dangerous alliances and other military commitments, the U.S. should adopt a new policy of strategic independence for the post-Cold War era. This would be based on three factors: a recognition that the Soviet threat has declined, a narrower and more rigorous definition of America's vital security interests, and the appreciation that other nations now have the economic strength to provide for their own defense needs without a U.S. subsidy.

By phasing out its global network of alliances and adopting a course of strategic independence, the U.S. radically could downsize its military establishment. The most important changes would include reducing the number of aircraft carrier battle groups from 14 to six and tactical air wings from 40 to 17; cutting the number of Army divisions from 18 to two and combining the remaining units with the Marine Corps in a new mobile strike force; scaling down the strategic arsenal from more than 12,000 warheads to 3,000-3,500; eliminating such unnecessary systems as the MX and Midgetman missiles, the B-2 Stealth bomber, and the C-17 transport plane; and placing greater emphasis on defending American territory and lives than on power projection in distant regions, which requires the development of an effective defense against ballistic missiles.

A Sizable Peace Dividend

Under a regime of strategic independence, the U.S. eventually could defend its legitimate security interests with a military force of only 905,000, compared with the 2,044,000 proposed in the Administration's 1991 budget—and the force of 1,635,000 contemplated in the revised 1995 projections. Adopting that strategy would enable the U.S. to reduce its military spending to $120,000,000,000 within five years. That is a sizable peace dividend by any definition. It not only would eliminate the alleged need for a tax increase to narrow the budget deficit, it could (and should) lead to substantial tax reductions. The American people have borne great risks and burdens throughout the Cold War; they now deserve to reap the benefits from the end of that long, twilight struggle.

"The U.S. economy remains almost twice the size of Japan's, nearly five times that of a united Germany, and larger . . . than the entire EC [European Community]."

The U.S. Will Remain an Economic Leader

Joel Kotkin

According to Joel Kotkin, the United States is likely to continue as the world's leading economic power through the twenty-first century. Kotkin argues that, contrary to the claims that the U.S. is in decline, America has maintained its position in the world economy. American leadership will continue, Kotkin contends, because the country has superior workers and vast resources. Kotkin is an international fellow in the school of business and management at Pepperdine University in Malibu, California.

As you read, consider the following questions:

1. According to Kotkin, what do European leaders foresee as the U.S. role in the world economy?
2. How does the author support his view that the United States has maintained its lead role in the world economy?
3. In the author's opinion, what factors may impede Asia's economic growth?

Joel Kotkin, "Reports of America's Death Are Greatly Exaggerated," *The Washington Post National Weekly Edition*, May 28-June 3, 1990. Reprinted with permission.

Until recently, most doomsday predictions of American economic decline were reactions to the rising power of Japan and other Pacific Rim nations. But now, dazzled by the spectacular events in Eastern Europe and the growing assertiveness of the continent's leaders, some Americans are adding a rendition of *Europe Uber Alles* [Europe Over All] to the more familiar bemoanings of the Asiatic peril.

Author and economist Walter Russell Mead, for instance, speaks of a new united Germany that "could push the United States out of Europe, into inglorious isolation in the Western Hemisphere." New York investment banker Jeffrey Garten of the Stamford Co. envisions a unified Europe, in tandem with Japan, dominating world money markets for decades because "America's strength is evaporating."

Out of the Picture?

For their part, our erstwhile European allies seem barely able to suppress their delight. Such conservative European leaders as former French prime minister Jacques Chirac and German Chancellor Helmut Kohl now speak openly about a future dominated totally by Europe and the Asian Pacific countries.

Further on the left, these perceptions are giving rise to a whole new school of post-North American geopolitics. Perhaps the most explicit of the new theorists is Jacques Attali, a leading adviser to French President Francois Mitterand and the odds-on choice to head the new $12 billion European Development Bank designed to aid the nations of Eastern and Central Europe in building free-market economies.

In his new book, *Lignes d' horizon,* a bestseller in France, and in recent interviews, Attali envisions a world breaking down into two main "cores"—one located between the European Community (EC) and the vast reaches of Soviet Russia; the other perched along the Pacific Rim. As for the United States— which is providing 10 percent of the European Development Bank's initial funding—Attali dismisses it as a pathetic ghost. "America," he said in an issue of *New Perspectives Quarterly,* "has become Japan's granary like Poland was for Flanders in the 17th century." He regards America as hopelessly behind Japan in virtually every economic field. The only region with a future is the West Coast, largely because it is "in the gravitational pull of Japanese financial power and geographic proximity."

While America turns "sadly inward," Attali sees Europe gaining strength. His proposed "European core"—including a democratizing Eastern Europe and the Soviet Union—could "overtake the elaborate Asian standard, and the values of European civil society—liberty and democracy—could stretch across the entire planet."

How credible is this Euro-chauvinistic vision? Its validity rests on assumptions of American decline and what Attali calls Europe's *"potentalite de development gigantesque"* [potential for enormous development]. Admittedly, the European economic growth rate has risen over the past few years. But most of Attali's presuppositions are about as solid as a soufflé.

America's share of the world economy—although far lower than its immediate post-war highs—has held steady over the past decade at between 22 percent and 24 percent, roughly the same as before World War II. Today the U.S. economy remains almost twice the size of Japan's, nearly five times that of a united Germany, and larger, by most measurements, than the entire EC.

Success Perceived as Failure

The question of America's future success in a global economy is too often confused with the issue of our regaining our postwar position as economic dictator to the world. That role is gone forever, and no one should wish it otherwise. The income of urban adults in the major industrialized countries is now practically uniform. That was the explicit objective of American statesmanship at the end of the war, the crowning adornment of our postwar foreign policy, a grand aim expressly adopted, pointedly pursued, and unambiguously attained. To seize upon that success as an index of relative "decline" is to miss the point.

Charles R. Morris, *The Atlantic Monthly*, October 1989.

Since it began recovering from the 1982 recession, U.S. economic growth has averaged 4 percent a year, two-thirds higher than West Germany's. Even since 1987—despite a "boom" prompted largely by in-migrations of Germans from the East as well as American and Japanese investments made to beat possible protectionism following European economic integration in 1992—economic growth in the United States has remained generally above the overall European levels.

Moreover, North America's share of manufacturing jobs in the non-socialist world held even throughout the 1980s (as did Japan's). The gainers during the decade were mostly among the industrializing nations of Asia; the only clear losers were the Europeans. In addition, European unemployment remains at nearly twice American levels; in Spain unemployment among those under age 25 had climbed to near 47 percent by the late '80s.

Nor is American industry becoming less competitive. In 1989 the United States overtook West Germany as the world's largest exporting nation. At the same time, American industrial productivity—which Attali claims is falling way behind Europe's—has been rising since the early 1980s at a rate somewhat higher than those on the continent. Today the cost of production in the United States is lower than in either Japan or West Germany. In fact, according to recent Bureau of Labor Statistics surveys, the American worker remains by far the most productive on earth. In 1988, U.S. gross domestic product per employed person (based on equivalent purchasing power) was 22 percent higher than Germany's, 17 percent above France and nearly 40 percent higher than Japan. And, as the *Economist* recently pointed out, the purchasing power of American workers remains 7 percent above their closest rivals, the Canadians.

The Perils of Integration

Ironically, perhaps the greatest threats to European growth are the policies likely to be adopted by the new Eurocrats such as Attali. If carried out in a free-market tradition . . . European integration in 1992 could well spark a renaissance. But many in Europe fear that the alliance will squander its opportunities by following the old French *dirigisme* [planned economy] dream of building "world competitors" through massive state subsidization and consolidation.

"We fear the commission will use its power to establish huge European enterprises—even if it means reduced competition," notes Rudiger Thiele, a top economic adviser to West German Chancellor Helmut Kohl. "There is a powerful tendency in this direction within the commission and every country. This is the great idea in Europe now."

If Thiele is correct, the first fruits of European integration may not be the doubling of growth promised by its promoters, but a spate of consolidations which, according to one recent private survey, could mean an initial loss of 500,000 jobs. Europe may be on the verge of repeating many of the same corporate pathologies that characterized American conglomeration in the 1960s and '70s—large, unfocused bureaucracies, unhealthy concentrations of market power and resistance to innovation.

As for Eastern Europe, the supposed savior and limitless market for the EC, problems also abound. These include, for example, a $60 billion clean-up cost for ecologically devastated East Germany, continuing political instability in Romania, Bulgaria and Yugoslavia, and the disintegration of the Soviet Union. With some of the world's highest per-capita debt rates, Eastern Europe, notes Columbia University Business School's James Rodgers, is more likely to be "the next South America rather than the next Southeast Asia."

Finally, with socialists and Greens now in control of the European parliament, yet other dangers lurk for a rebirth of continental enterprise. These include the imposition of a so-called "European Social Charter," a package of generous guarantees and accommodations for trade unions, which, according to the European Roundtable, "would bring serious risks to the competitiveness" of the Community.

American Strengths

Meanwhile, the Japanese find their stiffest competition not from Attali's European "core" but from the supposedly decadent Americans. Indeed, by the magic date of 1992, according to a recent survey by Dataquest, non-Japanese Asia will surpass Europe in the production of semiconductors, leaving the continent in a rather precarious fourth place. Europe—despite oft-repeated homilies about its well-educated workforce—also lacks the technical manpower to battle either Japan or North America. Even Germany boasts 40 percent *fewer* technical workers per million than the United States and only half as many as Japan.

Qualified for Leadership

In the global economic boom of the 1990s, human resources will be the competitive edge for both companies and countries. In this regard, no country is better positioned than the United States. The United States has the richest mix of ethnic groups, racial groups, and global experience that the world has ever known, and it is the *richness* of this mix that yields America's incredible creativity and innovation.

John Naisbitt and Patricia Aburdene, *Cato Policy Report*, May/June 1990.

At the same time, Asian powers are beginning to confront labor shortages, a decline in their fabled work ethic and a domestic consumption binge. Yet America remains a magnet for many firms and individuals abroad. Since 1970 the United States alone has attracted more than 11 million new *legal* immigrants—more than the rest of the world combined. Many of these newcomers, particularly from Taiwan, India and other Asian countries, are highly skilled additions to our technical workforce; and many of them—along with millions of illegal immigrants—provide much of the manual workforce that Japan and Taiwan now sorely lack.

In the future this immigration will provide North America with a critical demographic advantage over both Western Europe and Japan. Europe may seek to root out its estimated 8 million Third World immigrants—West Germany is offering incentives to get an estimated 1.5 million Turks out of the country—but its own populations are barely replacing themselves. A study reported in *American Demographics* projected that during the 1990s, the labor force of the United States and Canada will grow by 8.2 percent—more than twice the rate for Japan and Southern Europe and a full percent above Eastern Europe. The survey estimates that during the same period, Western Europe's workforce will decline by nearly 1 percent.

The Choice for Investors

Capital, too, has been flowing to North America. In part this flow is because of far greater reserves of developable land, making our continent among the least expensive places to invest in the advanced industrial world. Office and land costs in Los Angeles, for instance, are now as much as one-sixth of those in Tokyo and one-third the rates in major continental centers. For this and other reasons, America is consistently the first choice of investors from Japan, the Chinese diaspora, South Korea and Europe. Even the French invested nearly 25 percent more in the United States between 1986 and 1988 than they did in the "core" countries of Britain, Italy and West Germany combined. . . . North America's prospects are clearly far from hopeless. While Europeans, in their graceful old capitals, dream about a social democratic paradise in their regulated, crowded continent, while the Japanese and other Asians learn to enjoy affluence, no region is better positioned to embody mankind's dreams for the coming century.

"If the U.S. does not meet the challenge of new competition, it surely will . . . slip to number two in the world economy."

U.S. Economic Leadership Is Threatened

Abu K. Selimuddin

The United States, facing tough economic competition from Asia and Europe, can no longer take its leading role in the world economy for granted, argues Abu K. Selimuddin in the following viewpoint. Selimuddin points to a number of indicators, from America's trade deficit and loss of world markets to its poor national savings rate, to argue that the foundation of American economic superiority is weakening. Only by undertaking a serious effort to boost its economic competitiveness, the author concludes, can the United States remain number one. Selimuddin is a professor of business at Berkshire Community College in Massachusetts.

As you read, consider the following questions:

1. What are the defining characteristics of the world economy, in the author's opinion?
2. How has the growth of American manufacturing productivity compared to that of Japan and Germany, according to Selimuddin?
3. What does the author believe is wrong with American labor?

Abu K. Selimuddin, "Will America Become Number Two?" Reprinted from *USA Today* magazine, September 1989. Copyright © 1989 by the Society for the Advancement of Education.

World War II radically altered the fate and future of many countries. Nations that were once the strongest, such as Great Britain and France, came out of the war weakened economically and militarily. Their colonies, from which they previously derived economic power and strength, won independence. Japan and Germany lost the war, which left them in ruins. In contrast, it helped free America from the terrible grip of the Great Depression, which had lasted over a decade.

At the end of World War II, America emerged as the economic leader of the free world economy and has remained the undisputed champion since. In the 1950's and 1960's, the U.S. virtually had faced no fearful challenger. It was the number-one GNP [gross national product] producer in the world economy, and Americans enjoyed the highest standard of living, made possible by the largest per capita income in the world.

In international commerce, it enjoyed an absolute monopoly of market share by leading in world manufacturing exports. Trade deficit, national debt, and inflation were not the critical concerns worrying Americans then. The U.S. was also the biggest creditor and net exporter of capital across the globe. For example, through the Marshall Plan, America provided a total of $12,000,000,000 to the non-communist countries of Europe. Another $3,000,000,000 in grants and trade credits went to Japan to rebuild its war-devastated economy between 1945 and 1955. Encouraged by the success in Western Europe and Japan, the U.S. turned its attention to helping the Third World countries of Africa, Asia, and Latin America by becoming the most generous aid donor to the capital-poor countries of the free world.

A Competitive Global Economy

Today's global economy is much more competitive. Nations of the East—such as Japan and Asia's four "little dragons" (South Korea, Taiwan, Singapore, and Hong Kong)—and West have closed the gigantic lead in economic power once held by the U.S. America's domination of manufacturing exports and world market share is long gone. The U.S. now feels threatened by the shrinkage in its economic clout, which has been eroding since 1970.

In contrast, Japan already is enjoying the fruit of its "economic miracle" by being able to produce 70% of America's GNP. Most economic historians predict that Japan's per capita income will surpass America's by 20% at the turn of the century. By the 1980's, Japan's GNP was higher than the combined GNP's of Britain and France and it outproduced Britain in 1966 and France and Germany in 1967. Tokyo's stock exchange is the largest in the world, and most of the top banks in the world are situated in Japan. It is now the largest exporter of capital, made possible by its $1,000,000,000-a-day saving rate and trade surpluses estimated at $85,000,000,000 annually.

War-devastated West Germany also has made a comeback with strength and vigor. Its per capita income has risen to about $14,000, which is about 84% of America's, up from 40% in 1950. Germany enjoys a high saving rate and the second largest trade surplus after Japan.

© 1990 by Cartoonews, Inc. Reprinted with permission.

The European Economic Community [EEC] in its report, "The Economics of 1992," predicts a six percent growth in the Common Market's GNP. According to the experts, the elimination of internal barriers among EEC nations will make European products more attractive to their consumers than imports. American companies, which sell more to Europe than Japanese firms, are bound to experience more serious losses.

Asian Growth

Asia's "little dragons" have gotten bigger, better, and richer. They have high levels of education to absorb sophisticated technology; their growth rate averaged an impressive eight percent from 1984 to 1989, causing some shift of economic weight to the East; they are among the top 20% of manufacturing exporters in the world; and their total exports equal 80% of Japan's. Japan now imports from the "little dragons" twice what she did in the early part of this decade. All of them enjoy trade surpluses with America. They also have accumulated huge surpluses of yen, whose dramatic appreciation should give them extra impetus to enhance their competitive position relative to the U.S.

Thailand, China, India, and Indonesia also have great potential. Many other developing countries have projected annual growth rates of more than five percent. By contrast, in 1980, America exported $26,000,000,000 more to newly industrialized nations than it imported; in 1986, it imported $28,000,000,000 more than it exported.

What is also profoundly different today is the speed and scope of growth in world markets. Cheaper and faster transportation and information systems have expanded trade and travel. Interdependence among countries has been accelerated by a boom in foreign direct investment. Third World nations have been drawing increasing attention from Japan and America as cheap labor sources and consumer markets. Japan is making eyes at Asia's sleeping giant, China, by offering the Chinese a loan of over $5,000,000,000 to finance economic projects. Japan and China can derive enormous strength from each other by building an economic bridge between the world's most dynamic economy and the largest reservoir of labor and consumer markets.

Losing Security?

In the global competition of market-grabbing, the rise of the East may mean less economic security for the West.

Forty years ago, who would have imagined that America, the biggest and the best, would have to worry about its industrial competitiveness and ability to hold on to the number-one spot in the world economy? Yet, many experts, including the President's Commission on Industrial Competitiveness, have concluded that its capacity to compete in the world market is eroding.

"We are still number one, but we have come down a notch or two. The fear is that we may fall even further," warns Alan Greenspan, chairman of the Federal Reserve System. Several facts support this view:

Signs of the Slide

• While the U.S. share of global GNP has been falling since 1972, other countries, such as Japan, Germany, and Asia's "little dragons," were increasing theirs. In annual per capita income gain, Japan and Germany averaged 4.3% and 2.5%, respectively, between 1981 and 1989, while Asia's "little dragons" averaged a very impressive eight percent. In contrast, the U.S. had a 1.8% average increase during the same period.

• America is turning into a capital-poor country because of a dismally low rate of domestic saving. In 1986 and 1987, Americans saved only 2-2.5% of their disposable income. In contrast, Great Britain saved five percent, major industrialized nations averaged 10%, and the Japanese banked about 18%. America's capital-crunch is forcing the U.S. to sign more IOU's to get loans from Japan and others in order to keep expansion going.

• U.S. investment in plant and equipment during the 1980's was less than in the 1950's, 1960's, or 1970's, and its capital-labor ratio grew less quickly than any of America's major competitor nations.

• America is losing ground in manufacturing productivity to Japan and Germany. Its annual growth rate in manufacturing averaged 0.3% in the last five years, compared with 7.8% and 0.8%, respectively, for Japan and Germany.

Jobs and Products

• Japan is able to introduce new products faster than its competitors, constantly improve their quality, and adapt them to changing market environments. American firms do not make innovations incrementally. Instead, they tend to move from one production plateau to another. As a consequence, change takes more time and involves more risk.

• America's rising propensity to import and lack of competitiveness in exports have caused a mountainous deficit in trade balance—a negative export-import balance of 6.2%, while Japan and Germany grew 2.1% and 1.3%, respectively. Among the top 15 key manufacturing exportables, Japan led in automobiles, steel, telecommunications, instruments, textiles, semiconductors, and machine tools. Germany was first in petrochemicals, plastics, pharmaceuticals, and aluminum. In contrast, America led only in aircraft and computers, and its market share in the latter is down by seven percent since 1980. Blue-collar and rural employment are falling, partly as a consequence of the loss in manufacturing production and export.

• The U.S. is exporting jobs overseas. For example, in 1980, 6.9% of domestic consumer goods were imported, up from 5.4% in 1975; by 1987, 11.6% were imports. In capital goods, America imported 15% in 1980, compared with eight percent in 1975; by 1987, imports reached nearly 40% of total consumer products.

Not Meeting the Challenge

• America rapidly is losing its semiconductor market share to Japan. The takeover of semiconductor chip production raises the fear that the Pentagon may have to depend entirely on the Japanese for its needed chips for weapons. For example, six of the world's 10 largest semiconductor producers are now Japanese; a decade ago, only two were. Since 1980, America's share

of the world semiconductor market has declined from 60% to 40%, while Japan has doubled its share to 50%.
• Japanese auto makers are more cost efficient and productive than the U.S.'s. For example, the cost difference between an average American and a comparable Japanese car is now over $600. American man hours per car is 150, in comparison to 100 man hours in Japan. By 1995, the U.S. expects to reduce the man hours per car from 150 to 100, while Japan hopes to reduce it to 80.
• Japanese manufacturing facilities are newer and more modernized than American plants—10 years old, on average, as compared to 20 years in the U.S.

Living Beyond Our Means

U.S. consumers and corporations are living beyond their means because exports are not paying for the surge of imports. America's trade deficit, which reflects consumers' and businesses' debts, reached an all-time high of $175,000,000,000 in 1987. In contrast, Japan and Germany enjoyed surpluses of $75,000,000,000 and $45,000,000,000, respectively. These countries are recycling their accumulated trade surpluses by lending to American consumers, corporations, and government. They also are using these surpluses in buying pieces of America. Foreign investment in the U.S. amounted to $260,000,000,000 in 1987. By 1990, the estimated foreign ownership of America could stand at 10%, up by six percent from 1988. More foreign ownership will mean more influence on America's economic and political policy-making. The U.S. also will lose more economic clout in the world economy.

American Business

American business, with the exception of perhaps space and satellite technology, is no longer leading the world as it did 20 years ago. For example, in 1975, the first 15 places on the *Fortune* 500 list of the world's largest companies included 11 American corporations. Now there are only seven. Further, in the early 1970s, America's computer industry controlled 90 percent of the U.S. market. By 1990, Japan had surpassed it in many areas.

Werner Meyer-Larsen, *World Press Review*, January 1991.

Other bleak facts lead to prospects of a continuing decline:
• American workers put in less work-hours and are less productive than their counterparts in Japan and Germany. During the last decade, American labor productivity gain was 40% of Japan's and 60% of Germany's. Annual work hours per American are

1,700, compared to 2,400 in Japan.

- U.S. factory workers are the world's highest paid. In contrast, Koreans earn 15%, Taiwanese 17%, Brazilians 11%, and Japanese 70% of what Americans receive. Low hourly compensation, combined with productivity levels that match those in America, partly explains why the newly industrialized countries are gaining in competitiveness. In contrast, higher labor costs and lower productivity are pushing a number of U.S. manufacturing firms to move production overseas, causing loss of jobs and income at home. . . .

Financial Failure

- In the U.S., Federal debt has doubled since 1981 to a mind-boggling $2.8 trillion. The ratio of debt to GNP rose from 34.21% in 1980 to 55% in 1988. Interest fees on national debt is now three percent of GNP. This is dangerous for America's wealth. . . .
- Long the world's largest creditor and capital exporter, the U.S. is now the largest debtor in the global economy. America's net foreign debt is equivalent to seven percent of 1988's GNP. In the same year, Japan and Germany had net foreign assets of 8.5% and 10.5% of their respective GNP's. The power of Japan's growing economic might is well-demonstrated by its having budgeted $10,000,000,000 on foreign aid in 1989, displacing America, which committed $9,500,000,000, as the world's number-one aid donor. . . .
- America has fallen behind the Japanese in the global financial race. For example, the biggest Japanese investment bank, Nomura, has $1,000,000,000 more equity and 10 times more market value than America's largest, Merrill Lynch. Among the world's biggest commercial banks, the first four are Japanese-owned; the biggest U.S. commercial bank, Citicorp, is number five. International assets of American banks total $580,000,000,000, while Japan's are $640,000,000,000.

An Immediate Response Is Required

America has lost some business battles in the world economy, but not yet the major war. "The United States still earns and enjoys the world's highest real income per capita. If we call the U.S. level 100, . . . Canada is next to us, in the high 90's. Norway, West Germany, Sweden, and Switzerland are all below 90. Japan is scarcely yet at 80. . . . The Soviet Union is below 50," observes Nobel Laureate in Economics Paul A. Samuelson. Since 1973, the U.S. has added 35,000,000 new jobs; in contrast, the entire Common Market has created about 6,000,000 during the same time. Despite everything, America is still the locomotive to the free world economy.

However, one must not take comfort in thinking that the U.S.

always will be number one. What America needs to do—and do quickly—is sharpen its competitiveness in the global marketplace. If the U.S. does not meet the challenge of new competition, it surely will lose its leadership to the East and slip to number two in the world economy by the end of this century.

Ranking Priorities for a New World Order

This activity will allow you to explore the priorities you think are important to the United States in the establishment of a new world order. Your answers may differ from those of other readers, mirroring the complexity of international affairs.

Opinions about the best role for the U.S. in the new world order may vary among people with different international goals. For example, while the primary objective of the president of the United States is to promote American interests, the head of the United Nations may seek international cooperation as his or her first priority. Similarly, the president of a poor Third World nation such as Bangladesh may want the U.S. to give economic and food aid to help eliminate poverty.

The authors in this chapter offer several opinions regarding the role America should play in the new world order. The concerns listed on the following page mirror many of these opinions.

Part I

Working individually, rank the new world order concerns listed below. Decide what you believe to be the most important priorities for America's role in the new world order and be ready to defend your answers. Use number 1 to designate the most important concern, number 2 for the second most important concern, and so on.

_____ fighting communism in Latin America and Asia

_____ supporting democratic countries in the Third World

_____ encouraging cultural exchange between countries

_____ using the military to deter aggressor nations

_____ improving America's economy

_____ removing U.S. barriers to trade to increase economic cooperation

_____ reducing poverty in America

_____ supporting democratic political parties in Eastern Europe

_____ protecting U.S. citizens and companies abroad

_____ providing economic and food aid to the Third World

Part II

Step 1. The class should break into groups of four to six students. Students should compare their rankings with others in the group, giving reasons for their choices. Then the group should make a new list that reflects the concerns of the entire group.

Step 2. In a discussion with the entire class, compare your answers. Then discuss the following questions:

1. Did your opinion change after comparing your answers with those of other group members? Why or why not?

2. Consider and explain how your opinions might change if you were:

   a. a manager of an American multinational corporation

   b. the president of a poor, democratic country in Africa

Periodical Bibliography

The following articles have been selected to supplement the diverse views presented in this chapter.

Robert L. Brosage — "Time to Commit Politics," *Social Policy*, Spring 1990.

Ted Galen Carpenter et al. — "In from the Cold War," *Reason*, March 1991. Available from the Reason Foundation, 2716 Ocean Park Blvd., Suite 1062, Santa Monica, CA 90405.

John Lewis Gaddis — "Coping with Victory," *The Atlantic*, May 1990.

John Gray — "The Brazilianization of America," *Fortune*, August 27, 1990.

Stanley Hoffmann — "After the Cold War: What Should the U.S. Do?" *The Atlantic*, October 1989.

Michael T. Klare — "The U.S. Military Faces South," *The Nation*, June 18, 1990.

Robert Kuttner — "The Abyss," *The New Republic*, October 29, 1990.

Charles William Maynes — "America Without the Cold War," *Foreign Policy*, Spring 1990.

Sylvia Nassar — "It's Gloves-Off Time," *U.S. News & World Report*, December 25, 1989/January 1, 1990.

Paul Nitze — "America: An Honest Broker," *Foreign Affairs*, Fall 1990.

Joseph S. Nye Jr. — "The U.S.: Managing Global Responsibilities," *The World & I*, January 1991. Available from 2800 New York Ave. NE, Washington, DC 20002.

Colin L. Powell — "U.S. Foreign Policy in a Changing World," *Vital Speeches of the Day*, May 1, 1990.

Theodore C. Sorensen — "Rethinking National Security," *Foreign Affairs*, Summer 1990.

Stephen Van Evera — "The Case Against Intervention," *The Atlantic*, July 1990.

Ben J. Wattenberg — "How Bright Is America's Future?" *Reader's Digest*, August 1990.

William C. Westmoreland — "A Strong American Military," *The New York Times*, May 28, 1990.

What Role Will Economics Play in the New World Order?

THE NEW WORLD ORDER

Chapter Preface

Since the end of World War II, the level of international trade and investment has grown steadily: world trade expanded from $70 billion in 1950 to about $3 trillion in 1989. Many experts believe that the end of the Cold War will allow nations to participate in even more trade and join in a new period of economic cooperation and prosperity. After all, these analysts contend, with military and defense concerns greatly reduced by the passing of the Cold War, nations will be able to focus more on economic issues.

Experts who support this idea emphasize that several powerful economic and technological forces will bring the economies of the world together and encourage cooperation. Roger B. Porter, a U.S. government assistant for economic policy, believes that the growing number of multinational corporations and falling costs for international communication and transport will speed the trend toward global cooperation. Porter and others contend that these forces can help companies establish factories in foreign countries because computers, satellite communication, and fax machines make it easy to monitor operations at a plant thousands of miles away. Improvements in transportation allow products to be shipped quickly and inexpensively anywhere across the globe.

Some analysts, however, worry that not all nations will welcome increased international trade and investment. Individual countries may attempt to protect domestic jobs and industries from foreign competitors. For instance, Japan places restrictions on rice imports to protect its rice farmers. Restrictions such as these may increase as international trade increases. These actions could lead to trade protectionism, trade wars, or even trading blocs—groups of nations that trade freely among themselves but exclude the products of other countries. As *Los Angeles Times* reporters Doyle McManus and Robin Wright argue, "By the end of the 1990s, the world could be divided into three rival trading blocs grouped around the United States, Japan and the German-led European Community."

The viewpoints in the following chapter debate the role of economics in the new world order.

"In the new 'geo-economic' era not only the causes *but also the* instruments *of conflict must be economic."*

Economic Competition Will Replace Military Conflict

Edward N. Luttwak

From the wars of Alexander the Great to the two world wars of the twentieth century, military conflict has played a major role in international affairs. In fact, until the recent improvement in relations between the Soviet Union and the United States, the world trembled at the possibility that the two superpowers would repeat this historic pattern of warfare. In the following viewpoint, Edward N. Luttwak argues that, while conflict between nations will continue, it will no longer take on a military form. Instead, Luttwak contends, conflict will be played out in the realm of economics. The author is a scholar at the Center for Strategic and International Studies in Washington, D.C.

As you read, consider the following questions:

1. What effect did the Cold War have on international economics, according to Luttwak?
2. Why does the author think that international conflict will persist after the Cold War?
3. In the author's opinion, how will modern economic conflict differ from mercantilism?

Edward N. Luttwak, "From Geopolitics to Geo-Economics," © *The National Interest*, Summer 1990, no. 20, Washington, D.C. Reprinted with permission.

Except for those unfortunate parts of the world where armed confrontations or civil strife persist for purely regional or internal reasons, the waning of the Cold War is steadily reducing the importance of military power in world affairs.

The End of Conflict?

True, in the central strategic arena, where Soviet power finally encountered the *de facto* coalition of Americans, Europeans, Japanese, and Chinese, existing military forces have diminished very little so far. Nevertheless, as a Soviet-Western war becomes ever more implausible, the ability to threaten or reassure is equally devalued (and by the same token, of course, there is no longer a unifying threat to sustain the coalition against all divisive impulses). Either way, the deference that armed strength could evoke in the dealings of governments over all matters—notably including economic questions—has greatly declined, and seems set to decline further.

Everyone, it appears, now agrees that the methods of commerce are displacing military methods—with disposable capital in lieu of firepower, civilian innovation in lieu of military-technical advancement, and market penetration in lieu of garrisons and bases. But these are all tools, not purposes; what purposes will they serve?

If the players left in the field by the waning importance of military power were purely economic entities—labor-sellers, entrepreneurs, corporations—then only the logic of commerce would govern world affairs. Instead of World Politics, the intersecting web of power relationships on the international scene, we would simply have World Business, a myriad of economic interactions spanning the globe. In some cases, the logic of commerce would result in fierce competition. In others, the same logic would lead to alliances between economic entities in any location to capitalize ventures, vertically integrate, horizontally co-develop, co-produce, or co-market goods and services. But competitively or cooperatively, *the action on all sides would always unfold without regard to frontiers.*

If that were to happen, not only military methods but the logic of conflict itself—which is adversarial, zero-sum, and paradoxical—would be displaced. This, or something very much like it, is in fact what many seem to have in mind when they speak of a new global interdependence and its beneficial consequences.

Logic and Grammar

But things are not quite that simple. The international scene is still primarily occupied by states and blocs of states that extract revenues, regulate economic as well as other activities for various purposes, pay out benefits, offer services, provide infra-structures, and—of increasing importance—finance or otherwise sponsor the development of new technologies and new products. As territorial entities, spatially rather than functionally defined, states cannot follow a commercial logic that would ignore their own boundaries.

What logic then do they follow?

Do they seek to collect as much in revenues as their fiscal codes prescribe—or are they content to let other states or blocs of states tax away what they themselves could obtain? Since the former is the reality (that is, a zero-sum situation in which the gain of one is the loss of another), here the ruling logic is the logic of conflict.

Economic Hostility

The arguments for global cooperation in the maintenance of open markets will continue to be exceedingly strong. Yet they may not be strong enough to prevent prolonged bouts of economic hostility among the world's economic powers.

Raymond Vernon, *The World & I*, September 1990.

Do they regulate economic activities to achieve disinterestedly transnational purposes or do they seek to maximize outcomes within their own boundaries, even if this means that the outcomes are suboptimal elsewhere? Since the latter is the predominant, if not exclusive, reality, economic regulation is as much a tool of statecraft as military defenses ever were. Hence, insofar as external repercussions are considered, the logic of state regulation is *in part* the logic of conflict. As such, its attributes include the typically warlike use of secrecy and deception for the sake of surprise (as, for example, when product standards are first defined in secret consultations with domestic producers, long before their public enunciation).

The Logic of Conflict

Do states and blocs of states pay out benefits and offer services transnationally—or . . . do they strive to restrict such advantages to their own residents? Likewise, do they design infrastructures to maximize their transnational utility—or do they aim for domestically optimal and appropriately competitive configurations, regardless of how others are affected? Since the latter is the reality, the logic of state action is again *in part* the logic of conflict. (The competitive building of huge international airports in adjacent, minuscule, Persian Gulf sheikhdoms is an extreme example of such behavior, but such conduct is not uncommon in milder forms.)

Finally, do states and blocs of states promote technological innovation for its own sake—or do they seek thereby to maximize benefits within their own boundaries? Since the latter is the reality, the logic of conflict applies. (Three obvious examples are the obstacles that long delayed the introduction of Concorde flights into U.S. airports, Japanese barriers against U.S. supercomputers and telecommunications, and the development of rival High Definition Television formats.)

As this is how things are, it follows that—even if we leave aside the persistence of armed confrontations in unfortunate parts of the world and wholly disregard what remains of the Cold War—World Politics is still not about to give way to World Business, i.e., the free interaction of commerce governed only by its own nonterritorial logic.

Instead, what is going to happen—and what we are already witnessing—is a much less complete transformation of state action represented by the emergence of "Geo-economics." This neologism is the best term I can think of to describe the admixture of the logic of conflict with the methods of commerce— or . . . the logic of war in the grammar of commerce.

The Nature of the Beast

With states and blocs of states still in existence, it could not be otherwise. As spatial entities structured to jealously delimit their own territories, to assert their exclusive control within them, and variously to attempt to influence events beyond their borders, states are inherently inclined to strive for relative advantage against like entities on the international scene, even if only by means other than force. . . .

States will tend to act "geo-economically" simply because of what they are: spatially-defined entities structured to outdo each other on the world scene. For all the other functions that states have acquired as providers of individual benefits, assorted services, and varied infrastructures, their *raison d'etre* and the ethos that sustains them still derive from their chronologically first function: to provide security from foes without (as well as outlaws within). . . .

It is true, of course, that, under whatever name, "geo-economics" has always been an important aspect of international life. In the past, however, the outdoing of others in the realm of commerce was overshadowed by strategic priorities and strategic modalities. Externally, if the logic of conflict dictated the necessity for cooperation against a common enemy while, in contrast, the logic of commerce dictated competition, the preservation of the alliance was almost always given priority. (That indeed is how all the commercial quarrels between the United States and Western Europe—over frozen chickens, microchips,

114

beef, and the rest—and between the United States and Japan—from textiles in the 1960s to supercomputers in the 1980s—were so easily contained during the past decades of acute Soviet-Western confrontation. As soon as commercial quarrels became noisy enough to attract the attention of political leaders on both sides, they were promptly suppressed by those leaders—often by paying off all parties—before they could damage political relations and thus threaten the imperative of strategic cooperation.) Internally, insofar as national cohesion was sustained against divisive social and economic tensions by the unifying urgencies of external antagonisms, it was armed conflict or the threat of it—not commercial animosities—that best served to unite nations.

Not a Replay of Mercantilism

Now, however, as the relevance of military threats and military alliances wanes, geo-economic priorities and modalities are becoming dominant in state action. Trade quarrels may still be contained by the fear of the economic consequences of an action-reaction cycle of punitive measures, but they will no longer simply be suppressed by political interventions on both sides, urgently motivated by the strategic imperative of preserving alliance cooperation against a common enemy. And if internal cohesion has to be preserved by a unifying threat, that threat must now be economic. Such a reordering of modalities is already fully manifest in the expressed attitudes of other Europeans to the new undivided Germany, and even more so in American attitudes toward Japan. Mikhail Gorbachev's redirection of Soviet foreign policy had barely started when Japan began to be promoted to the role of the internally unifying Chief Enemy, judging by the evidence of opinion polls, media treatments, advertisements, and congressional pronouncements.

Should we conclude from all this that the world is regressing to a new age of mercantilism? Is that what "geo-economics" identifies, quite redundantly? Not so. The goal of mercantilism was to maximize gold stocks, whereas the goal of geo-economics (aggrandizement of the state aside) could only be to provide the best possible employment for the largest proportion of the population. In the past, moreover, when commercial quarrels evolved into political quarrels, they could become military confrontations almost automatically; and in turn military confrontations could readily lead to war.

In other words, mercantilism was a *subordinated modality*, limited and governed by the ever-present possibility that the loser in the mercantilist (or simply commercial) competition would switch to the grammar of war. Spain might decree that all trade to and from its American colonies could only travel in Spanish bottoms through Spanish ports, but British and Dutch armed merchantmen could still convey profitable cargoes to disloyal colonists in defiance of Spanish sloops; and, with war declared, privateers could seize outright the even more profitable cargoes bound for Spain. Likewise, the Dutch sent their frigates into the Thames to reply to the mercantilist legislation of the British Parliament that prohibited their cabotage, just as much earlier the Portuguese had sunk Arab ships with which they could not compete in the India trade.

The End of the Military Threat

"Geo-economics," on the other hand, is emerging in a world where there is *no superior modality*. Import-restricted supercomputers cannot be forcibly delivered by airborne assault to banks or universities in need of them, nor can competition in the world automobile market be assisted by the sinking of export car ferries on the high seas. That force has lost the role it once had in the age of mercantilism—as an *admissible* adjunct to economic competition—is obvious enough. But of course the decay of the military grammar of geopolitics is far more pervasive than this, even if it is by no means universal.

The Role of Economics

Events that are radiating outward from Germany to change the world highlight a domestic imperative for the United States: to adjust the instruments of its foreign policy and national security. Even though military power will still remain important, both economic instruments of foreign policy and underlying national economic strength and vitality will become more critical. Indeed, the events of 1989 have provided a basic lesson for America: The 1980s were marked by significant growth in spending on defense, but the 1990s—beyond the Cold War—will be dominated by economics.

Robert E. Hunter, *The World & I*, February, 1990.

Students of international relations may still be taught to admire the classic forms of *realpolitik*, with its structure of anticipatory calculations premised on the feasibility of war. But for some decades now the dominant elites of the greatest powers have ceased to consider war as a practical solution for military confrontations between them, because non-nuclear fighting would only be inconclusively interrupted by the fear of nuclear war, while the latter is self-inhibiting. . . .

For exactly the same reason, military confrontations were themselves still considered very much worth pursuing—and rightly so, for war was thereby precluded throughout the decades of Soviet-Western antagonism. More recently, however, the dominant elites of the greatest powers appear to have concluded that military confrontations between them are only dissuasive of threats that are themselves most implausible. It is that new belief that has caused the decisive devaluation of military strength as an instrument of statecraft in the direct relations of the greatest powers.

Hence, while the methods of mercantilism could always be dominated by the methods of war, in the new "geo-economic" era not only the *causes* but also the *instruments* of conflict must be economic. If commercial quarrels do lead to political clashes, as they are now much more likely to do with the waning of the imperatives of geopolitics, those political clashes must be fought out with the weapons of commerce: the more or less disguised restriction of imports, the more or less concealed subsidization of exports, the funding of competitive technology projects, the support of selected forms of education, the provision of competitive infrastructures, and more. . . .

An Opportunity for Mutual Benefits

Perhaps the pan-Western trade accords of the era of armed confrontation with the Soviet Union—based on the original General Agreement on Tariffs and Trade—may survive without the original impulse that created them, and may serve to inhibit the overt use of tariffs and quotas as the geo-economic equivalent of fortified lines. And that inheritance of imposed amity may also dissuade the hostile use of all other "geo-economic" weapons, from deliberate regulatory impediments to customs-house conspiracies aimed at rejecting imports covertly—the commercial equivalents of the ambushes of war. But that still leaves room for far more important weapons: the competitive development of commercially important new technologies, the predatory financing of their sales during their embryonic stage, and the manipulation of the standards that condition their use—the geo-economic equivalents of the offensive campaigns of war.

Today, there is a palpably increasing tension between the inherently conflictual nature of states (and blocs of states) and the intellectual recognition of many of their leaders and citizens that while war is a zero-sum encounter by nature, commercial relations need not be and indeed rarely have been. The outcome of that tension within the principal countries and blocs will determine the degree to which we will live in a geo-economic world.

"War, and potential war, will remain a feature of international politics."

Economic Competition Will Not Replace Military Conflict

Eliot A. Cohen

Eliot A. Cohen is a professor of international studies at Johns Hopkins University in Baltimore, Maryland. In the following viewpoint, Cohen challenges the notion that warfare is no longer practical for nations to pursue. As long as nations are motivated by fear, greed, and ambition, the author contends, warfare will continue to dominate international relations.

As you read, consider the following questions:

1. According to the author, what role will nuclear weapons play in international relations?
2. In Cohen's opinion, how will the spread of democracy affect the possibility of war between states?
3. What did Alexander Hamilton say about the chance for "perpetual peace"?

Elliot A. Cohen, "The Future of Force," *The National Interest*, Fall 1990. Copyright © 1990 Elliot A. Cohen. Reprinted with permission.

What direction should American strategy take? Indeed, does it have a future at all, or has the end of the Cold War and the apparent triumph of liberal democracy and capitalism in Eastern Europe rendered it obsolete? If the need for strategy—defined as the preparation and use of military power for the ends of policy—does persist, how should Americans prepare themselves to meet the challenges of the last decade of this century? . . .

For over forty years American strategy and defense planning has focused on the Soviet threat. That threat is disintegrating, and Soviet military power is undergoing a long-term and irreversible reduction. If so, one must ask where American defense planning should concentrate its attention henceforth, and how it should adapt to new challenges. Such a mammoth practical and conceptual task would be complex enough in any circumstances. It is made more difficult, however, by a variety of arguments to the effect that military force is no longer an important factor in world politics, that traditional considerations of *Machtpolitik* will lose or have lost their primacy; that force, in other words, is finished. . . .

Nuclear and Chemical Weapons

There are three core arguments for the dwindling importance of force in international politics. First, it is maintained that the development of the techniques of warfare have made military power increasingly unappealing as a tool of international politics; or, more extreme, that modern weapons have made military power *unusable* for purposes of foreign policy. Nuclear weapons create the kind of stalemate that perversely but blessedly created the long peace of the Cold War; chemical weapons serve as the poor man's atomic bomb; conventional weaponry including such modern refinements as cluster bombs, fuel-air explosives, and multiple rocket launchers make even that form of conflict too difficult to control. Not man's virtue, but his diabolical ingenuity in creating engines of destruction, has brought peace. Or has it?

Nuclear weapons probably—one cannot be certain about events that did not happen—prevented an all-out U.S.-Soviet war. But nuclear weapons have most assuredly not prevented the launching of wars, some quite large, against nuclear-armed states. The North Koreans and Chinese in the Korean War, the Vietnamese Communists in the Indochina War, the Arabs in the Yom Kippur War, and the Argentines in the Falklands War did not let their opponents' nuclear weapons stop them from using a great deal of force to secure their political objectives. Vast disproportions in firepower attributable to nuclear weapons did not prevent the Vietnamese from fighting a bitter frontier war with China, Afghan mountaineers from harassing Soviet invaders, or Palestinian and Shiite terrorists from raiding Israeli border settlements. And the real or potential existence of nuclear weapons has come very close to *inducing* warfare, as indicated by Soviet feelers about preventive war against China in the Nixon administration and the Israeli raid on the Iraqi Osirak reactor. Nuclear weapons exercise certain kinds of inhibiting effects on conflict, but in other cases they may provoke it—would the United States, indeed *should* the United States stand idly by if Muammar Qaddafi were to acquire an atomic bomb? . . .

Are chemical weapons the equivalent of nuclear weapons in their deterrent effects? One should not overdo the comparison, either in terms of destructiveness (bad weather can drastically reduce the impact of a chemical attack) or psychology. After Hiroshima and Nagasaki there was an altogether healthy taboo on the use of nuclear weapons, which we should attempt to preserve. Chemical weapons, in contrast, were used repeatedly during World War I and on many occasions since, including, it appears, in Southeast Asia. The Iraqi use of chemicals in the war with Iran was particularly chilling: chemical weapons were used openly and successfully (in both the tactical and strategic senses). No international sanctions followed their use. (Indeed, in that conflict the United States tilted toward the side that had used them.) Probably the day will come when the civilized nations will regret their failure to punish those who used such weapons. For we may be entering an age in which chemical weapons are used by more parties rather than fewer.

Conventional Warfare

Has conventional conflict become so terrible that man cannot wage it? The view has been pressed so many times in the past—from Ivan Bloch's dire predictions before 1914 of the slaughter that would ensue, to the terrifying predictions of annihilation through aerial bombardment in the interwar period—that a certain skepticism is warranted. Some modern weapons—highly precise long-range cruise missiles for example—appear to make violence more controllable. And other modern weapons contribute to the persistence of war, because they give the underdog a fighting chance. The Soviets discovered this unpleasant fact in battles with Afghan tribesmen who, despite their poverty and rudimentary educations, managed to master the use of Stinger missiles in a few weeks. Certain kinds of conventional weapons are now much easier to acquire than ever before, since Chilean, Chinese, and South African suppliers, among many others, ask few embarrassing questions about the uses of their cluster bombs, ballistic missiles, and long-range artillery.

What is almost certain is that we are entering a period of technological change in warfare so dramatic that it justifies the Soviet description: "the revolution in military affairs," a term they have applied to the invention of nuclear weapons, and before that, the advent of the tank and the airplane. It is a revolution brought about by a host of technologies, particularly those involving information processing. Although the Soviets have thought through some of its implications, neither they nor we can claim fully to understand it. What this means, however, is that war will take very different forms than it did in the past, not that it will cease to exist. . . .

Jack Ohman, *The Oregonian*. Reprinted with permission.

The technological arguments for the obsolescence of war are thus either flimsy or partial. A more persuasive case is made by those who point to the spread of free enterprise and liberal democracy, and the death of communism. They rightly scoff at those who contend that in principle the United States and Canada, newly-united Germany, and France will be potential military opponents once the overarching fear of the USSR has vanished. Small-scale fighting may go on in obscure corners of the world, they argue, but the advanced, secure, and liberal democracies of North America, Europe, and Australia will never contemplate armed conflict with each other. As liberal regimes spread, so too will the zone of peace. Meanwhile, the overwhelming preponderance of military power residing in the free world, and its irrelevance to political and economic disputes within that world, will debase traditional strategy to only marginal importance.

But the argument for peace through democracy needs to be qualified in many ways. It was, after all, the democratization of conflict in the nineteenth century that restored a ferocity to warfare unknown since the seventeenth century; the bloodiest war in American history remains the one fought between two (by today's standards flawed) democracies—the Civil War. Concentration camps appeared during another conflict between two limited democracies, the Boer War. World War I was launched by two regimes—Wilhelmine Germany and Austria-Hungary—that had greater representation and more equitable legal systems than those of many important states today. And even when modern liberal democracies go to war they do not necessarily moderate the scope of the violence they apply; indeed, sensitivity to their own casualties sometimes leads to profligate uses of firepower or violent efforts to end wars quickly. Shaky democracies fight each other all the time. In the spring of 1990, India and Pakistan came close, once again, to open warfare. We must remind ourselves just how peculiar the wealthy and secure democracies of the West are, how painful their evolution to stability and the horror of war with each other has been. Perhaps other countries will find short-cuts to those conditions, but it would be foolish to assume they will.

An Incomplete Victory

Moreover, although at the moment Western-style liberal democracy appears to be the most appealing form of government, we should not be complacent about its durability, especially where it is newly established. Will its global popularity withstand major economic setbacks, or even a prolonged failure to deliver the goods to developing nations eager to reach European, Japanese, and American standards of living? . . .

Liberal democracy gained victory in the Cold War by showing a persistence and a courage that many did not expect, and by delivering a prosperity that few could have imagined a half century ago. But the collapse of the Soviet empire owes as much, and perhaps more, to the fundamental hollowness and self-destructive nature of Marxism-Leninism. But other ideologies, as yet dimly foreseen, may pose threats equivalent to those of communism in its heyday, as may organized religions. Secular Western intellectuals, themselves immune to religious passion, may underestimate the power such beliefs exert not only on backward cobblers and peasant farmers, but on computer programmers, engineers, professors, and generals. . . .

A third and final argument for the obsolescence of force comes from the rise of global economic interdependence, and the general (or rather purported) decline in the autonomy and importance of the nation-state. Here again, an awareness of history inclines one to skepticism: Norman Angell traced this kind of interdependence before World War I and proclaimed that it made war impossible. In the 1970s a band of academic theorists put forward the same arguments, which crumbled in the face of wars in the Middle East and Soviet-supported conflicts in Africa and Asia. Of course, the case should not be overstated: "geo-economics," as Edward Luttwak terms it, *is* of rising importance, and so too are such novel problems as those of environmental pollution.

Ready to Fight

It is not possible to sustain the claim that the people in a democracy are especially sensitive to the costs of war and therefore less willing than authoritarian leaders to fight wars. In fact the historical record shows that democracies are every bit as likely to fight wars as are authoritarian states.

John J. Mearsheimer, *The Atlantic*, August 1990.

But just as it would be foolish to ignore the emergence of new transnational forces and agencies on the one hand, and difficult global problems on the other, it would be wrong to succumb to the fallacy of interpreting all international developments as portents of global peace. Political entities fight wars; indeed, it is the political character of warfare that distinguishes it from the violence of organized crime. War can do quite well in the absence of nation-states: empires, city-states, confederations, and aspiring subnational groups have all used warfare to preserve or aggrandize themselves. And as the Crown Prince of Jordan warned, we may see greater conflict because of the attempt to break up nation-states. Certainly, the crack-up of empires is rarely peaceful, and we stand on the verge of the dissolution of the world's greatest continental empire, the Soviet Union. The fissiparous tendencies of modern ethnic strife—in the USSR, Yugoslavia, Ethiopia, South Asia, and Lebanon—carry an implicit threat of violence. . . .

It is unlikely that new collective security arrangements—directed not against a potential enemy but against any and all potential aggressors—can replace the traditional forms of armament and alliances. The history of such pacts, and most notably of the League of Nations, is that they simply do not work. When the crunch comes, states either cannot agree on the definition of aggression, do not find it in their interests to oppose the aggressor, or simply do not have the stomach to use force. . . .

All three arguments for an era of peace—the horrific quality of modern military technology, the spread of democracy, and the rise of transnational issues and actors—contain important truths. But neither separately nor together do they warrant a general conclusion that military power is becoming obsolete, or that war will not be used by states and other political groups. The causes of war remain as they were described by Thucydides, namely fear, ambition, and the desire for gain. It is only appropriate to celebrate the spread of freedom in and the waning of the threat from the East. But it would be well to temper our optimism with Alexander Hamilton's unsparing assessment of human affairs. In the *Federalist Papers* No. 6, he warned those who would believe in the "paradox of perpetual peace" that men are "ambitious, vindictive, and rapacious." "Momentary passions, and immediate interests," he argued, "have a more active and imperious control over human conduct than general or remote considerations of policy, utility, or justice." And democratic governments are not immune from such drives. They too are "subject to the impulses of rage, resentment, jealousy, avarice, and other irregular and violent propensities." . . .

A Feature of International Politics

War, and potential war, will remain a feature of international politics. Its sources will be many and changing, from ethnic animosity to irredentism, from competition for power to religious fanaticism. Its stakes will include territory (including valuable offshore properties), water rights, and control of populations. It will result from traditional kinds of animosities, but also from the second and third order consequences of developments that are intrinsically unforeseeable. Economic depression, for instance, need not breed violence directly, but it may, as in the 1930s, abet the development of new forms of tyranny, or increase the likelihood of the resort to violence by desperate countries.

"The world will include many highly competitive capitalist economies, all prospering together."

The World Economy Will Benefit Many Nations

Edward Yardeni and David Moss

In the following viewpoint, Edward Yardeni and David Moss argue that international trade is becoming increasingly open and less regulated. The resulting competition in the international economy will lead to higher productivity and living standards, according to Yardeni and Moss. Furthermore, the authors assert, the prosperity of the world economy will spread as more countries, such as South Korea and Taiwan, industrialize. Yardeni is the chief economist of Prudential-Bache Securities, New York, a financial and investment services company. Moss is a history consultant for Prudential-Bache.

As you read, consider the following questions:

1. What role does the U.S. play in the world economy, according to Yardeni and Moss? How has this role changed?
2. Why do the authors believe that inflation will not accompany increased global prosperity?
3. In the authors' opinion, how is Japan changing to fit the global economy?

Edward Yardeni and David Moss, "New Wave Economics: Trends for the 21st Century." Reprinted from *USA Today* magazine, © January 1990 by the Society for the Advancement of Education.

The decline of America is a very popular subject. In his 1987 book, *Beyond Our Means*, Alfred Malabre, Jr., warned that "we've been living beyond our means—for so long, in fact, that now, sadly, it's beyond our means to put things right, at least in an orderly, reasonably painless manner." Paul Kennedy, a professor of history at Yale University, wrote a best-seller, *The Rise and Fall of the Great Powers*, based on the theme that "the United States now runs the risk, so familiar to historians, of the rise and fall of previous Great Powers, of what might roughly be called 'imperial overstretch.'" . . .

New Wave Economics

We argue that the pessimists are wrong. Americans do face all sorts of challenges as we approach the next century. The pessimists do play a very important role in our society by identifying the problems, but they tend to exaggerate. The forces of darkness always seem to be superior to the forces of light.

The pessimistic crowd has inspired us to reexamine the economy. We believe that it is time to change the way we think about it because the economy has changed. The business cycle framework is useful sometimes and downright useless at other times. Keynesian, monetarist, supply-side, rational expectations, and other models of the economy are too dogmatic, rigid, and simplistic.

As an alternative, we offer New Wave Economics, whose roots are in Adam Smith's *The Wealth of Nations*, published in 1776. In Smith's time, pessimism was as prevalent as it is today. Many essayists and pamphleteers were bemoaning the decline of Great Britain and predicting ruin for the country. Smith sought to discredit the pessimists of his day by demonstrating how free markets foster economic growth and increase the wealth of nations. New Wave Economics is an empirically based framework which examines several important new trends in the economy that largely have been ignored by the traditional models and the pessimists. New Wave Economics is not a radically new model of the economy or a theory which explains observed economic behavior. Rather, it is an interdisciplinary approach that extrapolates several important social, political, economic, and demographic trends visible today into the 1990's.

The resulting outlook for the U.S. and other capitalist economies is very upbeat, in stark contrast to the numerous dire predictions. Our optimistic forecast isn't intended to be a down-the-road scenario. Most of the trends we are projecting already are under way.

Market capitalism will continue to proliferate and flourish in the global economy. The prosperity created by the capitalist system is especially impressive in comparison to the stagnation of communist economies. The world economy will become more capitalistic as additional countries deregulate their economies. Increasingly, the competitive market will replace state ownership and central planning. In capitalist societies, public policies will become more effective by harnessing, rather than constraining, market forces. Deregulation will spur global competition, which will become even more intense as the capitalist world becomes increasingly multi-polar. The U.S. no longer dominates the capitalist world—Asian and European economies are as large as the North American economy. These markets will grow together, trade will expand, and more prosperity will result. Economic growth disciplined by global competition is not inflationary, so growth should be sustainable.

Capitalism never has been more dynamic. Capitalism produces change, which is occurring more rapidly. Intense global competition is the major cause of the faster pace of capitalism. Managerial and technological innovations are happening more frequently. Competitors are emerging in newly industrializing countries. Many companies are responding successfully to the challenges of dynamic market capitalism; business planners and managers are learning that, to survive and prosper in the New Wave world, they must adapt rapidly to the changes in the global marketplace. They recognize that their companies must produce and distribute goods and services in all the major capitalist markets. In the future, production will be almost as internationally mobile as financial capital. The proliferation of productive capacity around the world will intensify price competition, so inflation should stay low. To remain profitable, companies will continue to cut costs and increase productivity. Prosperity will create labor shortages, but businesses are more likely to boost capital expenditures than inflate their labor costs by bidding up wage rates. Capital spending and technological innovation should accelerate over the next several years in the industrialized economies.

The Power of the Market

The markets should do a much better job of regulating the capitalist economies than policymakers. Recessions should be less frequent and less severe than in the past. The booms and busts of the business cycle will remain a part of our economic lives, but market forces should dampen the booms. In the global credit markets, bondholders push yields up rapidly when they perceive an inflation threat. Such preemptive strikes reduce the likelihood that inflation will become a serious problem again. Therefore, severe busts no longer will be necessary to unwind the excesses caused by the booms since excesses won't be allowed to build in the first place.

In addition, capitalist economies are becoming more diversified and resilient to shocks such as the global stock market crash of

127

1987. Major industries can fall into recession without depressing over-all economic growth. Rolling recessions that are limited to certain industries are more likely to occur than economy-wide recessions.

Exchange rate movements can take quite a long time to fix trade imbalances among capitalist economies, but they do work eventually. The U.S. trade deficit should continue to narrow, another achievement of the automatic adjustment mechanism of the marketplace. . . .

Growth in the World Economy

International integration will create growth in the world economy. Fueling this is regional integration. As trade barriers within the European community and between the United States and Canada fall, new market opportunities are stimulating foreign investment. The opening of China, the Soviet Union, and Eastern Europe to the capitalist world will provide additional export markets for U.S. products, particularly capital goods and construction.

Victor D. Lippit, *Dollars & Sense*, January/February 1990.

Today, the capitalist world is evolving into three enormous, interdependent marketplaces: the North American bloc, which is moving toward a free-trade association between the U.S. and Canada; the newly industrializing countries of Asia, led by Japan; and, the unified economies of Western Europe, which, by 1992, will be the greatest example of economic deregulation in world history.

Economic borders are expanding dramatically and becoming less constrained by political borders. Markets are no longer national, but international. Trade is becoming freer. Competition within and among the capitalist blocs is intensifying. Challengers are cropping up within the newly industrializing nations; countries like Thailand and Malaysia are emerging as new competitors in the global marketplace; and, of course, tremendous potential exists in China and India.

The U.S. is not a loser in this arrangement. Rather, it prospers along with the other capitalist nations because Americans are responding successfully to the global competitive challenges. If the Asian and European blocs are prospering at a more rapid pace, a pessimist could conclude that America is in decline. However, this view is based on a wrong assumption—that the world economy is a zero-sum game. Competition does increase risk, but also raises the rewards enormously by expanding the global marketplace. The three capitalist blocs are huge markets that will continue to grow together.

Some pessimists foresee a grimmer scenario, with tremendous imbalances and tensions in the global economy. However, market forces are working. People are changing in response to the global competitive challenges and sharing a desire to prosper. Increasingly, they believe that capitalism is the means to that end. As trade becomes freer, the differences are likely to diminish. For example:

• Americans are working harder and productivity is growing at a faster pace, particularly in manufacturing. The threat of deindustrialization forced us to make our businesses more productive to compete in world markets. American companies are implementing Japanese cost-cutting techniques, and workers are settling for smaller wage gains so that their employers will stay in the U.S. Quality and the work ethic are making a comeback. Also, demographic forces should slow consumption and boost savings.

• As the Japanese have prospered, they've come to recognize that they can afford to improve the quality of their lives. They realize that they won't continue to prosper unless North Americans and Europeans are also. That's why they'll continue to support demands that they should consume and import more. Japanese companies responded to the soaring yen and plummeting exports by designing products that would be more appealing to their domestic customers. As the workweek gradually declines, their consumers will have more time to shop, increasingly at discount stores that sell only imported products. . . .

• South Korea's era of cheap labor rapidly is coming to an end. Its workers are proud of their country's successes in global markets and, not surprisingly, are demanding much higher wages (1987's average increase was 17%). . . .

The European Economic Community

The European Economic Community (EEC), which was established in 1958 and has grown from six to 12 members, is poised for a great leap forward. At a 1985 summit meeting in Milan, the EEC governments approved the Single European Act, which would create an open market by the end of 1992, promising to eliminate about 300 major economic barriers. Most significantly, these can be removed by "qualified majority voting" among ministers, rather than unanimity.

Why did the Europeans agree to such an unprecedented and extraordinarily ambitious deregulation plan? They feared that they were falling hopelessly behind the U.S. and Japan. For example, the U.S. created 28,000,000 jobs between 1970 and 1986, while the big Western European countries created next to none. Since 1957, a web of red tape and regulations gradually has spread throughout the EEC. A truck driver needs 35 pages of invoices, customs declarations, and import statistical surveys to carry a

load of goods from one end of the continent to the other. . . .
European leaders hope that freer markets might cure "Eurosclerosis."

If the plan succeeds, the European Economic Community will
be the world's greatest market. The potential is impressive:
320,000,000 consumers in the EEC, compared with 240,000,000
in the U.S. and 120,000,000 in Japan. In 1987, the EEC's gross domestic product was $4.2 trillion, almost equal to the U.S.'s and
well above the $2.7 trillion combined total of Japan, South Korea,
Taiwan, Hong Kong, and Singapore. . . .

The Pacific Century?

Across the Pacific, changes are just as significant as those under way across the Atlantic. The Europeans responded to the
global competitive challenge by adopting the Single European
Act, which targets the barriers to free trade that must be removed to create one market. In response to international pressures, the Japanese are making great progress in opening their
domestic economy to foreign competitors. The blueprint for the
deregulation of the Japanese economy is the 1986 Maekawa
Report, which recommended a historic transformation of Japanese society. . . .

The Maekawa Report proposed a revolutionary restructuring of
economic priorities including a radical deregulation plan based
on two premises: Japan must correct its trade imbalances to relieve international tensions which threaten to devastate its economy; and Japan is no longer poor, so it is time that the people enjoy the fruits of their country's prosperity. The Maekawa Committee recommended that Japan strive for economic growth led
by domestic demand instead of exports. Active efforts should be
made to encourage imports, particularly of manufactured
goods. . . .

Now, the Japanese are starting to worry about competition from
newly industrializing countries. In 1987, Japan became a net im-
porter of textile products for the first time in recent history.
Korean imports account for more than half of the total, causing
Japan's knitting industry to complain that the Koreans are dumping sweaters in Japan.

Meanwhile, the Koreans dramatically are expanding their capacity to produce steel, autos, and consumer electronics. Thailand
is emerging as a newly industrializing country. The Taiwanese are
making significant manufacturing investments in the Philippines.
Malaysia is a major supplier of semiconductors.

Will the next century be the Pacific century, as some fear? We
doubt it. More likely, it will be the New Wave century. There
won't be one preeminent economic superpower. Rather, the
world will include many highly competitive capitalist economies,
all prospering together.

4 VIEWPOINT

---

*"[The] internationalization of capital markets
and production increasingly constrains all
governments. . . . It also hurts ordinary
citizens."*

Only the Wealthy Will
Benefit from the World
Economy

Ronald Kwan

Many experts believe that the nations of the world are more
closely linked economically than at any other time in history. In
the following viewpoint, Ronald Kwan argues that this trend toward a more international economy increases the power of the
wealthy, often at the expense of the lower and middle classes.
When business owners can easily transfer their factories overseas, Kwan contends, they can use this power as a threat to
force workers to accept lower wages. The author is a doctoral
candidate in economics at Harvard University in Cambridge,
Massachusetts.

As you read, consider the following questions:

1. Why did Canada's attempt to lower interest rates fail,
   according to Kwan?
2. What does Kwan believe has been the most important cause
   of the growing international scope of business?
3. In the author's opinion, what are the consequences of the
   internationalization of capitalism?

Ronald Kwan, "Footloose and Country Free," *Dollars & Sense*, March 1991. Reprinted with
permission.

During the fall 1990 budget crisis, speculation raged over foreigners' increasing leverage over U.S. economic policy. A previously intransigent President George Bush had abandoned his "no new taxes" pledge shortly after U.S. representatives signed a trade agreement with Japanese officials. The pact called on the administration to take steps to eliminate the U.S. budget deficit.

For Canada's central bank, events in early 1990 left less room for speculation—except by currency traders. With Canada's economy slowing down, the bank attempted to stimulate the economy with a modest cut in interest rates. But the wealthy, seeking higher returns, began selling their Canadian investments and their Canadian dollars. The currency's value dropped three cents within a matter of days. To halt the capital flight, the central bank had to raise interest rates well above their previous levels, stifling consumer spending and business investment in plant and equipment. Canada fell quickly into a recession. By December 1990, unemployment had risen more than two percentage points to over 9%.

Capital Rules

Have the U.S. and Canadian governments lost the autonomy to determine their own monetary and fiscal policies? To some extent, yes. Does Japan now rule? No, capital rules.

Owners of capital have always been able to move their wealth across national boundaries, but they can now do so more freely than at any time since the end of World War II. This internationalization of capital markets and production increasingly constrains all governments, including those accustomed to calling their own shots on the international scene.

It also hurts ordinary citizens in more direct ways. Workers are pressured to accept lower wages or lose their jobs, as capitalists seek more favorable conditions elsewhere. Their communities are robbed of income, and their local governments are deprived of an adequate tax base. And taxpayers everywhere are left to foot the bill as transnational corporations (TNCs) use their global reach to shelter their profits.

While workers, communities, and government officials most commonly direct their wrath at foreign capitalists, particularly those from Japan, investors' nationality is not the most pressing issue facing U.S. communities or policymakers. Despite significant national differences in corporate styles and structures, capitalists tend to behave similarly regardless of their country of origin. German, Japanese, and British capitalists are generally just as anti-union when operating factories in the United States as their U.S. counterparts. And they are just as quick to sell off any government's bonds if the interest rate dips. All want the highest possible profits wherever they are, or wherever they have to go.

As capitalists gain greater power to go wherever they please, the key issue facing people in all countries is how to control capital to make it work for the whole population.

Agile, Mobile, and Hostile

Since the 1960s, capital increasingly has flowed across borders. The movement of capital has jumped dramatically, both as diversified purchases of stocks and bonds known as portfolio investment and as direct investment—controlling interest in physical assets like factories and real estate.

In 1970, U.S. citizens owned $166 billion in assets abroad (both portfolio and direct investment). By 1988 this had risen to $1,254 billion, an increase from 16% to 26% of the value of the U.S. gross national product. Foreigners, meanwhile, increased their ownership of U.S. assets from $107 billion in 1970 to $1,786 billion in 1988, a jump from 11% of U.S. GNP to 37%.

This globalization of capital makes it very difficult to even define capital's nationality. For example, with competition from other industrialized countries, exporters producing in the United States have lost much of their clout. But international companies headquartered in the United States have suffered no competitive decline at all. While the share of world manufactured exports produced in the United States dropped from 17.1% in 1966 to 13.4% in 1985, U.S. corporations' share increased from 17.3% to 18.3%. They hadn't lost business; they had simply shifted much of it to their subsidiaries in other countries. With U.S. corporations producing less and less in the United States, the gap between their interests and the interests of the U.S. people are now more glaring than ever.

Technology and Change

Why has capital become so footloose? Most simply, the U.S.-dominated postwar capitalist economy gave way to a more pluralistic world order, with other capital centers and other significant markets. The economies of Japan and the European countries regained their prewar strength, and newly industrialized countries like South Korea and Brazil began to compete in international markets. Capital began to surge across national boundaries seeking new markets and profits.

Perhaps the most commonly heard explanation for the increase in capitalists' freedom of movement is technological change. While technology's impact is often overstated, satellite communications permit portfolio investors in global financial markets to trade around the clock, making it almost as easy for a U.S. investor to trade German as U.S. bonds. This has increased the overall mobility of financial capital and permitted the rapid transmission of market crashes like the one in October 1987.

More important, faster and cheaper communications and transportation have allowed owners of transnational corporations to more closely control their direct investments in their far-flung foreign affiliates, enhancing their power. Lower transportation costs, combined with lower tariffs, have made it profitable for corporations to produce further from the products' ultimate destination. This permits them to shift or threaten to shift production when local labor unions or government officials act contrary to the company's interests.

Decontrolling Capital

Still, technology only facilitates capital mobility; it doesn't cause it. One of the most overlooked reasons for the increase in capitalists' freedom to move their wealth is the political dominance of international capitalists, who have used their power to implement free-market policies around the world.

Since World War II, governments have reduced or repealed much of the legislation designed to control capitalists' actions. At the end of the war, most countries had substantial restrictions on the movement of capital across borders, for conducting trade, to make investments, or simply to hold foreign currencies. While dominant U.S. financiers and large corporations favored unrestricted capital movement, weakened European capitalists sought to protect themselves from U.S. domination with a variety of policies designed to limit capital mobility.

Such controls had a macroeconomic rationale as well. They allowed progressive governments the autonomy to pursue full-employment policies and set appropriate interest rates free of the fear that the wealthy would take their capital abroad.

As large Japanese and European corporations recovered from the war, they sought to expand their investments beyond their own borders, and the alliance between domestic capitalists and advocates of progressive economic and social policies broke down. By the late 1970s, governments began to fully deregulate the movement of capital, urged on by the free-market ideology of monetarism and the ascension of Prime Minister Margaret Thatcher in Britain and President Ronald Reagan in the United States. . . .

Capital Constraints

One consequence of capitalists' growing international freedom is the constraint on national governments' ability to stimulate their economies through expansionary fiscal and monetary policies. If a government tries to spur economic activity by loosening monetary policy, expanding credit, and lowering interest rates, foreign and domestic owners of financial capital, seeking higher interest rates elsewhere, can leave. This limits the funds available in credit markets, raising interest rates and reducing or eliminating the intended effect of the original policy. Such capital flight also lowers the value of the domestic currency, which fuels inflation by raising the costs of imported goods. In the face of capital flight, most central banks back away from expansionary monetary policies, as the Bank of Canada did within hours of its modest interest-rate reduction in early 1990.

"REMEMBER — IT'S MY BALL...
So YOU HAVE TO PLAY BY MY RULES!"

© Simpson/Rothco. Reprinted with permission.

Fiscal policy is also constrained. When governments raise taxes on corporations and on the wealthy or they expand social programs, the rich can simply move their money elsewhere. In 1981, the newly elected French government of Socialist Francois Mitterand felt the sting of international capital. The government increased spending on social benefits to families, the unemployed, and retirees; announced plans to expand public employment and investment; and moved to nationalize some major industries. This led to faster growth in France. But the wealthy began to take their money out of France, forcing the government to devalue the franc three times in 18 months. By June 1982, the French government effectively gave in, limiting social transfers and public spending in favor of policies to promote business investment and household saving. . . .

Another consequence of the globalization of capital markets is the rise in currency speculation, which increases the volatility of both interest and exchange rates. Currency trading now measures in the hundreds of billions of dollars *per day*, as speculators seek to profit from short-term shifts in exchange rates. Even before Canada's central bank lowered interest rates, currency speculators forced the Canadian dollar down a full cent by selling off their Canadian holdings in anticipation of the move.

The Tax Scandal

Governments are further limited in how they can tax corporations. If they raise tax rates, capitalists can easily shift their profits elsewhere. TNCs often illegally evade taxes by recording profits in low-tax jurisdictions such as Panama.

Moreover, since overseas profits are only taxed by the U.S. government when they are received by the U.S. parent, TNCs can legally avoid paying U.S. corporate income taxes in two ways. They can reinvest the profits abroad, or they can judiciously time the so-called repatriation to coincide with losses from their domestic operations, reducing their total tax bills. . . .

Such corporate tax avoidance has helped persuade governments all over the world to lower their corporate tax rates in an effort to get TNCs to report and retain profits in their respective countries. Between 1984 and 1990, the U.S. government cut the corporate income tax rate from 51% to 39%. The average rate for the United States, Japan, Germany, France, Canada, and the United Kingdom fell from 51% to 43% over the same period.

Foreign-owned companies also pay little in U.S. taxes on their U.S. operations. A February 1990 *New York Times* investigation reported that U.S. subsidiaries of foreign companies have doubled their gross income in the 1980s but have seen virtually no increase in their U.S. tax bills. According to a 1990 congressional investigation, foreign-owned companies commonly engage in transfer pricing: One foreign parent charged its subsidiary $250 per television set, but charged only $150 to an unrelated company. According to the *Times*, foreign companies may owe the IRS [Internal Revenue Service] as much as $13 billion.

Such corporate tax evasion leaves the rest of us holding the fiscal bag, with higher payroll taxes and reduced social services.

Who Is Us?

Political economist Robert Reich, in a *Harvard Business Review* article entitled "Who Is Us?," concluded that, contrary to popular opinion, "us" should not include U.S. corporations producing abroad, but it should include subsidiaries of foreign companies producing in the United States.

In fact, neither type of transnational corporation is "us." U.S. and foreign corporations that operate globally have fewer long-term interests in common with the U.S. communities in which they produce than they once did. TNCs now have less stake in a community's infrastructure, education, training, or health care. And they are less concerned with maintaining good labor relations. If the local community and work force don't ante up with direct or indirect subsidies or contract concessions, then the TNC can shift production elsewhere. The threat of capital flight is now just as real in Flint, Michigan, as it is in Morelos, Mexico.

Fleck Manufacturing Inc., for example, a Canadian auto parts supplier with a plant in Ontario, recently purchased a factory in Nogales, Mexico. It then offered its Ontario workers a raise of just 22 cents an hour, warning that if they struck for more, Fleck would close the plant. The workers balked, and Fleck shut the plant. . . .

Taking Action

Whether it be labor actions or government measures, citizens will have to take direct action to respond to the increasing freedom now enjoyed by the wealthy. The free flow of capital across national boundaries is not technologically inevitable. It springs from the domination of government policy by transnational business interests. To limit the destructive effects of capital flight on workers, communities, taxpayers, and government institutions, citizens will have to exercise control over the prerogatives of capitalists.

"The world economy is so interlinked . . . that it is increasingly difficult to differentiate between American, Japanese and European 'success.'"

The Economies of the World Are Unified

Kenichi Ohmae

Kenichi Ohmae, one of Japan's most prominent management consultants, is the managing director of McKinsey & Company, an international consulting firm. He has authored several books on international trade and economic issues, including *Triad Power*, *The Borderless World*, and *Fact and Friction*. In the following viewpoint, Ohmae argues that corporations are becoming less tied to a particular country and are more integrated into the world economy. The successful corporations of the future, the author predicts, will operate in more than one country and produce goods for consumers around the world.

As you read, consider the following questions:

1. In the author's opinion, what three countries or regions form the basis of the world economy?
2. What does Ohmae believe is the relationship between the Japanese and American economies?
3. What is the biggest threat to the world economy, according to Ohmae?

Kenichi Ohmae, "Beyond Friction to Fact: The Borderless Economy," *New Perspectives Quarterly*, Spring 1990. Reprinted with permission.

When Sony purchased Columbia Studios, the American headlines screamed "Japan invades!"

"Invading," or its Japanese countercharge, "bashing," typifies the way in which the front page of both US and Japanese newspapers discuss the two nation's relations. The financial pages of the same papers, however, discuss the same issue in terms of "joint-ventures" or "corporate tie-ups."

At the end of the 20th century, the politically-charged terms of the front page have come to reflect a fiction rooted in the 19th-century mindset of the nation-state; the business links and their terminology reflect the reality of today's borderless economy.

The Great Global Triad

Today, the world stands not only at the threshold of a quantum leap in material wealth, but at the threshold of global social regeneration. Unfortunately, the acrimony of the current debate—where fiction overrides fact and results in the friction of nationalist emotions—threatens to derail the momentum toward this promising future. The economies of the great global Triad—the US, Japan and Europe—are already so interwoven that loosening a few threads could unravel the entire cloth and expose us all to depression.

The world economy is so interlinked by the open trading system through which the large transnational companies operate that it is increasingly difficult to differentiate between American, Japanese and European "success." We are no longer strangers, but insiders in each other's lands.

IBM [International Business Machines] Japan has over 1,000 corporate affiliates and more than 19,000 employees in Japan. Texas Instruments is Japan's most competitive producer of semiconductors. Estee Lauder is Japan's most successful cosmetics manufacturer. In fact, the top 2,000 American companies operating in Japan have a production value greater than the US-Japan trade deficit.

The Source of Wealth and Security

To an increasing extent, Detroit is Tokyo and vice-versa. Ford owns about 25 percent of Mazda. General Motors is the largest shareholder in Isuzu, at 34 percent, and owns five percent of Suzuki. Chrysler owns 25 percent of Mitsubishi. Both Nissan and Toyota have established major auto plants in the US. Honda even exports cars back to Japan from plants in the US and is rumored to be moving its world headquarters to Los Angeles.

In Europe, Ford and GM each share about 12 percent of the European market; their production facilities there compete handily with Renault, Volkswagen and Fiat. Mitsubishi and Daimler-Benz are negotiating a plan of "intensive cooperation" in automobile technology, aerospace and microelectronics.

It is difficult to designate the nationality of these successful global insider corporations—they fly the flag of their customers, not their nation. They thrive on the loyalty of the denationalized consumer. Their rise or fall rests on the harsh judgement of the consumer over which car, VCR or personal computer to buy.

International Corporations

The last time I looked, IBM was still making $9 billion in revenues in Japan, Coke was making more money in Japan than in the United States, and Proctor & Gamble had come up with a new, thin absorbent diaper—colored pink for girls and blue for boys—that had increased its market share in Japan from 10 percent to 20 percent.

And the last time I looked around the U.S., Ford was building a new car using American workers and managers, but also new manufacturing and management techniques borrowed from Mazda. Ford owns 25 percent of Mazda. The last time I looked, state government officials in the U.S. were still boarding planes for Tokyo seeking new Japanese investment in their states. And a Japanese food and beverage company had bought a minority interest in the Birmingham Barons—an American minor league baseball team.

Jim Manzi, speech at Tokyo Fujitsu Conference, March 13, 1990.

The links of the great Triad economy are the source of wealth and security in this interdependent world. Recognizing the emergence of the Triad marketplace, and active participation in it, is key to the enduring prosperity for any nation. Insiders will prosper and grow strong; protectionists and outsiders will wither because they will be unable to earn the allegiance of consumers with plenty of alternative choices in the global supermarket.

The borderless economy has two aspects: global commonality and regional differences.

As national boundaries lose significance for both consumers and corporations, the commonalities of the Triad become more important than national differences.

At the same time, the interests of regions within national boundaries have very distinct attributes, tastes and needs. This means, for example, that Osaka might compete with Tokyo and California with New York.

To be successful, the transnational corporations of the Triad must adopt a strategy of "global localization," as Sony's Akio Morita has phrased it, or, as I prefer, a strategy of "insiderization" with a "multilocal" approach.

Although these terms sound like oxymorons, they simply mean

that successful companies will base their strategies on an appreciation of the unique character and needs of regions within national borders.

Differences and Similarities

Over the past two decades, most Japanese companies have learned to differentiate their markets in the US by regional attributes. For example, they have seen that subcompact cars sell best in the heavily urbanized regions of New York and southern California while larger, in some cases more luxurious, cars fit the taste of consumers in the Midwest and the South.

By contrast, most US businesses still view Japan from 12,000 miles away through the looking-glass of the gray bureaucrats of Tokyo known as Japan, Inc. Naturally, at that distance, Japan's regional consumer patterns are about as distinguishable as the Milky Way.

But global localization does not mean the endless search for differences because, already, the commonalities across the Triad economy are far greater than the unique attributes of localities. In our management consulting work, for example, 80 percent of what applies in the US works as well in Germany. And the consumer desires of the Japanese *shinjinrui*—the generation younger than 30—are far more similar to the same generation in Los Angeles or Paris than they are different.

Corporate Decisions

Today corporate decisions about production and location are driven by the dictates of global competition, not by national allegiance. Witness IBM's decision to transfer 120 executives and the headquarters of its $10 billion per year communications business to Europe, a move that is partly symbolic—a recognition that globalization must take companies beyond their old borders—and partly practical—an opportunity for IBM to capitalize on the expected growth in the European market.

Robert B. Reich, *Harvard Business Review*, March/April 1991.

As national borders continue to erode, what will emerge? The winners of the future will not be nations, but regions such as Alsace Lorraine, Wales, Kansai, Orange County or North Carolina. The winning corporations of the future will be those that serve the global consumer well—whatever their national origin. Sony, with its hardware headquarters in Tokyo, its entertainment headquarters in Los Angeles and its telecommunications headquarters in New York or Europe comes to mind.

And what of politics? Politicians around the world will have to turn their energies away from preservation of the status quo to the more important mission of creating a political framework for the borderless economy.

The European vision does not extend beyond 1992. The Japanese have no vision: we have been meekly hiding behind America's nuclear umbrella, implementing the obsolete assignments of General Douglas MacArthur. The NATO [North Atlantic Treaty Organization]-Warsaw structure, and America's sense of mission, have lost their *raison d'etre* without the Cold War.

A borderless economy inside a political vacuum spells peril. Without a new framework, the danger is that new villains will be created to put flesh on the old skeleton. Without the Russians as an arch-rival, might the Japanese or the Germans be cast in that role by an America without a mission?

The Borderless Economy

A xenophobic scenario such as this is what most threatens our full passage to the borderless economy of the future. Only the creation of a political culture that reconciles the schizophrenia between citizen and consumer can clear the way.

"A new world may well be emerging, or rather an old world may be coming back from the dead. I am talking of a world of trading blocs."

The Economies of the World Will Dissolve into Trading Blocs

Walter Russell Mead

Walter Russell Mead is a scholar of international economics at the World Policy Institute in New York City and the author of *Mortal Splendor: The American Empire in Transition.* In the following viewpoint, Mead warns that, after winning the Cold War, the U.S. is in danger of becoming an inferior economic power. The international economy may break into three rival trading blocs, the author contends, with the United States a member of the poorest and most troubled one.

As you read, consider the following questions:

1. What were the two pillars of American strategy after World War II, according to the author?
2. In Mead's opinion, what nations will comprise the three rival trading blocs?
3. Why does the author think that the American trading bloc would be the weakest?

It is too often forgotten that the American strategy after World War II had *two* pillars. One was, of course, the policy of containing Soviet expansionism in Europe and the Third World. However, in the years immediately following World War II, the primary goal of our diplomacy—the original foundation of our postwar strategy—was the creation of the international financial system designed at the conference of forty-four states and nations held at the New Hampshire resort of Bretton Woods. It was at Bretton Woods in 1944—more than in Warsaw and Budapest and Bucharest in 1989—that the United States won the Cold War.

In 1944 and the years that followed, Americans had three goals for the postwar economic order. *First*, we insisted that we would be in charge. As we had all the gold and all the goods, this seemed like a reasonable position to take, and those nations that considered it unreasonable were in no position to do much about it. Our *second* demand was for the creation of a truly global trading system. The wholly *international* economy was our idea—a bold, new idea. The nations of Europe had traditionally preferred their own trading blocs to a global system regulated by international rules of trade. Countries like England and France had grown by building overseas empires, carving up the world in a way that guaranteed each imperial power its own source of raw materials and its own markets. American strategists came to believe that such systems blocked economic growth and eventually caused wars. And they were right. . . .

Encouraging Rapid Growth

The *third* American postwar goal was the establishment of a growth-oriented world economy. Generally speaking, economic policymakers have to choose either slow growth with minimal inflation or faster growth with the risk of greater inflation. Compared with other major countries, the United States wants a little more growth, even if we have to take the inflation. Countries like Germany, on the other hand, are more willing to accept slow growth if it will keep the inflation rate at or near zero. . . .

In the 1940s, history gave the United States the opportunity to shape a world economic order to its liking, and we did so. It was global- and growth-oriented. . . . This system worked not only for us; it led to an unprecedented global boom. What was good for the United States turned out to be good for the world. It was as players in this new U.S.-engineered global economy that the nations of Western Europe and Japan rebuilt their shattered economies and reached the position they are in today—one in which they are no longer obliged to accept our leadership.

Western Europe and Japan are back, and their preferences are beginning once again to shape the world's economy. A new world may well be emerging, or rather an old world may be coming

144

back from the dead. I am talking of a world of trading blocs. This would be a world of slow growth. It would be a world in which we would not fit comfortably.

In my darker moments, I envision a world made up of three rival blocs: a Euro-bloc based in the Western European nations of the Common Market and now expanding to include Hungary, Poland, and others in Eastern Europe; an East Asian bloc dominated by Japan and including Korea, Thailand, and the other free market industrializing nations of the region; and the American bloc, dominated by the United States, augmented by Canada, and incorporating Latin America.

Europe and Japan

Since the economic shocks of the 1970s, some observers have predicted a world economy divided into regional blocks; . . . the consolidation of Europe and the rise of Japan may point in that direction.

Miles Kahler, *Foreign Affairs*, Fall 1990.

Most of the Euro-bloc countries never really liked the American idea of a global system. The British fought us tooth and nail over "Imperial Preference"—their system of tariff protection to keep their empire together—and with the other nations of Western Europe have been reluctant to open their markets to goods manufactured in the Orient. Europe pressed to keep Japan from becoming a party to the General Agreement on Tariffs and Trade (GATT)—the treaty that, beginning in 1948, laid down a code of international economic conduct aimed at reducing tariffs and opening markets. And even today the nations of Western Europe impose tight restrictions on Japanese-made autos and other imports.

Trading Blocs

The Europeans have a logical alternative to a global economy, one that becomes more compelling as the Soviet-bloc countries of Eastern Europe move toward market economies. Schematically, it would work like this: Western Europe can import its raw materials from Africa and the Soviet Union, and its fuel, increasingly, not only from the Middle East but also from the USSR. It can place its low-wage industries in the former Soviet-bloc countries. (The average monthly industrial wage in Poland in January 1990 amounted to thirty-seven dollars a month.) The wealthy Western European countries can continue to specialize in high-technology and service industries, marketing these goods and services from the Urals to the Atlantic.

In this new, post-Cold War world, the Western European nations will have very little need of, or interest in, goods and services from Asia or the Americas. Europe already produces huge agricultural surpluses, and with the increase in agricultural productivity that can be expected with the liberalizing of Eastern Europe, the continent's food supply will only increase. It is true that developments in American and Japanese technology have tended to outpace those of European manufacturers. But the gap has been closing fast. The European consortium that designed and built the Airbus is challenging American dominance of civil aviation, and Europe is also pushing into space. Europe is determined to develop its high-tech industries, and the record of German, French, and British science suggests it will succeed.

The Other Side of the World

On the other side of the world, a new East Asian bloc is rising. Its outlines are already clear. Japan will import raw materials and low-end manufactured products from South Korea, Thailand, and China while exchanging manufactured goods for oil with the Middle East. In addition, Japan will export capital, capital goods, and high-technology products to all these markets—and to some degree to Australia, New Zealand, the United States, and Latin America—in exchange for food and raw materials (and American films and rock videos).

Like the Euro-bloc, the East Asian bloc will aggressively protect its own markets for cutting-edge products, limiting America's role as far as possible to the export of raw materials. Raw materials already form a higher percentage of U.S. exports to Korea than of Korean exports to the United States. This is, from the Asian point of view, an appropriate division of labor and a model for the future transpacific relationship.

The third major bloc is the weakest and most troubled. It is, unfortunately, ours. America's protectionists and neo-isolationists seem to think that a protected Pan-American bloc could strengthen the U.S. economy, but they are sadly mistaken. There aren't enough customers in it. Economically, the United States and Canada are too much like twins to grow rich trading largely with each other. Latin America is in a prolonged economic decline. From 1981 to 1987, to cite just one figure, imports to Argentina, Mexico, and Brazil—the three largest economies in Latin America—fell 36 percent. Latin America is a region of depressed consumption, political instability, and chronic underdevelopment. Moreover, Latin America does not seem particularly eager to tie its future to the United States. . . .

In a world of rival blocs, the Asian and European blocs are almost certain to be more appealing to the Latin Americans than one dominated by the gringos; our bloc, along with all its other weaknesses, will be full of defectors and aspiring defectors. . . .

The future does not have to be this bleak. But we will have to change the way we think about foreign policy. For the last fifty years we have waged foreign policy in the spirit of Jeane Kirkpatrick and General George Patton; now we need to move in the spirit of Ginger Rogers and Fred Astaire. Peace is a complicated dance in which partners change rapidly. It is a dance at which the United States has never excelled. . . .

The national interest is the key to our position in this strange new world of peace. Those interests have not changed much since colonial times: We want a world that is open to peaceful commerce, and one that is open to growth.

We can no longer impose these values on the rest of the world, but they remain persuasive. France, for instance, does not want an insular Europe if it means German domination. Korea feels the same way about Japan. Our interest in growth continues to be shared by developing nations.

Nothing Inevitable About the Future

There is nothing inevitable about the future. But . . . the United States will need to stop gloating about winning the Cold War and start to assess, soberly, its place in the global economy. Of this I see little sign.

Distinguishing Between Fact and Opinion

This activity is designed to help develop the basic reading and thinking skill of distinguishing between fact and opinion. Consider the following statement: "In 1985, the European Economic Community approved the Single European Act, which would create an open market by the end of 1992." This is a factual statement because it can be checked by looking at news and magazine articles that describe the event. But the statement "An organized European Economic Community has resulted in less autonomy for the individual European nations" is an opinion. Many people may disagree that European autonomy has decreased. Others might argue that even if there has been a loss of autonomy, an organized Economic Community is not the cause.

When investigating controversial issues it is important that one be able to distinguish between statements of fact and statements of opinion. It is also important to recognize that not all statements of fact are true. They may appear to be true, but some are based on inaccurate or false information. For this activity, however, we are concerned with understanding the difference between those statements which appear to be factual and those which appear to be based primarily on opinion.

Most of the following statements are taken from the viewpoints in this chapter. Consider each statement carefully. *Mark O for any statement you believe is an opinion or interpretation of facts. Mark F for any statement you believe is a fact. Mark I for any statement you believe is impossible to judge.*

If you are doing this activity as a member of a class or group, compare your answers with those of other class or group members. Be able to defend your answers. You may discover that others come to different conclusions than you do. Listening to the reasons others present for their answers may give you valuable insights into distinguishing between fact and opinion.

O = opinion
F = fact
I = impossible to judge

1. In 1987, pay increases given South Korean workers averaged 17 percent.
2. For more than forty years, American strategy and defense planning has focused on the Soviet threat.
3. Nuclear weapons prevented an all-out U.S.-Soviet war.
4. International cooperation will create growth in the world economy.
5. Opening China, the Soviet Union, and Eastern Europe to the capitalist world will provide additional export markets for U.S. products.
6. Intense global competition is the major cause of the faster pace of life in capitalistic countries.
7. The outlook for the U.S. and other capitalist economies is very positive.
8. America no longer leads the world in the production of steel and automobiles.
9. Smaller Asian nations like Thailand and Malaysia are increasing their share of the new global marketplace.
10. Twenty-eight million jobs were created in the United States between 1970 and 1980.
11. The internationalization of the world economy pressures all workers into accepting lower wages or facing unemployment.
12. Capitalists want the highest possible profits they can achieve.
13. Since World War II, governments have repealed much of the legislation designed to control capitalists' actions.
14. Foreign companies should pay the Internal Revenue Service as much as $13 billion in back taxes.
15. IBM has more than one thousand corporate affiliates and more than nineteen thousand employees in Japan.
16. Ford owns 25 percent of Mazda, General Motors owns 34 percent of Isuzu, and Chrysler owns 25 percent of Mitsubishi.
17. What is good for the United States is good for the world.
18. Latin America, a region of depressed economies and chronic underdevelopment, figures little in the new world order.
19. The United States, Europe, and Asia are the world's three leading economic regions.
20. In 1988, U.S. citizens owned $1.254 trillion in assets abroad, in both stock portfolios and direct investments.
21. Japanese investment in America, Europe, and Asia increased during the 1980s.

Periodical Bibliography

The following articles have been selected to supplement the diverse views presented in this chapter.

C. Michael Aho and Bruce Stokes — "The Year the World Economy Turned," *Foreign Affairs*, vol. 70, no. 1, 1990/91.

Norman A. Bailey — "The World Economy in the 1990s," *The World & I*, January 1990. Available from 2800 New York Ave. NE, Washington, DC 20002.

C. Fred Bergsten — "The World Economy After the Cold War," *Foreign Affairs*, Summer 1990.

Zbigniew Brzezinski — "Europe and Amerippon: Pillars of the Next World Order," *New Perspectives Quarterly*, Spring 1990.

Business Week — "It's a Global Game," March 5, 1990.

Jim Devine — "Fool's Gold: A Response to Victor Lippit," *Dollars & Sense*, March 1990.

Jeff Faux — "Labor in the New Global Economy," *Dissent*, Summer 1990.

Selig Harrison and Clyde V. Prestowitz Jr. — "Pacific Agenda: Defense or Economics?" *Foreign Policy*, Summer 1990.

William R. Hawkins — "Politics over Economics: Thinking About Trade and Industry," *The World & I*, October 1989.

Miles Kahler — "The International Political Economy," *Foreign Affairs*, Fall 1990.

Paul Kennedy — "Economic and Military Security: How We Can Have Both," *Vital Speeches of the Day*, July 15, 1989.

Robert Kuttner — "Block That Trade," *The New Republic*, April 17, 1989.

Victor D. Lippit — "The Golden '90s," *Dollars & Sense*, January/February 1990.

Walter Russell Mead — "The World Economic Order," *Dissent*, Summer 1990.

Joseph S. Nye Jr. — "Soft Power: Redefining Power in a New Global Age," *Foreign Policy*, Fall 1990.

Roger B. Porter — "Conflict and Cooperation in the Global Marketplace: A Healthy Competition," *Vital Speeches of the Day*, January 1, 1991.

Raymond Vernon — "Maintaining an International Economy," *The World & I*, September 1990.

How Will the End of the Cold War Affect the World?

THE NEW WORLD ORDER

Chapter Preface

The end of the Cold War brought improved relations between the U.S. and the Soviet Union, the dismantling of the Berlin Wall, the reunification of Germany, and a series of mostly nonviolent revolutions that led to democratic governments in Czechoslovakia, Poland, and other Eastern European states. The wave of peaceful and democratic change in Eastern Europe has led some observers optimistically to predict a future world order marked by peace and democracy. As professor of politics Lee Edwards writes, "Once-communist countries are implementing democratic reforms and free market systems. Continents that were locked in protracted conflict are now joined in cooperative ventures. Nations that were hopelessly divided are now uniting."

Whether the future can deliver on such high hopes is unknown. There are many potential barriers to a peaceful democratic world, including a rise in conflict between different ethnic and religious groups, a resumption of historical animosities between countries, and cultural misunderstandings between countries and regions. Some examples of these barriers include battles between ethnic groups in the Soviet Union and Yugoslavia and the rise of Islamic fundamentalism in the Middle East that has led to antagonism toward the U.S. and other Western democracies.

One other source of future conflict is the persistent economic inequality between the industrialized nations and the impoverished countries of the Third World. Indeed, some observers argue that Third World nations could suffer the most from the end of the Cold War. With the end of the competition for ideological followers, the Soviet Union and the United States will abandon the Third World as unimportant. Journalists Doyle McManus and Robin Wright agree, writing that "The end of the Cold War . . . [has] created a . . . nightmare for much of the developing world: the fear not merely of being left behind, but of possibly being forgotten entirely."

The viewpoints in the following chapter examine these issues as they relate to the future shape of the post-Cold War world.

"Democracy has not only spread dramatically but it also seems to be growing at an accelerating pace."

The End of the Cold War Will Bring a New Era of Democracy

Joshua Muravchik

In recent years a growing number of countries have moved from authoritarian to democratic governments, including Poland and Czechoslovakia in Europe, Brazil and Argentina in Latin America, and South Korea and the Philippines in Asia. In the following viewpoint, Joshua Muravchik predicts that such changes in the world's nations are likely to continue. He refutes arguments that some societies are incapable of democracy, and urges that the U.S. work to encourage the spread of democracy worldwide. Muravchik is a resident scholar at the American Enterprise Institute, a Washington, D.C.-based think tank. This viewpoint is taken from his book *Exporting Democracy: Fulfilling America's Destiny.*

As you read, consider the following questions:

1. What three reasons does Muravchik give to argue that the international spread of democracy benefits the U.S.?
2. How does Muravchik respond to the argument that countries like Japan are not as democratic as the U.S.?
3. What point is the author trying to make in examining the last two hundred years of world history?

Joshua Muravchik, "New Dominions for Democracy," *The American Enterprise* magazine, January/February 1991. Copyright © 1991, Joshua Muravchik. Reprinted with permission from *The American Enterprise* magazine.

Almost without trying, America won the Cold War. We won not by the strength of arms or the skill of diplomats, but by virtue of the power of the democratic ideas on which our system of government is based and on the failure of the communist idea. We should now work to advance the democratic cause. Although exporting democracy will never be easy, it will grow easier with communism's dissolution. There are at least three important reasons why we should concentrate on continuing its spread.

The first is empathy with our fellow humans. Democracy does not make everyone happy, but it does deliver on its promise to allow, in our forefathers' brilliant phrase, the pursuit of happiness. Some people will never find their own happiness no matter how free they are to pursue it, but more people find happiness through their own pursuit than when it is defined for them by others.

Second, the more democratic the world, the friendlier America's environment will be. True, some democratic governments have been nuisances for the United States. Those of Sweden, India, France, and Costa Rica have at times played that part. But none has ever been our enemy. We could live comfortably indeed in a world where our worst antagonists were an Olaf Palme, a Charles de Gaulle, an Indira Gandhi, or an Oscar Arias.

Third, the more democratic the world, the more peaceful it is likely to be. Research has shown that war between democracies has almost never occurred in the modern world.

It is also advantageous for America to be democracy's advocate, even apart from the benefits of creating a more democratic world, because playing this role enables America to rally support for its policies and actions from large numbers of people both at home and abroad.

Can Democracy Spread?

These arguments lose their force, however, if as some believe there is no practical prospect for the further spread of democracy. If democracy can thrive only in rich countries, or Western countries, or English-speaking countries as some suggest, then it has already spread about as far as it can. To work for its extension would be futile. Nor would advocacy of democracy win America much credit if everyone could see that the cause had already reached its farthest horizon.

The skeptics of democracy's prospects come from all points on the political spectrum. . . .

The conservative commentator Irving Kristol says: *We should not pretend in our foreign policy statements that we can look forward in the near future to democracy conquering the world. The world is not like that. I am not one of those who are thrilled by the success of democracy in Argentina or in the Philippines or . . . Korea. I am a betting man, and I will lay odds that democracy will not survive in those countries. The preconditions for democracy are complex—certain strong cultural traditions, certain strong cultural attitudes. So far as I can see, those countries do not have them, and therefore, a democracy in any of them would shortly be discredited and be replaced by some sort of authoritarian regime of either the left or the right.*

Kristol's views are not much different from those of political scientist Robert Packenham, who describes himself as part of the leftish "revisionist" school of historical interpretation. He probably agrees with Kristol about few other topics. He wrote: *The chances for liberal democracy in most Third World countries in the foreseeable future are not very great; and the chances that the United States can be effective in advancing the cause of democracy through positive action are probably even smaller. The attempt to promote liberal constitutionalism is often both unrealistic from the point of view of feasibility and ethnocentric from the point of view of desirability.*

Left or right, the skeptics of democracy all speak in tones of wisdom and experience, rebuking democratic globalists for their juvenile enthusiasm. In particular, the skeptics point to the record of the many new nations created in the decolonization that followed World War II. Most were endowed at their birth with democratic constitutions, but democracy failed to take hold.

Special Cases?

For all their pretensions to dispassionate empiricism, the skeptics tend to be dogmatic. They ignore a wealth of evidence that contradicts their wisdom. Germany and Italy are not Anglo-Saxon countries. Japan is not a Western country. And India is certainly not a rich country. Democracy flourishes in each. True, many poor and non-Western countries are not democratic. True, democracy does not come easily, and it has often been destroyed. But this does not prove the skeptics' case that democracy is virtually impossible outside the First World. One need not believe that universal democracy can come easily to believe that such examples as Japan and India show the reasonableness of working for democracy's growth in non-Western, nonrich countries.

The skeptics sometimes reply that Japan, or one of the other late-developing or non-Western democracies, is not really democratic. Japanese politics, they point out, has long been dominated by one party, with factional divisions based not on ideology but on personality. Relations within each faction, moreover, are rigidly hierarchical. In short, the texture of Japanese politics differs markedly from the democratic norm that derives from the American or British experience. Indeed, it differs in some of the very things that we feel define democracy, such as egalitarianism.

155

In this argument, the critics are coming at the democratic globalists from opposite directions. They often say that it is absurd to expect other societies to adopt or imitate American structures. ("Democracy U.S.-style cannot be exported," says Howard Wiarda.) Surely this is a straw man, because no serious commentator advocates that U.S.-style democracy be reproduced in exact detail. (The efforts 40 years ago of some overly zealous occupation officials to impose U.S.-style federalism on Japan despite that nation's legal unity and ethnic homogeneity quickly fell by the wayside.) Then these same critics turn around and dismiss the use of Japan as an example of Asian democracy because its structures so differ from our own that they ought not to be labeled democratic.

Steve Kelley. Reprinted with permission.

What the Japanese have, not surprisingly, is Japanese-style democracy rather than American-style democracy. This is exactly what they ought to have. Its personalistic factions and emphasis on loyalty and hierarchy reflect Japanese culture. These features may seem repugnant to us, but the system retains the essential features of democracy: namely, the main government officials are chosen in honest, open, competitive elections, and the citizens enjoy the right to hear and take part in unfettered political discourse. These features are the bedrock of what democratic globalists want to universalize. The fact that they may be achieved within a myriad of legal and conventional forms is more than tolerable; it is desirable.

Counting the Democracies

Another retort of the skeptics is that Japan and India are special cases, the one having been democratized at gunpoint by the American (officially the Allied) occupation, the other by decades of British tutelage. Perhaps so, but each country in the world is a special case, in some sense unique. And Japan and India, though powerful examples, are not the only ones to which democratic globalists can point. Freedom House each year publishes "Report on Freedom," which rates every country in the world on a scale of one to seven in terms of its political freedoms and civil liberties and then groups them into three broad categories: free, partly free, and not free. In its January 1990 report, Freedom House found that 61 of the world's 167 sovereign states deserved to be called free. Thirty-nine percent of the world's people live in these countries, a higher percentage than ever before. The proportion living in free countries has crept steadily upward in recent years, although the share of the world's population living in the advanced Western countries has declined.

Of Freedom House's list of free countries, nine are in Latin America, twelve in the Caribbean, fourteen in Asia and the Pacific, three in Africa, and one in the Middle East. In other words, 39 free countries lie outside North America, Europe, Australia, and New Zealand. Many of these 39 besides Japan and India can be called special cases. Israel, for instance, is not entirely a non-Western country. Some Pacific countries in this list are small. Some Caribbean ones are prosperous, and some have a heritage of British tutelage. But given the numbers, can all of these be dismissed as special cases? Thirty-nine countries constitute a substantial portion of the non-European, non-Anglo-American world. How many such exceptions are required before we can dismiss the skeptics' denial that democracy can work in such countries? The list includes a wide variety of countries, showing that democracy can exist under many different conditions. Significantly, although some are prosperous, many on the list are poor. Twelve of the 39 have a per capita annual gross national product of less than $1,000—India, the Philippines, Bolivia, Botswana, and the Dominican Republic are among them.

Further, the argument that many of these non-Western democracies are special cases, even if true, implies less than first appears. Many non-Western countries that are not among these 39 but are among the partly free might also be considered special cases. Turkey is a European country; Pakistan shares India's tutelary history; the Republic of China is prosperous; and so on. The point is the United States could fashion a busy program of fostering democracy abroad simply by focusing on such countries. A substantial part of the world might be democratized before we exhausted the "special cases."

As much as these tabulations dramatize the growth of democracy, they in fact understate it. For one thing, they have not yet caught up with the changes in the communist world. Poland and Hungary are counted in this survey as partly free, as is Nicaragua. East Germany (the reunification of Germany is not recognized), Czechoslovakia, Bulgaria, Romania, the U.S.S.R., and Mongolia are all counted as not free. Yugoslavia is listed as partly free. Nor did the 1990 survey record some changes outside the communist world. Thus, it lists Namibia as partly free and Panama as not free.

The Growing Appeal of Democracy

The Freedom House data also do not measure the enormous growth of prodemocracy sentiment in countries that are still far from being democratic. In Nepal, South Africa, Mozambique, Nigeria, and Haiti, popular pressures have led to promises or processes of democratic reform. Elsewhere, democratic movements have been cruelly repressed, as in Burma, but how long will the repression succeed?. . .

Driven by the American model, the democratic idea steadily increased in appeal through the nineteenth century but then suffered a decline after World War I, under the challenge of philosophies that seemed newer and more promising. Now, after a 70-year detour, democracy again seems to capture the imagination of intellectuals, students, and workers in all corners of the world. Even the Arab world, which has seemed least affected by global democratization and which alone possesses a still-vibrant rival ideology in Islam, has begun to feel the tremors. . . .

Yet the recent surging of the democratic tide leaves many skeptics unmoved. Outside America and Europe, democracy has its ups and downs, they say. Today's rise is tomorrow's fall. Latin America, they say, has had elected governments that reverted to dictatorships. While they boast a long historical memory, the skeptics forget the record of their own forebears. Many of the doubts expressed about the prospects of today's fledgling democracies were expressed a few decades ago about democracies now considered stable and enduring. As World War II drew to its end and America began to contemplate what to do with Japan, President Harry Truman received a briefing from Joseph Grew, the State Department's leading Japan expert, who had served there as U.S. ambassador until the war. Grew told him that "from the long-range point of view, the best we can hope for is a constitutional monarchy, experience having shown that democracy in Japan would never work."

When the Western occupation of West Germany ended in

1952, the eminent political scientist Heinz Eulau toured that country and wrote despairingly about the prospects for democracy there. "German politics is . . . grounded not on democratic experience but on a deep emotionalism. . . ."

Democracy and Peace

A tide of democratic change is sweeping the world, not only in the once-monolithic communist regions but also in a wave that started in Mediterranean Europe in the mid-1970s and spread to Latin America, Asia, Africa and, even, South Africa.

Remarkably, the current demise of communism and the movement toward democracy have come not in the aftermath of destructive war but in an unprecedented half-century of global peace. Indeed they come at a time when the Cold War has ended, regional conflicts from Central America to Southeast Asia have abated, and Europe, the very powder keg of global wars from the late eighteenth to the mid-twentieth centuries, has moved into a historic process of economic and political unification.

Dankwart A. Rustow, *Foreign Affairs*, Fall 1990.

Doubts about the suitability of democracy have in the recent past extended all the way to America itself, or at least to parts of it. As Senator Strom Thurmond explained to the Harvard Law School in 1957: *Many Negroes simply lack sufficient political consciousness to spur them on to participate in political and civic affairs. I might point out here that a great number of those who lack this political consciousness probably also lack certain other qualities prerequisite to casting a truly intelligent ballot, and thus that the cause of good government would not necessarily be served by a sudden vast swelling of the registration lists through artificial politically-inspired stimuli.*

Within a few years after the adoption of the Voting Rights Act, however, Senator Thurmond had reevaluated the level of Negro political consciousness to the extent of announcing his decision to become the first southern senator to hire a Negro professional staff member. Why should today's skepticism about democracy in Latin America or Asia prove any more perspicacious than that of a couple of generations ago about Japan, Europe—or South Carolina?

Democracy is fragile and needs time to take hold. It would be amazing if the current democratic momentum were unbroken by disappointments and reversals here and there. Many states where democracy is now entrenched once experienced failures at establishing democratic rule: France, for example. Many newer nations are likely to have similar experiences. But history shows a gradual and ragged advance of democracy. Indeed, to call democracy's growth gradual may concede too much to the skeptics. When modern democracy was born in 1776, the free population of the United States was not much more than 2 million. The electorate, all-male and in some states qualified by property ownership, amounted to less than 1 million. Today, according to Freedom House's figures, more than 2 billion people live in democratic countries. In short, over the past 200 years, while the population of the world has grown six times larger, the population of the world that is self-governing has increased 2,000-fold.

A Historical Pattern

We may gain some perspective by considering the world in arbitrary 50-year intervals. In the world of 1800, one democracy existed, the small United States of America. The French Revolution, though inspired in part by America, had failed to establish democratic government. If we look next at 1850, America had been joined in the democratic camp by Belgium, Switzerland, and to some extent England, which had an elected government although a majority of males still lacked the franchise. By 1900, England was almost fully democratic. France too was a democracy. Italy, the Low Countries, and Scandinavia were all in varying degrees democratic or well on their way to being so. By 1950, all of Western Europe, except Iberia, was democratic, including West Germany, although its elected government still functioned under the aegis of the Allied occupation. The same was true for Japan. Newly independent India was democratic, as were Israel and Lebanon.

The next half-century interval, beginning in the year 2000, is still a decade away. Today, we find all of Western Europe democratic, with inroads being made into Eastern Europe. We also find nearly all of Latin America and the Caribbean democratic, as well as many of the Pacific island states and large areas of Asia. By the year 2000, some of the 61 countries that Freedom House called free in 1990 may have fallen off the list, but this list may also expand over these years. In this 200-year interval, democracy has not only spread dramatically but it also seems to be growing at an accelerating pace.

The spread of democracy will come about not through the influence of American power or by the exact imitation of American institutions but by the recognition and acceptance of those profound and humane ideals on which America was founded.

"The worldwide move toward democracy is beset by . . . major challenges."

A New Era of Democracy Is Uncertain

Doyle McManus and Robin Wright

Doyle McManus and Robin Wright are reporters for the *Los Angeles Times*. In the following viewpoint, they argue that despite the movement toward democracy in Eastern Europe and elsewhere, the worldwide spread of democracy is not a certain development. Economic problems, ethnic rivalries, and cultures that seem incapable of adopting democratic principles may slow or reverse the trend toward democracy, they reason.

As you read, consider the following questions:

1. Why does Yuri Shchekochikhin believe Russians are not ready for democracy?
2. What three major challenges does democracy face in the world, according to McManus and Wright?
3. Why are some people in developed nations dissatisfied with democracy, according to the authors?

By all rights, Yuri Shchekochikhin, a 39-year-old Russian playwright, should be a very happy man. His plays are winning wide acclaim; the newspaper column he writes is avidly read. He has even been elected to the new Soviet Parliament. Most important, his ardent cause—the advent of democracy—is closer to fruition than ever before.

Yet Shchekochikhin, like many of his countrymen, is deeply depressed.

"The situation is terrible," he declared, chain-smoking his way down Kalinina Prospekt, one of Moscow's tree-lined boulevards. "I am worried about a right-wing coup, a military coup. . . . We are heading for terrible trouble."

Russians simply are not ready for democracy, the new Parliament member complained. His constituents besiege him for help in getting jobs, or apartments, or telephones. "People here still want a good czar to fix everything," he said.

These should be heady days for Moscow's democrats. The city is a madcap bazaar of new political movements, from Liberal Democrats, Social Democrats, Christian Democrats and Constitutional Democrats to Monarchists, Pacifists, Greens and even Blues ("the color of outer space," an official explained).

But when Shchekochikhin and his wife, Nadia, welcome friends to their cramped apartment for a dinner of lamb stew and endless bottles of vodka, their conversation returns time and again to the same discomfiting paradox: Their hopes have never been higher, and they have never been more afraid.

Democracies Under Strain

And the Russians aren't alone. Around the world, from Prague's Hradcany Castle to the Royal Palace of Katmandu, an extraordinary uprising of popular will has swept communist and other authoritarian governments from power, seemingly resolving the central political struggle of the 20th Century in favor of capitalism and democracy. But instead of a golden age of stable, humane politics, most newly democratic countries find themselves beset by insecurity and fear.

In Latin America, rightist dictatorships have given way to popularly elected presidents, only to see democracy's luster dimmed by economic stagnation. In Eastern Europe, a string of communist dictatorships have fallen, but some countries are already feeling what a leader of Poland's Solidarity movement called "the totalitarian temptation."

"The tide is coming in now; I think the tide will go out," said Brent Scowcroft, President George Bush's national security adviser. "A lot of [the new democracies] will not survive the strains of societies trying to cope with very difficult problems."

The worldwide move toward democracy is beset by three major

challenges:

• Where prosperity seems beyond reach, as in Eastern Europe and Latin America, citizens may despair of elected governments. Empty grocery shelves and unemployment tempt some to trade freedom for promises of order and security—whether a return to military strongmen in Latin America or a resurgence in Eastern Europe not of Stalin-style communism but of authoritarian populism.

By Dana Summers © 1989, Washington Post Writers Group. Reprinted with permission.

• From the Soviet Union to the Middle East and Asia, democracy's tolerance for pluralism and diversity often collides with religious beliefs and other traditional values—sometimes bending democratic principles into almost unrecognizable shapes. Russia, for example, appears headed down a zigzag path toward a Slavic combination of democracy and authoritarianism; other Soviet republics may invent their own variations, too. One consequence: ideological friction among nations, while less acute than during the Cold War, is unlikely to disappear.

• Even in the stable and prosperous West, there's a growing consensus that democracy needs renewal, but no agreement on how to go about it. In parts of Western Europe, the radical right and the radical left have shown worrisome bursts of strength. And in the United States, polls find Americans troubled by the shortcomings of their own political system. On both continents, new movements and pressure groups are seeking to make government more responsive.

In the 1990s, all these prospects may become sources of concern for Americans, who have long believed that the spread of democracy helps ensure world peace because democratic governments rarely go to war with each other. The promotion of democracy around the world was a major goal of U.S. foreign policy during the 1980s. Now, as democracy is being threatened, Americans may find themselves debating whether—and how—to step in and help.

The turn of the 1990s marked a political epoch: the collapse of Marxism and the virtual dissolution of the left-vs.-right spectrum that defined Western politics for more than a century. But the change may not be over yet.

The old political alignments are taking new forms, from Russia's Democrats, Greens and Blues to Israel's Zionists—from South Africa's white minority to the Arab world's Muslim majority.

"As long as people are people, democracy, in the full sense of the word, will always be no more than an ideal," Czechoslovakia's President Vaclav Havel said in his speech to the U.S. Congress in February 1990. "One can approach it as one would the horizon in ways that may be better or worse, but it can never be fully attained. In this sense, you, too, are merely approaching democracy."

Economic Priorities

With luck, Daman Dhungane, a middle-aged lawyer from Katmandu, may some day be remembered as the James Madison of the Himalayas. A member of the commission that drafted the first democratic constitution for Nepal's 1,200-year-old monarchy, he trekked from jungle valleys to the slopes of Mt. Everest asking his countrymen what their charter should say.

He got responses Madison never contemplated.

"All they say is 'Airplanes,'" Dhungane recalled. "Everyone wants an airfield and an airplane, plus seeds and fertilizer. How can we write that into the constitution?"

Dhungane's dilemma is emblematic of a predicament facing many of the world's new democracies: From Asia to the Andes, citizens want fundamental liberties, but they often judge a government first on how well it delivers the goods—airplanes and fertilizer, jobs and prosperity.

From that standpoint, the new democracies face tough times.

Throughout the 20th Century, when economic troubles hit countries with weak democratic institutions, the result was frequently democracy's collapse. The regimes that followed were authoritarian and sometimes bellicose—from Germany's Hitler to Latin America's generals. Nowhere is the problem more stark—or more heartbreaking—than in Poland and Argentina, whose peo-

164

ples struggled to escape from tyranny, only to be handed the painful legacy of economic misrule.

In both countries, the old political struggle between left and right has been put aside. Now, the question is whether citizens will keep faith in democracy through hard times, or surrender to the promises of new authoritarian demagogues.

Eastern Europe

Poland opened the way for democracy in Eastern Europe through the epic, decade-long struggle of the Solidarity movement. Now . . . economic hardship has stripped democracy of some of its allure.

An economic austerity program, after an initial period of success, stunned Poles with its severity; more than 1 million found themselves suddenly unemployed, and the price of bread more than tripled. Almost overnight, the language of politics changed from celebration to recrimination.

"What shape will political life take here?" asked Adam Michnik, one of Solidarity's leading intellectuals. "It will not be . . . the rebuilding of a Western European state with division into left and right. It will be a conflict of two political cultures: on one side the culture of European liberalism and the other, nationalist, authoritarian and conservative.". . .

Elsewhere in Eastern Europe, Czechoslovakia and Hungary, which had longer histories of democracy before World War II, are suffering the same ills, only to a lesser degree. Bulgaria, Romania and Yugoslavia, with a more meager democratic heritage, are doing even worse. . . .

Argentina

Far across the Atlantic from Eastern Europe, South America is waging its own struggle to stay democratic. A continent once run by so many generals that military rule became known as "the Latin model" now boasts an unbroken string of elected civilian governments. And after a long wave of economic disasters turned the 1980s into what Latins call "the Lost Decade," most governments—whatever their original political stripe—now proclaim that protectionism and state management of the economy were wrong.

"We in South America are enacting a true epic," said Argentina's former president, Raul Alfonsin, who restored democracy after seven years of military rule.

"This has occurred in the framework of the worst [economic] crisis we have suffered in this century. This thoroughly gives the lie to those who suggest that democracy is not viable in countries that don't have a given level of well-being or economic growth."

But the democracy Alfonsin restored in Argentina is now in danger of collapsing because of economic chaos. In 1989, inflation soared to more than 3,000%, hungry mobs looted supermarkets, and Alfonsin lost his bid for reelection.

His successor, the populist Carlos Saul Menem, launched economic reforms so stringent that they shocked his own followers. Menem's program initially drove inflation down to only 5% per month—but then, just as in Poland, conditions turned worse again. Today, inflation is back up to 15% per month and thousands of Argentines are applying to emigrate back to Spain and Italy, the countries their grandparents left in search of a better life.

The Durability of Democracy

Although at the moment Western-style liberal democracy appears to be the most appealing form of government, we should not be complacent about its durability, especially where it is newly established. Will its global popularity withstand major economic setbacks, or even a prolonged failure to deliver the goods to developing nations eager to reach European, Japanese, and American standards of living?

Eliot Cohen, *The National Interest*, Fall 1990.

"There is a danger that behind this disenchantment there could come . . . a pre-Nazi climate, a climate that would allow all the authoritarian sectors to move us backward," Alfonsin said sadly. Political scientist Atilio Boron is more bitter. "You can save democracy only when you can show that democracy matters and that democracy works," he said. "Alfonsin said that with democracy, people would eat, people would find their [kidnapped] children and people would be cured. None of that came true. . . . Democracy for us has been nothing.

"If democracy does not work in Latin America, then the way is open for fundamentalist messianic leadership . . . an ultra-nationalist right-wing movement," he said. . . .

Democracy and Islam

It was one of the most democratic elections ever held in the Arab world. The campaigning was spirited; the vote count was honest. For the first time, women were allowed to vote. The winner: an alliance of Islamic fundamentalists who believe democracy is legitimate only if it obeys the dictates of the Holy Koran.

The members of Jordan's new Parliament, elected in that vote in 1989, promised to respect democracy, Islam and the monarchy of King Hussein, all at the same time. Most of them also openly rejected secular, Western values—the values most Americans think of as part and parcel of democracy.

"We accept democracy," said Laith Shubeilat, a soft-spoken civil engineer who is one of the newly elected fundamentalists. "We do not accept liberal democracy. . . . The values of society should be Islamic."

One of the basic goals of Islamic democracy, he said, is to make Muslim values the moral standards of Jordanian society and Muslim religious law the basis of civil jurisprudence. Otherwise, he complained in a thoroughly modern metaphor: "We are Muslim hardware being reprogrammed to carry Western software."

From Muslim Jordan to Buddhist Burma, ordinary people have stood up with courage and persistence to demand the same things: democratic government and an economy that works. But while the demand has been universal, the chosen solutions are not.

As a result, in the decade ahead, the banner of democracy may unfurl over forms of government the West will find hard to accept or even understand.

In much of Asia, Africa and the Middle East, the democratic ideals first developed in 18th Century America and Europe still conflict with more traditional views of life. In the Middle East, the main political struggle is not between left and right, but between Islamic and secular. In East Asia, it is between the Confucian tradition of hierarchical authority and newer, more populist challenges. In Africa, it is between tribal and nationalist forms of political life.

In the Soviet Union, where the stakes are highest of all, the contest is between the traditional Russian desire for a strong central authority and the growing centrifugal tendencies toward pluralism.

"Right now, we're in a wave of democratic advances," Scowcroft said. "I don't think they'll last everywhere, because there are many societies, in many parts of the world, in which a society based on the individual . . . is kind of anathema. An individual is nothing as an individual; he only gets identity as part of a group of some kind or another, whether it's religious or cultural or ethnic. So I'm not sure that democracy is going to sweep the world.". . .

Extremist Groups in Germany

On paper, the Germans of 1990 have everything: roaring prosperity, a stable democracy and, now, reunification. So why are some of them unhappy with the new post-modern order?

Spokesmen for the neo-Nazis, the anarchists and radical Greens offer vaguely similar answers, despite enormous differences in their ideologies: somehow, parliamentary democracy doesn't satisfy all the hungers of people caught up in a confusing, changing world. Some Europeans still yearn for causes and ideologies more consuming than market capitalism. . . .

167

The upsurge of extremist politics is not confined to Germany. In France, the rightist National Front won almost 12% of the vote in elections for the European Parliament in 1989, largely by stirring hatred of non-European immigrants. In Italy, local neo-fascist parties have been gaining respectability and support. Even in the United States, former Ku Klux Klan leader David Duke won a surprising 44% of the vote in 1990 for a U.S. Senate seat from Louisiana.

Democracy and the Soul

There is more going on here than simple racism or xenophobia. French historian Emmanuel Todd believes these movements are, in large part, reactions to the larger strains of adjustment as societies move into the 21st Century. Paradoxically, he argues, as the traditional quarrels between left and right die down, fringe movements gain more support.

"The existence of the National Front [in France] is quite typical of the situation where the politics are becoming centrist," he said. "The existence of the National Front . . . is not so much connected with the intensity of the immigration problem; it's much more connected with the speed of the transformation in society itself."

Both the new European right and the Greens, he suggested, have risen to provide "disoriented individuals and groups threatened by economic changes a chance to express their anguish."

An Unsatisfactory Ideology

But there is yet a deeper problem, a philosophical one: is democracy satisfying to the soul?

The two totalitarian ideologies of the 20th Century, communism and fascism, were both utopian creeds born of dissatisfaction with the existing democratic order (abetted, of course, by economic distress). There are some who suggest that the same bleak mood could arise again.

"Liberalism has won, but it may be decisively unsatisfactory," wrote Allan Bloom, the conservative social philosopher at the University of Chicago, referring to "liberalism" in the broad sense of democratic secularism.

"It appears that the world has been made safe for reason as understood by the market, and we are moving toward a global common market, the only goal of which is to minister to man's bodily needs and whims," he wrote.

And in such a future, he argued, a rebirth of fascism cannot be counted out. "If an alternative is sought there is nowhere else to seek it," Bloom wrote. "I would suggest that fascism has a future, if not *the* future."

"A world of spreading democratic ideology and practice offers some significant possibilities for spreading peace."

The End of the Cold War Will Lessen Worldwide Conflict

Bruce Russett

Bruce Russett is the Dean Acheson Professor of International Relations and Political Science at Yale University in New Haven, Connecticut. He is the editor of the *Journal of Conflict Resolution* and has written many books, including *Controlling the Sword: The Democratic Governance of National Security*. In the following viewpoint, he argues that the end of the Cold War could usher in a new era of peace. Because democratic countries historically have almost never gone to war with each other, Russett predicts that the spread of democracy will result in a more peaceful world.

As you read, consider the following questions:

1. What two apparent facts does Russett discuss at the beginning of the viewpoint?
2. Why do democratic states avoid war, according to the author?
3. What is the main difference between domestic and international politics, according to Russett?

Bruce Russett, "Politics and Alternative Security: Toward a More Democratic, Therefore More Peaceful, World," in *Alternative Security: Living Without Nuclear Deterrence*, Burns H. Weston, editor. Boulder CO: Westview Press, 1990. Reprinted with permission.

Two apparent facts about contemporary international patterns of war and peace stare us in the face. The first is that some States expect, prepare for, and fight wars against other States. The second is that some States do *not* expect, prepare for, or fight wars *at least against each other*. The first is obvious to everyone. The second is widely ignored, yet it is now true on an historically unprecedented scale, encompassing wide areas of the earth. In a real if still partial sense, peace is already among us. We need only recognize it, and try to learn from it. . . .

Peace Among Democracies

I am referring to the peace among the industrialized and democratically governed States, primarily in the northern hemisphere. These States—members of the Organization for Economic Cooperation and Development (OECD: Western Europe, North America, Japan, Australia, and New Zealand), plus a few scattered less industrialized democratic States—constitute a vast zone of peace, with more than three quarters of a billion people. Not only has there been no war among them for almost 45 years, . . . there has been little expectation of, or preparation for, war among them either. By war I mean large-scale organized international violence with at least 1,000 battle deaths (by a conventional social science definition). In fact, even much smaller-scale violence between these countries has been virtually absent. The nearest exception is Greece and Turkey, especially with their brief and limited violent clashes over Cyprus. They are, however, among the poorest countries of this group and only sporadically democratic.

In the years before 1945, many of them fought often and bitterly, but always when at least one of the States in any warring pair was ruled by an authoritarian or totalitarian regime. Despite that past, war among them is now virtually unthinkable. What seemingly had been the most permanent enmities—for instance, between France and Germany—have for the past two or three decades appeared well buried. Individual citizens may not love each other across national boundaries, but neither do they expect the other's State to attack nor do they wish to mount an attack on it. Expectations of peace are thus equally important; these peoples make few preparations for violence between them; peace for them means more than just the prevention of war through threat and deterrence. This condition has been characterized as a "security community" or as "stable peace." By the standards of world history this is an extraordinary achievement.

Explanations for Peace

It is not easy to explain just why this peace has occurred. Partly it is due to the network of *international law and institutions* deliberately put into place to make a repetition of the previous world wars both unthinkable and impossible. But that network is strongest in Western Europe, often excluding the countries in North America and the Far East; even in the strongest instance the institutions typically lack full powers to police and coerce would-be breakers of the peace—and, as we shall see, even powerful institutions alone cannot guarantee peace if the underlying preconditions of peace are lacking.

In part it is due to favorable economic conditions associated with advanced capitalism. Fairly steady economic growth, a high absolute level of prosperity, relative equality of incomes within and across the industrial States, and a dense network of trade and investment across national borders all make resort to violence dubious on cost-benefit grounds; a potential aggressor who already is wealthy risks much by resorting to violence for only moderate gain. But the condition of peace among these rich States has not been endangered by periods of postwar recession and stagnation, and in other parts of the world, especially Latin America, there are democratic States that are not wealthy but still at peace with one another.

Partly too, peace is the result of a perceived external threat faced by the industrialized democracies. They maintain peace among themselves in order not to invite intervention by the communist powers. Where peace among them is threatened, it may be enforced by the dominant hegemonic power of the United States. But the external threat also has waxed and waned without affecting the peace among these States. Indeed, their peace became even more stable during the 1970s and 1980s, the very time when the Cold War abated and Europeans, especially, ceased to have much fear of Soviet attack. All these explanations, therefore, are at best only partial ones, and we are driven back to observing that the period of peace among the highly industrialized States essentially coincides with the period when they all have been under democratic rule. . . .

Peace and Democratic States

With only the most marginal exceptions, democratic States have not fought each other in the modern era. This is perhaps the strongest non-trivial or non-tautological statement that can be made about international relations. The nearest exception is Lebanon's peripheral involvement in Israel's "War of Independence" in 1948. Israel had not yet held an election, so Melvin Small and J. David Singer did not count it as a democracy. Other exceptions are truly marginal: in 1849 between two States both briefly democratic (France and the Papal States), and Finland against the western allies in World War II (nominal only because Finland's real quarrel was with the USSR). In the War of 1812 with the United States, Britain's franchise was sharply restricted, as was the Boer Republic's in its attempt to preserve its indepen-

171

dence against Britain in 1898.

By democratic State I mean the conditions of public contestation and participation, essentially as identified by Robert Dahl, with a voting franchise for a substantial fraction of male citizens (in the Nineteenth and early Twentieth centuries and wider thereafter), contested elections, and an executive either popularly elected or responsible to an elected legislature. While scholars who have found this pattern differ slightly in their definitions, agreement on the condition of non-war among democracies ("liberal," "libertarian," or "polyarchic" States) is now overwhelming. This simple fact cries out for explanation: what is it about democratic government that inhibits people from fighting one another? . . .

Distribution of International Wars, 1945-88

| | Fought in | | |
Fought by	OECD countries	Communist countries	Less developed countries
OECD countries	0	1	7
Communist countries	0	3	3
Less developed countries	0	1	19

Source: Melvin Small and J. David Singer, *Resort to Arms: International and Civil Wars* (Beverly Hills, CA: Sage, 1982), updated to 1988. Includes all interstate and colonial wars (not civil wars) with over 1,000 battle deaths.

There are powerful norms against the use of lethal force both within democratic States and between them. Within them is of course the basic norm of liberal democratic theory—that disputes can be resolved without force through democratic political processes, which in some balance are to ensure both majority rule and minority rights. A norm of equality operates both as voting equality and as certain egalitarian rights to human dignity. Democratic government rests on the consent of the governed, but justice demands that consent not be abused. Resort to organized lethal violence, or the threat of it, is considered illegitimate and unnecessary to secure one's legitimate rights. Dissent within broad limits by a loyal opposition is expected and even needed for enlightened policy-making, and the opposition's basic loyalty to the system is to be assumed in the absence of evidence to the contrary.

All participants in the political process are expected to share these norms. In practice, the norms do sometimes break down, but the normative restraints on violent behavior—by State and citizens—are fully as important as the State's monopoly on the legitimate use of force in keeping incidents of the organized use of force rare. In fact, the norms are probably more important than is any particular institutional characteristic (two party/multi-party, republican/parliamentary) or formal constitutional provision. Institutions may precede the development of norms. If they do, the basis for restraint is likely to be less secure.

Democracy did not suddenly emerge full-blown in the West; nor did it emerge by any linear progression. Only over time did it come to mean the extension of a universal voting franchise, formal protection for the rights of ethnic, racial, and religious minorities, and the rights of groups to organize for economic and social action. The rights to organize came to imply the right to carry on conflict—non-violently—as by strikes, under the principle that both sides in the conflict had to recognize the right of the other to struggle, so long as that struggle was constrained by law, mutual self-interest, and mutual respect. The implicit or explicit contract in the extension of such rights was that the beneficiaries of those rights in turn would extend them to their adversaries. . . .

Winners and Losers

Politics within a democracy is seen as largely a non-zero sum enterprise: by cooperating, all can gain something even if all do not gain equally, and the winners today are restrained from crushing the losers; indeed, the winners may, with shifting coalitions, wish tomorrow to ally with today's losers. If the conflicts degenerate to physical violence, either by those in control of the State or by insurgents, all can lose. In international politics—the anarchy of a self-help system with no superordinate governing authority—these norms are not the same. "Realists" remind us of the powerful norms of legitimate self-defense and the acceptability of military deterrence, norms much more extensive internationally than within democratic States. Politics between nations takes on a more zero-sum hue. True, we know we all can lose in nuclear war or in a collapse of international commerce, but we worry much more about comparative gains and losses. The essence of realist politics is that even when two States both become more wealthy, if one gains much more wealth than the other it also gains more power potential to coerce the other; thus the one that is lagging economically only in relative terms may be an absolute loser in the power contest.

Theories of International Relations

The principles of anarchy and self-help in a zero-sum world are seen most acutely in "structural realist" theories of international relations. Specifically, a bipolar system of two great States or alliances, each much more powerful than any others in the international system, is seen as inherently antagonistic. The nature of the great powers' internal systems of government is irrelevant; whatever they may work out with or impose on some of their smaller allies, their overall behavior with other great powers is basically determined by the structure of the international system and their position in that structure. Athens and Sparta, the United States and the Soviet Union, all are doomed to compete and to resist any substantial accretion to the other's power. . . .

Yet democratic peoples . . . sense that somehow they and other peoples *ought* to be able to satisfy common interests and work out compromise solutions to their problems, without recourse to violence or threat of it. After all, that is the norm for behavior to which they aspire within democratic systems. Because other people living in democratic States are presumed to share those norms of live and let live, they can be presumed to share their moderate behavior in international affairs as well. That is, they can be respected as self-governing peoples and expected to offer the same respect to other democratic countries in turn. The habits and predispositions they show in their behavior in internal politics can be presumed to apply when they deal with like-minded outsiders. If one claims the principle of self-determination for oneself, normatively one must accord it to others perceived as self-governing. Norms do matter. Within a transnational democratic culture, as within a democratic nation, others are seen as possessing rights and exercising those rights in a spirit of enlightened self-interest. Acknowledgment of those rights both prevents us from wishing to dominate them and allows us to mitigate our fear that they will try to dominate us.

Realism has no explanation for the fact that certain kinds of States—namely, democratic ones—do not fight or prepare to fight one another. One must look instead to the liberal idealist vision of Immanuel Kant's *Perpetual Peace*, embodied also in Woodrow Wilson's vision of a peaceful world of democratic States. This same vision inspired US determination to root out fascism and establish the basis for democratic governments in West Germany and Japan after World War II (and partly also explains, and was used to justify, interventions in Vietnam, Grenada, Nicaragua, and so on). . . .

A Shift Toward Democracy

The end of World War II brought in its wake the demise of colonial empires; it brought a degree of self-determination to the formally colonized peoples. Unfortunately, that self-determination was often highly restricted, limited in part by ties of economic and military neo-colonialism. Self-determination also was often limited to the elites of the new States, as the governments installed were frequently authoritarian and repressive—anything but democratic. Yet there has been, since the mid-1970s, some evolution toward greater democracy in large parts of what is called the Third World. In 1973 only two Spanish- or Portuguese-speaking States in South America were governed by democratic regimes (Colombia and Venezuela); [in 1990] only two are ruled by military dictatorships (Paraguay and, in transition, Chile). Democracy remains fragile and imperfect in many of them, but the relative shift away from authoritarian rule is palpable.

A Zone of Peace

The East-West rivalry during the four decades of Cold War was of a very traditional sort: two great alliance systems struggling for predominance. As in great-power rivalries of the past, military instruments and tacit or explicit threats of force have been central elements. Meanwhile, however, the currency of weapons and the threat of force have vanished almost entirely from relations among the other developed, industrialized states. Despite heavy historical legacies such as long-standing Franco-German antagonism, since the 1950s the use of force between France and the Federal Republic of Germany has been inconceivable. Similarly, it strains the imagination to put forward any plausible scenario involving the use of force between France and a reunified German state. Liberal democratic states, as Princeton University professor Michael Doyle has convincingly argued, do not make war on one another, bitter though their disputes may sometimes become.

Richard H. Ullman, *Foreign Policy*, Fall 1990.

This shift shows up statistically on a worldwide basis. A long-term observer of political rights and civil liberties, Raymond Gastil, has carried out, over this period, a project of rating countries according to their degree of "political freedom." His rating is not meant to reflect a broad definition of human rights that includes, for example, the so-called second generation economic rights to employment or the satisfaction of basic physical needs. Rather, it addresses first generation rights: electoral practices, the accountability of the executive and legislature, judicial procedures, and freedom of expression and association—in short, dimensions of the traditional political definition of democracy. For some of his purposes, Gastil uses two scales of seven points each; for others he collapses these complex judgments into three categories of States: free, partly free, and not free. The distribution of States in these three categories has varied over time.

By this evaluation, there has been a substantial decline in the number of strongly authoritarian (not free) States and a similarly substantial increase in the number of partly free States, especially if 1973 is used as the base year. These trends can be seen in many parts of the world: the demise of dictatorships in Greece, Portugal, and Spain in Europe; Gastil's recent characterization of Hungary, Poland, and even the Soviet Union with scores in the "partly free" range; improvements he noted in China (as of 1988, and still overall "not free"); and shifts in several large, important countries elsewhere. Does this analysis imply something more, that if the shift toward democracy does continue, we would then move into an era of international peace? If all States were democratic, could we all live in perpetual peace? Does a solution lie in creating a world where all countries are governed by democratic practices? In principle, this would both rid the world of aggressive behavior of some kinds of autocratic regimes and deprive democratically governed peoples of a normatively legitimate target for jingoism.

A serious reservation, however, must concern interpretation of the word "creating." The argument here does *not* imply that the route to ultimate perpetual peace is through wars, or threats of war, to make other countries democratic. . . .

A second temptation, related to the first, may be to define "democracy" too narrowly and ethnocentrically, equating it too readily with all the particular norms and institutions of the Western parliamentary tradition. . . .

It is inexcusably ethnocentric to imagine that other peoples are inherently incapable of autonomy and self-government, to declare them unsuited for democracy. Although it is myopic to overlook or idealize the ways in which many Third World governments, for instance, oppress their own peoples, it is equally ethnocentric to imagine that their ways of insuring autonomy and self-determination will be exactly like ours or to require the full panoply of Western forms. In terms of the vision here, what is important is to support democratic governments where they exist and to recognize and reinforce a worldwide movement toward greater popular control over governments, rather than to specify the endpoint in detail for each case.

Conclusion

Whatever the faults of Western liberal (bourgeois) democracy, a world of spreading democratic ideology and practice offers some significant possibilities for spreading peace. Those possibilities can be enhanced by attention to implementing a broad definition of human rights and institutionalizing greater information flows. Human rights and information constitute elements both of greater global democratization and of direct and indirect contributions to international peace. In a world of imperfect democratization, such measures can help reduce those imperfections and compensate for some of them in the avoidance of war.

4

"The prospects for international peace are not markedly influenced by the domestic political character of states."

The End of the Cold War Will Not Lessen Worldwide Conflict

John J. Mearsheimer

John J. Mearsheimer chairs the department of political science at the University of Chicago. In the following viewpoint, he argues that there is no reason to believe wars cannot break out between democratic states. He argues that the countries of Europe have a long tradition of warfare, and that historical animosities and struggles for power and influence could lead to future wars after the U.S. and the Soviet Union withdraw.

As you read, consider the following questions:

1. Why does Mearsheimer believe the Cold War will be missed?
2. What flaws does the author perceive in arguments that say democratic countries will not engage in war?
3. What examples of wars or near-wars between democracies does Mearsheimer describe?

John J. Mearsheimer, "Why We Will Soon Miss the Cold War," *The Atlantic*, August 1990. Reprinted with permission.

Peace: it's wonderful. I like it as much as the next man, and have no wish to be willfully gloomy at a moment when optimism about the future shape of the world abounds. Nevertheless, my thesis in this essay is that we are likely soon to regret the passing of the Cold War.

To be sure, no one will miss such by-products of the Cold War as the Korean and Vietnam conflicts. No one will want to replay the U-2 affair, the Cuban missile crisis, or the building of the Berlin Wall. And no one will want to revisit the domestic Cold War, with its purges and loyalty oaths, its xenophobia and stifling of dissent. We will not wake up one day to discover fresh wisdom in the collected fulminations of John Foster Dulles.

We may, however, wake up one day lamenting the loss of the order that the Cold War gave to the anarchy of international relations. For untamed anarchy is what Europe knew in the forty-five years of this century before the Cold War, and untamed anarchy—Hobbes's war of all against all—is a prime cause of armed conflict. Those who think that armed conflicts among the European states are now out of the question, that the two world wars burned all the war out of Europe, are projecting unwarranted optimism onto the future. The theories of peace that implicitly undergird this optimism are notably shallow constructs. They stand up to neither logical nor historical analysis. You would not want to bet the farm on their prophetic accuracy.

Testing the Theories of War

The world is about to conduct a vast test of the theories of war and peace put forward by social scientists, who never dreamed that their ideas would be tested by the world-historic events announced almost daily in newspaper headlines. This social scientist is willing to put his theoretical cards on the table as he ventures predictions about the future of Europe. In the process, I hope to put alternative theories of war and peace under as much intellectual pressure as I can muster. My argument is that the prospect of major crises, even wars, in Europe is likely to increase dramatically now that the Cold War is receding into history. The next forty-five years in Europe are not likely to be so violent as the forty-five years before the Cold War, but they are likely to be substantially more violent than the past forty-five years, the era that we may someday look back upon not as the Cold War but as the Long Peace, in John Lewis Gaddis's phrase.

This pessimistic conclusion rests on the general argument that the distribution and character of military power among states are the root causes of war and peace. Specifically, the peace in Europe since 1945—precarious at first, but increasingly robust over time—has flowed from three factors: the bipolar distribution of military power on the Continent; the rough military equality between the polar powers, the United States and the Soviet Union; and the ritualistically deplored fact that each of these superpowers is armed with a large nuclear arsenal.

Tom Meyer. Reprinted with permission.

We don't yet know the entire shape of the new Europe. But we do know some things. We know, for example, that the new Europe will involve a return to the multipolar distribution of power that characterized the European state system from its founding, with the Peace of Westphalia, in 1648, until 1945. We know that this multipolar European state system was plagued by war from first to last. We know that from 1900 to 1945 some 50 million Europeans were killed in wars that were caused in great part by the instability of this state system. We also know that since 1945 only some 15,000 Europeans have been killed in wars: roughly 10,000 Hungarians and Russians, in what we might call the Russo-Hungarian War of October and November, 1956, and somewhere between 1,500 and 5,000 Greeks and Turks, in the July and August, 1974, war on Cyprus.

The point is clear: Europe is reverting to a state system that created powerful incentives for aggression in the past. If you believe (as the Realist school of international relations theory, to which I belong, believes) that the prospects for international peace are not markedly influenced by the domestic political character of states—that it is the character of the state system, not the character of the individual units composing it, that drives states toward war—then it is difficult to share in the widespread elation of the moment about the future of Europe. The year 1989 was repeatedly compared to 1789, the year the French Revolution began, as the Year of Freedom, and so it was. Forgotten in the general exaltation was that the hope-filled events of 1789 signaled the start of an era of war and conquest. . . .

Is War Obsolete?

Many students of European politics will reject my pessimistic analysis of post-Cold War Europe. They will say that a multipolar Europe, with or without nuclear weapons, will be no less peaceful than the present order. Three specific scenarios for a peaceful future have been advanced, each of which rests on a well-known theory of international relations. However, each of these "soft" theories of peace is flawed.

Under the first optimistic scenario, a non-nuclear Europe would remain peaceful because Europeans recognize that even a conventional war would be horrific. Sobered by history, national leaders will take care to avoid war. This scenario rests on the "obsolescence of war" theory, which posits that modern conventional war had become so deadly by 1945 as to be unthinkable as an instrument of statecraft. War is yesterday's nightmare.

The fact that the Second World War occurred casts doubt on this theory: if any war could have persuaded Europeans to forswear conventional war, it should have been the First World War, with its vast casualties. The key flaw in this theory is the assumption that all conventional wars will be long and bloody wars of attrition. Proponents ignore the evidence of several wars since 1945, as well as several campaign-ending battles of the Second World War, that it is still possible to gain a quick and decisive victory on the conventional battlefield and avoid the devastation of a protracted conflict. Conventional wars can be won rather cheaply; nuclear war cannot be, because neither side can escape devastation by the other, regardless of what happens on the battlefield. Thus the incentives to avoid war are of another order of intensity in a nuclear world than they are in a conventional world. . . .

Is Prosperity the Path to Peace?

Proponents of the second optimistic scenario base their optimism about the future of Europe on the unified European market coming in 1992—the realization of the dream of the European Community. A strong EC, they argue, ensures that the European economy will remain open and prosperous, which will keep the European states cooperating with one another. Prosperity will make for peace. The threat of an aggressive Germany will be removed by enclosing the newly unified German state in the benign embrace of the EC. Even Eastern Europe and the Soviet Union can eventually be brought into the EC. Peace and prosperity will then extend their sway from the Atlantic to the Urals.

This scenario is based on the theory of economic liberalism, which assumes that states are primarily motivated by the desire to achieve prosperity and that leaders place the material welfare of their publics above all other considerations, including security. Stability flows not from military power but from the creation of a liberal economic order. . . .

One Flaw

This theory has one grave flaw: the main assumption underpinning it is wrong. States are not primarily motivated by the desire to achieve prosperity. Although economic calculations are hardly trivial to them, states operate in both an international political and an international economic environment, and the former dominates the latter when the two systems come into conflict. Survival in an anarchic international political system is the highest goal a state can have.

Proponents of economic liberalism largely ignore the effects of anarchy on state behavior and concentrate instead on economic motives. When this omission is corrected, however, their arguments collapse for two reasons.

Competition for security makes it difficult for states to cooperate, which, according to the theory of economic liberalism, they must do. When security is scarce, states become more concerned about relative than about absolute gains. They ask of an exchange not "Will both of us gain?" but "Who will gain more?" They reject even cooperation that will yield an absolute economic gain if the other state will gain more, from fear that the other might convert its gain to military strength, and then use this strength to win by coercion in later rounds. Cooperation is much easier to achieve if states worry only about absolute gains. The goal, then, is simply to ensure that the overall economic pie is expanding and that each state is getting at least some part of the increase. However, anarchy guarantees that security will often be scarce; this heightens states' concerns about relative gains, which makes cooperation difficult unless the pie can be finely sliced to reflect, and thus not disturb, the current balance of power.

Interdependence, moreover, is as likely to lead to conflict as to cooperation, because states will struggle to escape the vulnerability that interdependence creates, in order to bolster their national security. In time of crisis or war, states that depend on others for critical economic supplies will fear cutoff or blackmail; they may well respond by trying to seize the source of supply by force of arms. There are numerous historical examples of states' pursuing aggressive military policies for the purpose of achieving economic autarky. One thinks of both Japan and Germany during the inter-war period. And one recalls that during the Arab oil embargo of the early 1970s there was much talk in America about using military force to seize Arab oil fields. . . .

The Cold War and Peace

Bipolarity, an equal military balance, and nuclear weapons have fostered peace in Europe over the past 45 years. The Cold War confrontation produced these phenomena; thus the Cold War was principally responsible for transforming a historically violent region into a very peaceful place. . . .

The demise of the Cold War order is likely to increase the chances that war and major crises will occur in Europe. Many observers now suggest that a new age of peace is dawning; in fact the opposite is true.

John J. Mearsheimer, *International Security*, Summer 1990.

Take away the Soviet threat to Western Europe, send the American forces home, and relations among the EC states will be fundamentally altered. Without a common Soviet threat or an American night watchman, Western European states will do what they did for centuries before the onset of the Cold War—look upon one another with abiding suspicion. Consequently, they will worry about imbalances in gains and about the loss of autonomy that results from cooperation. Cooperation in this new order will be more difficult than it was during the Cold War. Conflict will be more likely.

In sum, there are good reasons for being skeptical about the claim that a more powerful EC can provide the basis for peace in a multipolar Europe.

Under the third scenario war is avoided because many European states have become democratic since the early twentieth century, and liberal democracies simply do not fight one another. At a minimum, the presence of liberal democracies in Western Europe renders that half of Europe free from armed conflict. At a maximum, democracy spreads to Eastern Europe and the Soviet Union, bolstering peace. The idea that peace is cognate with democracy is a vision of international relations shared by both liberals and neoconservatives.

This scenario rests on the "peace-loving democracies" theory. Two arguments are made for it.

First, some claim that authoritarian leaders are more likely to go to war than leaders of democracies, because authoritarian leaders are not accountable to their publics, which carry the main burdens of war. In a democracy the citizenry, which pays the price of war, has a greater say in what the government does. The people, so the argument goes, are more hesitant to start trouble, because it is they who must pay the bloody price; hence the greater their power, the fewer wars.

The second argument rests on the claim that the citizens of liberal democracies respect popular democratic rights—those of their countrymen, and those of people in other states. They view democratic governments as more legitimate than others, and so are loath to impose a foreign regime on a democratic state by force. Thus an inhibition on war missing from other international relationships is introduced when two democracies face each other.

Flawed Arguments

The first of these arguments is flawed because it is not possible to sustain the claim that the people in a democracy are especially sensitive to the costs of war and therefore less willing than authoritarian leaders to fight wars. In fact the historical record shows that democracies are every bit as likely to fight wars as are authoritarian states, though admittedly, thus far, not with other democracies.

Furthermore, mass publics, whether in a democracy or not, can become deeply imbued with nationalistic or religious fervor, making them prone to support aggression and quite indifferent to costs. The widespread public support in post-Revolutionary France for Napoleon's wars is just one example of this phenomenon. At the same time, authoritarian leaders are often fearful of going to war, because war tends to unleash democratic forces that can undermine the regime. In short, war can impose high costs on authoritarian leaders as well as on their citizenry.

The second argument, which emphasizes the transnational respect for democratic rights among democracies, rests on a secondary factor that is generally overridden by other factors such as nationalism and religious fundamentalism. Moreover, there is another problem with the argument. The possibility always exists that a democracy, especially the kind of fledgling democracy emerging in Eastern Europe, will revert to an authoritarian state. This threat of backsliding means that one democratic state can never be sure that another democratic state will not turn on it sometime in the future. Liberal democracies must therefore worry about relative power among themselves, which is tantamount to saying that each has an incentive to consider aggression against another to forestall trouble. Lamentably, it is not possible for even liberal democracies to transcend anarchy.

Problems with the deductive logic aside, at first glance the historical record seems to offer strong support for the theory of peace-loving democracies. It appears that no liberal democracies have ever fought against each other. Evidentiary problems, however, leave the issue in doubt.

First, democracies have been few in number over the past two centuries, and thus there have not been many cases in which two democracies were in a position to fight with each other. Three prominent cases are usually cited: Britain and the United States (1832 to the present); Britain and France (1832-1849; 1871-1940); and the Western democracies since 1945.

Second, there are other persuasive explanations for why war did not occur in those three cases, and these competing explanations must be ruled out before the theory of peace-loving democracies can be accepted. Whereas relations between the British and the Americans during the nineteenth century were hardly blissful, in the twentieth century they have been quite harmonious, and thus fit closely with the theory's expectations. That harmony, however, can easily be explained by common threats that forced Britain and the United States to work together—a serious German threat in the first part of the century, and later a Soviet threat. The same basic argument applies to relations between France and Britain. Although they were not on the best of terms during most of the nineteenth century, their relations improved significantly around the turn of the century, with the rise of Germany. Finally, as noted above, the Soviet threat goes far in explaining the absence of war among the Western democracies since 1945.

Third, several democracies have come close to fighting each other, suggesting that the absence of war may be due simply to chance. France and Britain approached war during the Fashoda crisis of 1898. France and Weimar Germany might have come to blows over the Rhineland during the 1920s. The United States has clashed with a number of elected governments in the Third World during the Cold War, including the Allende regime in Chile and the Arbenz regime in Guatemala.

Last, some would classify Wilhelmine Germany as a democracy, or at least a quasi-democracy; if so, the First World War becomes a war among democracies.

No Guarantee of Peace

While the spread of democracy across Europe has great potential benefits for human rights, it will not guarantee peaceful relations among the states of post-Cold War Europe. Most Americans will find this argument counterintuitive. They see the United States as fundamentally peace-loving, and they ascribe this peacefulness to its democratic character. From this they generalize that democracies are more peaceful than authoritarian states, which leads them to conclude that the complete democratization of Europe would largely eliminate the threat of war. This view of international politics is likely to be repudiated by the events of coming years.

"Ironically the superpowers' agreement about things is causing many Third World people even greater concern than the conflict did."

The End of the Cold War Will Harm the Third World

Vanessa Baird

The waning of the Cold War has been marked by improved relations between the United States and the Soviet Union and by the overthrow of communist governments in Eastern Europe. In the following viewpoint, Vanessa Baird argues that these developments could have a negative impact on Third World countries in Africa, Latin America, and Asia. She asserts that because developed nations will concentrate more on their own affairs and on helping Eastern Europe, they will give less development assistance to the Third World. Less aid will mean continued poverty and hunger in the Third World, she maintains. Baird writes for the *New Internationalist*, a British magazine that covers issues of poverty and Third World development.

As you read, consider the following questions:

1. What form of North-South trade does Baird predict will increase?
2. What form of international dictatorship dominates in the Third World, according to the author?
3. What policies does Baird recommend concerning the Third World?

Vanessa Baird, "East Meets West, North Forgets South," *The New Internationalist*, September 1990. Reprinted with permission of New International Publications.

The German tourists were sitting outside a boulevard cafe, sipping beers and relaxing in the oblique golden glow of an autumn sun. Suddenly a man with a small black beard and a large white smile sauntered across and gave the nearest tourist a slap on the back.

'Congratulations! Congratulations!'

The tourist smiled in a bemused but friendly way. Her friends looked on nonplussed.

'You've done it. You've got rid of that Wall,' the man explained. 'I'm from Brazil . . . but I feel so happy for Europe today. Well, for the world . . .'

The Berlin Wall had started coming down that morning. A long collective nightmare seemed to be coming to an end. It was impossible not to feel elated. This very special breakthrough appeared to open up a new era of peace. One could dream of Cold War nuclear arsenals fading into the mists of history. One hardly dared believe it.

A few metro stops from the cafe was the Avenue d'Iena and the Paris branch of the World Bank. This was the setting for an international conference on world development media organized by the United Nations.

Making People Care

We—about 60 journalists from many different countries—spent the two days discussing everything from ideology to marketing. But our central concern was: how do you get people to care about what is happening on the other side of the world? How do you make it relevant to their lives? What we wanted people to care about, of course, was global injustice and inequality—and inevitably there were attacks on the International Monetary Fund (IMF) and the World Bank (in whose comfortable seats we were awkwardly sitting).

But in the evenings the talk kept drifting back to the events that were so dramatically unfolding a few hundred miles away in Eastern Europe. We were as excited as anyone by the changes— but we had a sneaking suspicion that the Third World was going to lose out as a result.

The sparks from Eastern Europe have begun to land in the Third World. For most Westerners the Cold War conjured up visions of ranged missiles facing each on either side of the Iron Curtain. But it was in the Third World that the Cold War was actually fought—in Vietnam and Korea, Cambodia and Ethiopia, Nicaragua and Afghanistan, to name but a few sad locations.

Superpower backing in local conflicts not only prolonged war— it also gave tyrants the power to commit atrocities against their own populations with relative impunity. So one effect of the international thaw can only be good for the Third World: the superpowers are beginning to withdraw support from some of their most repellent allies. . . .

The shifting sands of the post-Cold War world have made life dangerously unpredictable for Third World leaders who do not have a base of popular support. They can no longer exploit Cold War rivalries and cannot rely upon superpower support when they put down domestic rebellions.

Poor Countries Ignored

For decades, underdeveloped countries could extract aid and favors from the superpowers because the global rivals competed for influence in the humblest of capitals. Now, with the U.S.-Soviet rivalry ebbing and the industrialized countries preoccupied with their own economic competition, the poorer nations may be ignored in the stampede for greater wealth.

Doyle McManus and Robin Wright, *Los Angeles Times*, December 11, 1990.

But there is a flip side to the end-of-the-War euphoria. Ironically the superpowers' agreement about things is causing many Third World people even greater concern than the conflict did.

There is an old African saying that goes: 'When elephants fight it is the grass that suffers.' It was commonly used to describe how Cold War conflict affected the Third World. The new 'old African saying' doing the rounds is: 'And when elephants make love, grass suffers also.'

Sweetening the love-making of East and West is the dream of mutual benefit. The East will provide the West with investment opportunities and cheap labour close to home. The West will provide the East with badly needed cash for economic reconstruction.

Losing Aid

Not surprisingly, the Third World loses out. Aid funds are already being redirected to the East from the developing nations of the South. The US has cut its economic support to the Third World from $545 million in 1989 to $350 million in 1990 to allow for emergency funds for Eastern Europe. According to United States Agency for International Development official Mark Edelmann, sub-Saharan Africa is likely to suffer further cuts because these countries have no effective lobbying in Washington. 'No one gets more unless someone gets less,' he observed.

Both the British and Australian governments claim that aid for Eastern Europe will not come out of overseas development budgets. But the current climate in the Northern corridors of power does not augur well for the South. US Senator Robert Dole, for

187

example, is calling for major cuts in the $330 million in aid which goes to the Philippines, Pakistan, Egypt, and Turkey. [British Prime Minister] John Major has spoken out against funding 'white elephant' development projects in Africa.

The general sense is that 'we have done enough for the Third World.' In fact Western aid to the Third World as a percentage of GNP [gross national product] has been steadily dropping over the past 25 years—only the high profile given to this 'charity' has increased. . . .

The Soviet bloc, meanwhile, is far too preoccupied with its own problems to pay attention to those of its old allies in the South, Angola and Mozambique.

Trade and Investment

The Third World has another worry: what will be the effect of detente on North-South trade and investment? If the rich countries can invest in Eastern Europe—with its offer of skilled labour at just two dollars an hour—will it bother to invest in the South? If it can trade with the East—will it bother to trade with the South?

The message from the US to Latin America has been clear—either join the free-market party or stay out in the cold. In his 'Americas Initiative' President George Bush has outlined his plan to establish a hemisphere-wide free trade zone. The backyard is getting very big indeed.

The Americas Initiative would entail more deregulation, public-spending cuts and an opening up to the world economy. A regional investment fund would be earmarked for countries carrying out privatization programmes. The social and political cost of such an IMF-style programme is well-known. It squeezes the poor hardest.

The shift of attention from South to East is a convenient one for Westerners to make. The problems of the Soviet bloc had nothing to do with colonial exploitation and unfair commodity prices. The West does not feel responsible for—nor guilty about—the mess created there. Rather it can gloat and patronize as it welcomes its prodigal sisters and brothers back to the common, white European fold. Third World countries, meanwhile, face the prospect of having to compete with Eastern Europe—and see it as another big stick the rich world can use against them.

Dirty Business

There is one form of North-South trade which is likely to see a sharp increase, however: the dumping of toxic waste on the Third World.

The scale of the former Soviet Bloc's pollution and environmental degradation problems have shocked the world. But they have sent a special chill down the spines of Third World ecologists. If Eastern Europe is to be 'cleaned up' to meet Western European standards where will the substitute dumping grounds be? East Germany, for example, earns more than $620 million a year from taking Western industrial filth.

Says Indian ecologist Vandana Shiva: 'We in the Third World anticipate that the consolidation of market democracy across the entire North will have very high environmental costs for us . . . it is the Third World that will bear the ecological costs of the industrialism and consumerism in the North including the costs of 'cleaning up' Eastern Europe.'

Mikhail Gorbachev's comment to his people that it is important to maintain relations with the South because the latter is a supplier of cheap materials, has not exactly added to confidence. The tune is that familiar one of neo-colonialism—sung now in East-West unison.

Fighting Dictatorships

The news is not all grim. Back in December 1989 Mobutu Sese Seko, the infamous dictator of Zaire, was having dinner when news of the trial and execution of his comrades in corruption, Nicolae and Elena Ceausescu of Romania, was broadcast on television. In some consternation he abandoned his guests.

Mobutu was right to be worried. The revolutionary success of the citizens of Bucharest, Prague and Leipzig was an inspiration to people in many African countries who had almost given up hope of ousting their own corrupt or repressive leaders. Dictatorships of 40 years' standing could be toppled almost overnight. The unimaginable suddenly seemed possible—or at least worth a try.

And Africans have given it a go. Riots, protests and calls for multi-party democracy have rocked capitals across the continent, from Algeria in the north to Zambia in the south. President Kenneth Kaunda of Zambia has faced a coup attempt and leaders of single-party regimes in Zaire, Tanzania, Benin and Ivory Coast have had to promise to allow opposition parties to stand in the next elections.

'The changes in the Soviet Union, Eastern Europe and South Africa,' says Zambia's former defence minister Arthur Wina, 'have woken us up from years of indifference and despondency. We are sitting in an atmosphere of real emergency.'

Eastern Europe provided the trigger, but at the root of the discontent was a continent-wide, long-term economic crisis. Africa's huge debt burden to the rich world and the harmful impact of IMF-imposed austerity programmes are largely to blame. And this, ironically enough, is the product of Western capitalism—not of the lack of Western-style democracy.

In this euphoric year of revolutions, multi-party democracy may look like a panacea, but it may prove to be little more than a placebo. National dictatorship as a system of government seems to be disappearing from the face of the globe—in Latin America in the 1980s, then in Eastern Europe and now in Africa.

But a form of international dictatorship is growing unchecked—that of the market. Its police are the bureaucrats and technocrats of the financial institutions of the rich—GATT [General Agreement on Tariffs and Trade], the IMF, the World Bank. Their track record of concern for people in the poorer part of the world is appalling.

A Larger Third World

Will the new democrats of the East stand up for the Third World in the international community? They may well find that they have more in common when Eastern Europe splits in two. A tiny handful of Eastern European countries (East Germany, Hungary, Poland) will be selected to join the First World, while the majority will find themselves becoming part of a larger Third World—one in which the free market fails to meet even the most basic needs.

No Third World Peace Dividend

In general, the 1990s are likely to see increased competition rather than cooperation between Southern countries; and this may well not be confined to peaceful competition. Environmental scarcities such as access to secure water supplies may spark armed conflict. The ending of the Cold War between the superpowers may have the benefit of pressuring their proxies in regional conflicts in such Southern locations as Angola to reach agreement with one another, and may lead to a more rational allocation of foreign aid as the West no longer finds it necessary to prop up the corrupt 'friendly' regimes of strategically located countries like Zaire and the Sudan; but it will probably not deliver a peace dividend in the South. Not only will there be large quantities of second-hand weaponry on the market, but established arms suppliers will be looking for new outlets for their deadly exports. And Southern countries themselves, such as Brazil and China, have discovered that the weapons trade can be a major source of foreign-exchange earnings.

John Ravenhill, *International Affairs*, April 1990.

The world has been shaken up—and provides the chance to take a fresh look at ways in which global relations might be put on a more equal footing. Events in Eastern Europe have thrown up a plethora of new possibilities:

• A substantial chunk of the huge NATO [North Atlantic Treaty Organization] and Warsaw Pact savings on defence ($467 billion if 1989 spending were halved) could be allocated for Third World development. Third World people bore the brunt of the Cold War.

They should at least reap some of the benefits of its ending.

• The IMF managed very fast to mobilize large sums from its reserve capital fund for Eastern Europe. Now it could do the same for the Third World by using money from this fund to write off IMF debt arrears. This would help stem the flow of $110 billion a year from the South to service its debts to the North.

• International agreements on prices for Third World commodities have in the past been hampered by Eastern-bloc reluctance to partake. Now there is no excuse. And commodity-price agreements are far more crucial to Third World economic recovery than aid.

One World

• Last, but not least, the democracies of the North should start work on a form of democracy they prefer to ignore—ecological democracy. That means respecting the life in other regions—and not dumping the toxic rubbish created by excessive consumption habits on less fortunate people in the Third World.

The world we have known for the past four decades has shattered. Between the shards are growing flowers of democracy. But having a choice of parties for which to vote is not enough.

What we all have to do is grasp this chance to promote the idea of One World—before we find that the North-South divide has been cast in the scrap concrete of the Berlin Wall.

"The move toward democracy and open markets in Eastern Europe is not a threat to the countries of the erstwhile Third World."

The End of the Cold War Will Not Harm the Third World

Richard E. Bissell

Richard E. Bissell is assistant administrator at the U.S. Agency for International Development. In the following viewpoint, he refutes the argument that the end of the Cold War will be disastrous for the Third World. Bissell argues that a country's economic success depends more on internal economic policies than outside assistance, and he asserts that an increasing number of Third World nations are reforming their economies and governments in positive ways. Bissell argues that the whole concept of a Third World dominated and exploited by wealthy nations is outdated and should be discarded in the post-Cold War era.

As you read, consider the following questions:

1. What ideology united the Third World in the 1970s, according to Bissell?
2. According to the author, what important changes occurred in Third World nations in the 1980s?
3. Why does Bissell believe there is no real conflict between Eastern European and Third World countries?

Reprinted from "Who Killed the Third World?" by Richard E. Bissell, *The Washington Quarterly*, vol. 13, no. 4, Autumn 1990 by permission of The MIT Press, Cambridge, Massachusetts. Copyright © 1990 by the Center for Strategic and International Studies and the Massachusetts Institute of Technology.

One of the most dramatic theories has been that the East-West thaw is eliminating U.S. and Western interest in the Third World. Leaders of developing countries have a nightmare: that the industrialized countries are sealing up their collective hearts, picking up their aid purses, and heading off for Eastern Europe. In this nightmare, the poor and hungry of the Third World are left alone, beside the road, without resources and without a cause to attract attention from the rest of the world. The scenario is a dramatic one, heightened by a series of diplomatic events in 1990, and made more poignant by a sense of revolutionary good news about emerging democracies yielding such bad news for the majority of mankind.

The problem is that this nightmare is only half true. The Third World, as a political movement, has disintegrated; it was on its deathbed, however, well before the liberalization of Eastern Europe. It is important to understand why and how, so the industrialized world can respond positively to the opportunities in both Eastern Europe and the developing countries of Latin America, Asia, and Africa.

The Rise of Third-Worldism

The Third World movement has its origins in a specific phase of independence for most post-colonial less-developed countries (LDCs). In the early phases of independence, most countries experienced a heady nationalism, born out of a misplaced confidence that a new state automatically could succeed to the authority and resources of the colonial power as easily as it raised a new flag. For Africa and Asia, the effort to create a Third World coalition reflected an awareness that arrived a few years after each state's independence—that in fact each country did not possess the economic and political resources to move international events greatly. Even India, the subcontinent giant with enormous resources, embraced the bargain of the disaffected newly independent at the inaugural meeting of the nonaligned states at Bandung in 1957 in order to gain a place on the world stage. . . .

Who joined the Third World? By coining the name, adherents clearly expected it to include countries not in the First (capitalist) or Second (socialist/Communist) Worlds. Did that mean China could be admitted? China was certainly a member until it obtained its permanent Security Council seat in 1971; then it became unclear. Other countries on the periphery caused dilemmas—South Korea, Turkey, and Israel, among others—but none were important enough to unsettle the vision that came to be known as the Group of 77 (G-77), for the number of initial members. The number, which actually grew in subsequent years despite the fixed appellation, mattered because it was greater than the combined votes of the East and West blocs at the United Nations (UN). Thus was born the idea of the automatic majority in the UN General Assembly, and the illusion of power that held sway in much of the 1970s.

As the Third World movement was political in origin, it required an ideology to maintain it. Given the great diversity of states in the movement, it was unlikely to have a spontaneous ideological worldview based on historical experience. Therefore, the movement looked for an ideology that would explain what its members did share in common: powerlessness, poverty, and a need to get their issues on the international agenda. The members needed to explain to their own people and to the world why their political independence had not delivered them from difficulty. Independence, it turned out, had been a chimera, and it was not clear why.

Dependency Theory

The answer was found in the social structural analysis of the "dependency school" of both East and West. This analysis placed the Third World in a structurally inferior position on the periphery of global affairs, and thus established a myth-structure in which the LDCs were only pawns and a worldview commanding structural transformation. Economically, the world was seen as driven by the historical advantages of [domination] by the industrialized countries and their multinational corporate minions. Politically, criticism focused on the hegemony allegedly established by the powers of the First and Second Worlds in the wake of World War II. The central theme of third-worldism was the inability and futility of individual LDCs taking control of their future until a radical change had been wrought in the international power balance. In the West, this sometimes was called "third world socialism," owing to the major redistributive element in the ideology. The emphasis on the redistribution to the poorer nations of economic goods in terms of capital and income was matched in a less tangible way by calls for a political reordering to give at least equality, if not dominance, to the Third World agenda. . . .

The 1970s

The 1970s were driven by a desire in the First World to accommodate the Third World agenda. "North-South" meetings became a staple of international life. UN power structures were amended to accommodate the interests of the majority. Meetings of the UN Conference on Trade and Development (UNCTAD), where demands for changes in global economic structures were explored, were unceasing. Western equity holdings in the Third World were reduced. Nationalizations in key sectors attempted to ensure that Third World governments never again would be threatened by multinational companies operating in their countries.

194

At the end of the decade, however, a visceral stocktaking occurred. For the men, women, and children of the developing countries, there had been few improvements in the standard of living. Certainly, the gap in the quality of life between the developed and the developing countries was growing, although government officials seemed to be doing well with frequent trips to New York and Geneva. The problems of governance in the LDCs and their internal economies were worsening. Basic government and social services were disintegrating. There were more palms to grease with bribes. The stocktaking in the West was more dramatic, based on decisive events. The double ratcheting of oil prices in 1973 and 1980 raised enormous alarm that the West's economic influence was dissipated. The emergence of premodern political systems, as represented by the caricature regimes of Idi Amin in Uganda and the ayatollah in Iran, suggested to the West that it was time for another approach. The decisive years for all sides were 1979 and 1980, when forces emerged to push aside the Third World agenda.

Aid and Poverty

One thing we have learned is that foreign aid doesn't permanently cure poverty. Countries do it on their own or don't. Culture matters. So do competent governments with popular support that pursue sensible economic policies. When conditions are favorable, foreign aid can help.

The recognition of this reality is a further reason why the idea of the Third World no longer makes sense. The concept of a Third World implicitly presumed that all poor nations could be made wealthier with the correct doses of outside money and advice. This was a wild exaggeration.

Robert J. Samuelson, *Newsweek*, July 23, 1990.

Hindsight shows clearly what was not understood at the beginning of the 1980s—or since then, by many. No vote was taken in an international body to disband the Third World. Rather, the Third World lost its adherents. Defections from the cause increased during the 1980s. Events disproved the value of its ideology. Politically, the international community chose contexts other than third-worldism to address a series of issues where sensible compromises were reached without the North-South confrontations of the 1970s. In effect, the developing countries discovered what can be achieved through cooperation rather than confrontation with the rest of the world. To be sure, several successes were needed to show how it was done.

The first significant sign of the erosion of third-worldism was a decision by an increasing number of states to internationalize their economies. The export-driven growth in East Asia, demonstrating that poor countries did not inevitably lose in the existing international structure, challenged the rest of the developing countries. In looking closely at the growing Asian economies, others realized that internal measures were as important as international networks. When leaders asked how to get advice on internal reforms, they found that they had well-trained individuals in senior positions and access to advice from the World Bank and the International Monetary Fund. The gradual adherence of those leaders to internal reforms was essential, and although the rewards of such reforms were not always instantaneous, leaders learned that they were essential for the eventual satisfaction of the people's desire for an improved quality of life.

Reform took on many different hues. In some cases, the focus was on relations with the external world—moving from an overvalued exchange rate to an undervalued one, simplifying regulations, eliminating tariffs and controls that were disincentives for exports, and allowing indigenous companies to keep foreign exchange earnings for the import of new technology. In all cases, internal reform was essential to establish confidence in the long-term future of the economy and the social system. . . .

Diminishing Unity

As each country in the Third World coalition began to measure its own ability to build domestic confidence and open linkages abroad, the elements of unity among the LDCs began to diminish. First, some countries were successful in their economic reforms, and thus began to move away from poverty. With the injection of assistance from the World Bank, regional development banks, and bilateral donors in support of these reforms, economic growth began to pick up, most visibly after the global recession of 1981-1982. The United States and others aggressively maintained a policy line in favor of open markets, ensuring export opportunities for developing countries even as the U.S. trade deficit continued to grow. . . .

The 1980s also eroded third-worldism's tolerance and even support of nondemocratic regimes. The opening up of economies required the opening up of societies generally. Much of the Third World rhetoric had dwelt on the inefficiency of multiparty systems, unguided pluralism, and the dangers of empowering people at the grass roots. In the 1960s and 1970s, politics had been an elite sport; in the 1980s, the requirements of mobilizing popular support for economic reforms compelled a more broad-based politics. Thus, President Ronald Reagan's speech at Westminster in 1982 on democracy-building found a remarkable resonance. The subtle change in the focus of the United States from the rights of the prominent few to the participatory freedom of the people at large, helped catalyze a profound political transformation of the international policy community. Free elections were held first in Latin America. The rapid weakening of the Leninist models in China and the Soviet Union accelerated the change, reaching avalanche proportions by 1989, when the countries of the Third World already had realized that their societies had to choose between democratization and collapse, both political and economic.

Changing Soviet Policy

Just as Moscow has accepted indigenously supported political change in Eastern Europe, it has also accepted such change in the Third World. The Soviets accepted the results of the February 1990 Nicaraguan elections, in which the pro-Soviet Sandinista government was displaced by a pro-American one. Moscow has also accepted the complete disappearance of the Marxist regime in South Yemen, which in May 1990 voluntarily merged with (and submitted to being ruled by the leader of) non-Marxist North Yemen. Nor has Mikhail Gorbachev done anything to prevent the increasingly Western orientation of once-Marxist Mozambique. In line with his policy toward all the East European countries where peaceful change took place, Gorbachev since 1989 has not acted to prevent peaceful political change in the Third World, even if this has meant the dissolution of a Marxist regime. And just as he did nothing to prevent the violent downfall of the Marxist regime in Romania, he appears less than fully committed to preventing the Marxist regime in Ethiopia from meeting with a similar fate.

Mark N. Katz, *The Washington Quarterly*, Winter 1991.

The latest payoff of reform was the steady integration of the economies of the developing world into international trading regimes. Internal reform required external reform at a later stage, although as recently as 1986, one informed observer could comment that "Third World states will still find great difficulty adopting a capitalist international trading system or confining themselves to a trading strategy in world politics." In retrospect, it is clear that the difficulty encountered by most developing countries was merely perceptual—failing to recognize the major trade opportunities of the 1990s. This too has changed. For example, former trade hard-liners, such as India and Brazil, have shown interest in new approaches to intellectual property rights. This is hardly surprising now that India is a major exporter of computer software, based on the third-largest pool of software programmers in the world. Likewise, Mauritius has developed textile and computer industries that are competitive worldwide; with those sectors as leaders, economic growth is rising by nearly 10 percent annually. There are still major problems with agricultural monocultures devoted to tropical crops. Countries are learning, however, that they should not rely solely on cocoa, sugar, or coffee, and where they must, that they must add value to products in order to pick up the processing markup. Ecuador, for instance, ships tons of shrimp each year, but only recently began to break into the precooked shrimp market in Europe. Other countries will follow in food processing and agribusiness. . . .

In the 1990s we live in a world different from that of 1960, 1970, or 1980. International solidarity no longer is organized along North-South lines. The old division between "haves" and "have-nots" is muddied, not least by the many "somewhat-haves" and countries with a mixture of both.

What Succeeds Third-Worldism?

Some would argue that the failure of third-worldism was that rhetoric does not fill stomachs. In a way, that is true, although even in the 1970s, there was a significant flow of funds to the LDCs. The enormous flow of public sector borrowing from commercial banks produced statistics that indicated all was well. Unfortunately, such flows funded a kind of economic development that was neither broad-based nor sustainable. It was narrowly based in being siphoned off by the first hands to touch the money (namely, those in government). It was unsustainable because the private sectors in the LDCs effectively were being strangled. Well-motivated governments could feed people for a year, but few in the 1970s created the markets and institutions to feed a generation.

The real failure of the Third World movement was psychological. By blaming the rest of the world for the ills of the LDCs, people were left feeling powerless. This was convenient for the autocratic leaders of most LDCs, but it was logically wrong, and an increasing number of people came to recognize that it was morally wrong as well. To deprive people of their ability and rights to control their lives was a clear transgression of striking social and political consequence. Those who made short-term gains out of such an ideology were overthrown in the 1980s. . . .

It is no coincidence that the demise of the Third World movement occurred during a decade of strengthening democracy. The determination of the Reagan administration to support democracy-building around the world, first in Central America and Eastern Europe, but also in Namibia and elsewhere, implied the downfall of third-worldism. . . .

The Third World and Eastern Europe

This brings us full circle to the mistaken thesis raised at the beginning of this article. The move toward democracy and open markets in Eastern Europe is not a threat to the countries of the erstwhile Third World. The most important mobilization occurring in both regions is internal, not external. The power to mobilize resources is far greater within any country than outside it. Foreign aid can be only a catalyst, and not a solution in itself. It can stabilize an economy, but the long-term investment in a society must be generated overwhelmingly from within. The movement toward democracy in all regions is a crucial step in raising confidence in government and a stable economy. It is only one step, with many to follow, but it is the most important and necessary one. Democracy is contagious, as well demonstrated in Eastern Europe and in Latin America, and remaining nondemocratic forces are right to feel threatened by global popular democratic aspirations.

Confidence in the Future

The race for free markets also is essential for long-term development. It will be tempting for some people to demand immediate payoffs from economic change. Bread riots will occur. The most important change has come, however, when people have focused on the long term and on economic change for their children's generation. That is an investment mentality that bespeaks a confidence in the future of a society. The rest of the world can provide a catalyst for that confidence, with small amounts of money, but it can never create the confidence. Each government and its private sector institutions must earn that confidence from its own people, which is a protracted process. In this, there is no competition between Eastern Europe and the developing countries. All countries are involved in a process of generating and maintaining the confidence of their peoples. Today, they reinforce one another, across national boundaries, with a spirit of self-determination and direction, in sharp contrast to the "solidarity" of blame and recrimination so pervasive in the Third World era.

Recognizing Statements That Are Provable

We are constantly confronted with statements and generalizations about social and moral problems. In order to think clearly about these problems, it is useful if one can make a basic distinction between statements for which evidence can be found and other statements which cannot be verified or proved because evidence is not available, or the issue is so controversial that it cannot be definitely proved.

Readers should be aware that magazines, newspapers, and other sources often contain statements of a controversial nature. The following activity is designed to allow experimentation with statements that are provable and those that are not.

The following statements are taken from the viewpoints in this chapter. Consider each statement carefully. *Mark P for any statement you believe is provable. Mark U for any statement you feel is unprovable because of the lack of evidence. Mark C for any statement you think is too controversial to be proved to everyone's satisfaction.*

If you are doing this activity as a member of a class or group, compare your answers with those of other class or group members. Be able to defend your answers. You may discover that others will come to different conclusions than you do. Listening to the reasons others present for their answers may give you valuable insights in recognizing statements that are provable.

P = provable
U = unprovable
C = too controversial

1. The year 1989 was marked by major political changes in Eastern Europe.

2. The world is entering a new era of peace and prosperity.

3. Democracy in Latin American countries will probably not survive very long.

4. As long as people are people, true democracy will remain only an ideal.

5. In France the right-wing National Front won 12 percent of the vote to the European Parliament.

6. Demonstrations for democracy have occurred in recent years in the countries of China, Nigeria, and Nepal.

7. Research has shown that war between democracies has almost never occurred in the modern world.

8. The Kellogg-Briand Pact of 1928 which outlawed wars among nations did not succeed in ending war.

9. Since 1973 military dictatorships have perished in Greece, Spain, and Argentina.

10. Americans will soon regret the passing of the Cold War.

11. The foundation of peace in Europe has not been democracy, but the stability brought on by the Cold War standoff between the U.S. and the U.S.S.R.

12. The most peaceful period in European history since 1648 in terms of wars fought and people killed has been the last forty-five years.

13. The world will be a more peaceful place if more countries were democracies.

14. U.S. aid to Third World countries fell from $545 million in 1989 to $350 million in 1990.

15. The revolutions in Eastern Europe will cause many people in America and Europe to forget about the Third World.

16. Foreign aid cannot be a solution to Third World poverty.

17. The term "Third World" encompasses wildly diverse countries.

Periodical Bibliography

The following articles have been selected to supplement the diverse views presented in this chapter.

Mark Falcoff — "First World, Third World, Which World?" *American Enterprise*, July/August 1990.

Francis Fukuyama — "The End of History?" *The National Interest*, Summer 1989.

Paul Hockenos and Jane Hunter — "Thaw in Cold War Freezes Out Third World," *In These Times*, August 29-September 11, 1990.

Samuel P. Huntington — "No Exit: The Errors of Endism," *The National Interest*, Fall 1989.

Geoffrey Kemp — "Regional Security, Arms Control, and the End of the Cold War," *The Washington Quarterly*, August 1990.

Michael Ledeen — "The Second Democratic Revolution," *The American Spectator*, October 1990.

John Lukacs — "The Stirrings of History," *Harper's Magazine*, August 1990.

Edward N. Luttwak — "The Shape of Things to Come," *Commentary*, June 1990.

Robert J. Myers — "After the Cold War," *Society*, March/April 1991.

Dankwort A. Rustow — "Democracy: A Global Revolution?" *Foreign Affairs*, Fall 1990.

Wolfgang Sachs — "What Next?: The Post-Cold War World," *The Utne Reader*, November/December 1990.

Robert J. Samuelson — "End of the Third World," *Newsweek*, July 23, 1990.

Jill Smolowe — "Don't Call Us, Friend, We'll Call You," *Time*, March 15, 1990.

Leonard R. Sussman — "The Distance to Democracy," *World Monitor*, February 1991.

Steve Tesich — "Breaking Away from Ourselves," *The Nation*, March 18, 1991.

Leon Wieseltier — "Propositions for a Postcommunist World," *Harper's Magazine*, December 1990.

What Role Will International Organizations Play in the New World Order?

THE NEW WORLD ORDER

Chapter Preface

The dramatic improvement in relations between the United States and the Soviet Union since the mid-1980s has led some observers to predict a new era of effectiveness for international organizations. With the Cold War behind them, these experts argue, the Soviet Union and the United States can work together to aid international organizations in achieving common objectives. According to former United Nations under secretary general Brian Urquhart, the end of the Cold War has allowed the UN, for example, "to make notable progress in peace-making and peace-keeping tasks."

Yet the end of the Cold War may also lead to new impediments for international organizations. For instance, some experts believe that without the unifying threat of the Soviet bloc, former allies such as Europe, Japan, and the United States may clash over economic issues, making more cooperation through international organizations unlikely. Furthermore, some analysts contend that international organizations which owed their existence to the Cold War, such as the North Atlantic Treaty Organization, are obsolete.

The viewpoints in the following chapter debate how the end of the Cold War affects the future role of international organizations in world affairs.

"The United Nations has become a vital forum in addressing multinational interests and concerns."

The United Nations Can Solve International Problems

Richard S. Williamson

The United Nations (UN), founded in 1945, is an international organization with 159 member countries. The stated purposes of the UN are to maintain international peace and to achieve international cooperation in solving global problems. Richard S. Williamson argues in the following viewpoint that the UN has successfully worked for peace in the past and that the importance of the UN is increasing. The United Nations, Williamson contends, is well-suited to address the concerns that arise as nations become more linked to each other economically. The author is the former United States assistant secretary for international organization affairs.

As you read, consider the following questions:

1. What are some of the United Nations' problems, according to the author?
2. In which areas can the United Nations be particularly effective, in the author's opinion?
3. Why does the author believe that the UN should be concerned about human rights issues?

Richard S. Williamson, "Toward the 21st Century: The Future for Multilateral Diplomacy," *Department of State Bulletin*, December 1988. Public Domain.

I firmly believe that as we look toward the 21st century, multilateral diplomacy will be of growing importance to the United States in pursuing its national interests and for other nations in pursuing theirs.

Global Issues

Profound changes are underway in the world—changes in virtually every subject from science to superpower relations. As a result, the "member state" itself has undergone a redefinition. That is because the issues confronting us, whether they be political, economic, or scientific in nature, transcend national borders.

A number of factors are increasing national interdependency. Scientific, economic, and political matters are global in dimension and enormous in extent. They are outstripping the traditional means by which governments dealt with them. The speed at which information flows—whereby, in an instant, a computer in New York can exchange information around the globe by tying in with another computer—has already created a global marketplace. The amount of money that changes hands in the global financial market in 1 day exceeds $1 trillion—more than the entire annual budget of the U.S. Government. Such flows transcend national boundaries and can overwhelm rigid economic policies.

Facing every nation is a variety of emerging problems of great urgency which transcend the national borders. We can see this today in a number of environmental issues. Emissions from factories in one nation cause trees to die and lakes to be polluted in another nation. Floods in Bangladesh are caused by deforestation in upriver countries. Rain forests are cleared for development in one region, and the climate is changed throughout the Western Hemisphere. Chlorofluorocarbons are released in several countries, and the "greenhouse effect" in the earth's atmosphere is apparent.

Actions which were once viewed as strictly national or domestic are being perceived as having international repercussions. Nations are becoming more aware that we must work together within the global community to better understand the many implications which our individual actions will have for all our societies in the decades ahead. . . .

The Importance of the United Nations

When the United States emerged on the world stage, diplomacy was conducted country to country, bilaterally. Suspicious of broader multilateral entanglements, the United States rejected entry into the League of Nations after World War I.

Following World War II, however, traditional American idealism heartily embraced the work in San Francisco in 1945 to create a world assembly. The UN Charter embodies the ideals and moral goals of our own Constitution. Despite frustrations with the organization, the United States has remained firm in its commitment to the United Nations as an important forum in helping governments take collective action for addressing global problems and challenges. We have demonstrated our commitment by consistently supporting the United Nations morally, financially, and politically.

The United Nations was founded to keep the peace, to promote political self-determination, to foster global prosperity, and to strengthen the bonds of civility among nations. By subjugating the individual interests of member states to the greater good of the world community, the United Nations was to speak with the voice of moral authority, its greatest power. Over the past 40 years, however, as the voice of the United Nations has become louder, its moral authority has been weakened by the trends toward double standards, loose rhetoric, bloc voting, and petty politicization.

Critical International Problems

[The United Nations] enables the international community to assemble, analyze, and evaluate data; understand issues and problems; and clarify the options available to states for joint and several action. In this way, it is able to begin to deal with the new social problems that arise from rapid economic and technological transformations. Thus it is also able to respond to serious problems such as the growing threat of drug trafficking and abuse, and the AIDS pandemic. Without the United Nations, it would be difficult to find an international method to turn the highest levels of knowledge and experience into action on critical international problems.

Javier Perez de Cuellar, *Social Education*, September 1989.

Much progress has been made in addressing these problems, but there is still an important need to take a realistic look at the United Nations as it actually is. What are its limitations and its capabilities? What do we need to do in seeking broader multilateral solutions to the challenges of today so that the United Nations is better able to fulfill its mandate in the world of tomorrow?

I have tried to stress here important questions not confined to bilateral solutions. There are important issues that transcend national borders and must be considered in a global context. Two such issues—refugee assistance and human rights—are ones for which the United Nations has become a vital forum in addressing multinational interests and concerns.

Throughout history, people have fled injustice, war, drought, and famine. More than 100 million people have been uprooted from their homes since World War I, making the 20th century what has been called "the century of refugees and prisoners.". . .

We must not forget that the root cause of mass refugee flows is the denial of fundamental human rights. The care of refugees is an international concern and the responsibility of every country and each individual, with equitable burdensharing.

While the initial focus of refugee assistance is on short-term material assistance for basic life-sustaining needs, an important element of assistance efforts is the search for more lasting solutions to refugee problems. Such solutions include the fostering of voluntary repatriation, when that is appropriate, local integration in the country or region of asylum, and, finally, resettlement in third countries.

Refugees have no political influence. If the international community fails to speak for them, their cause will be lost in darkness, and the violation of human rights will go on endlessly. And it is in the United Nations that the international community can rise up and speak with one voice, a voice of moral and political authority. We, as members of the international community, have been tasked to share the burden of supporting multilateral, bilateral, or private efforts to achieve more durable refugee solutions wherever they are possible.

Human Rights

Another continuing challenge for UN member states as we look toward the 21st century is human rights. The protection and promotion of basic human rights and fundamental freedoms are among the principal purposes of the United Nations set forth in its Charter and in the Universal Declaration of Human Rights.

A reason for the primacy of human rights in the United Nations is that its founders recognized from the bitter experience of the Second World War that those governments that abuse the rights of their own citizens are more likely to abuse the rights of citizens of other countries. Promotion of the respect for human rights is thus linked to the United Nations' basic purpose of keeping the peace. . . .

We see the United Nations with its various organs as the preeminent global organization in the area of human rights. The need to address human rights violations in multilateral forums is also linked to the efforts to help avoid new mass flows of refugees.

In our view, no state may hide behind the argument of national sovereignty in the area of human rights. The world community has made clear that human rights are matters of international concern. As in the case of all manmade institutions, the United Nations often carries out its tasks in an imperfect way. But the United Nations can and does have an impact with respect to protecting human rights. It is like a hoe—by itself useless, but in the hands of the gardener, it can make the earth productive and help it yield fruit. Its principal tool is its ability to generate publicity and investigate a specific situation of human rights abuses or promote thematic human rights issues. . . .

With all of its flaws, the United Nations remains the only body of its kind in the world. It is the only arena where the tortured and abused of the world have an opportunity to lay forth their cases and stand some chance of having the world community act on their behalf. . . .

Conflict Resolution

Since the first UN peacekeeping effort in Palestine in 1948, peacekeeping operations have become an important technique in international conflict management. We face a unique and exciting opportunity for the United Nations in the peacekeeping area. . . . The United Nations is moving center stage in helping to resolve significant regional conflicts that have cost many lives and, in some cases, been tinderboxes with the potential to explode into major power confrontations.

At a time of such major UN involvement in making positive contributions for peacekeeping, it is incumbent upon us to study the reasons events have joined to create this opportunity. . . . If we are unrealistic in our expectations, or fail to be hard-headed in our analysis of the apparent success and progress of UN peacekeeping, we will endanger future potential for the United Nations as a peacekeeping tool.

The fact of the matter is that the United Nations cannot and should not seek to impose solutions on parties. Rather, once the parties have—through exhaustion, their own cost-benefit analysis, or other reasons—reached a stage where it is time for the conflict to end, the United Nations can provide an invaluable role as a facilitator to this process. Whether by bridging a gulf of remaining differences or merely providing a graceful exit, and/or providing domestic justification that the respective governments can use with their own situation at home, the United Nations has a role. It does not impose peace. However, it can act as a midwife, a helpful facilitator, a promoter of peace. This is a limited role, but it is an enormously important role. . . .

Global Problem Solving

As with conflict resolution, the UN system is uniquely able to help governments take collective action, when governments have a unity of purpose and political will. In recent years, the ability of the United Nations and its specialized agencies to respond quickly and effectively to global problems has taken on new importance.

At the International Atomic Energy Agency (IAEA), for example, important work is done on nuclear nonproliferation, assurance of supply, and nuclear safety. The IAEA responded fully and constructively to the nuclear accident at Chernobyl, helping to analyze the causes of the accident, contain the fallout, and draft international conventions to deal with future nuclear accidents.

At the Secretary General's initiative, 138 countries met in 1987 and declared the elimination of drug abuse and illicit trafficking a universal priority. We are moving toward a strong new antidrug trafficking convention. . . . Stronger UN drug control programs will follow to address this serious international problem.

Another excellent example of global problem-solving can be found in the World Health Organization (WHO). WHO has led the fight to eradicate smallpox, developed programs targeting the health of children, and has been aggressively coordinating the global response to the problems of AIDS [acquired immune deficiency syndrome].

The Pressures for Interdependence

The pressures for interdependence have never been clearer. Destructive weapons have attained global reach. Atmospheric pollution, the greenhouse effect, acid rain, the spread of chlorofluorocarbons, tropical deforestation, and Chernobyl-type accidents respect no frontiers. The things we make and buy, the money we use and borrow, and the data we transmit flow in ever larger quantities across national borders. . . .

Somehow, without losing their national identity, the nations of the world must learn to hang together (in Ben Franklin's words) if our problems are not to spin out of control.

Only the United Nations, associating 159 states of every political stripe and region, can serve as a vehicle for this development.

David Popper, *The Humanist*, January/February 1990.

Finally, we should also note the significant problem-solving undertaken by other UN agencies like the International Maritime Organization and the International Civil Aviation Organization. These have both been in the vanguard of the global fight against international terrorism. . . .

Gathering Place for the World

Among the foremost arenas for multilateral diplomacy is the United Nations. The UN system is important to the world community and to the interests of its individual member states. Debates in the United Nations set the international agenda for much of the world. These debates legitimize and delegitimize issues on the world stage and focus world attention, often establishing the framework for progress.

In the areas of peacekeeping, human rights, and the vital work of the specialized agencies, we can see an increasing number of opportunities on the horizon for effectively utilizing the diplomatic benefits of the United Nations as a gathering place for the world.

At the same time, we must continue to take a realistic look at the United Nations as we approach the next century. We must not allow the euphoria felt in some quarters to blind us to the political realities which are intertwined within the multilateral arena. . . .

Faith and Commitment

In order to be forward-looking about the United Nations, we must be able to take a long look back—back to the United Nations as it was intended to be by its founders. The future of multilateral diplomacy, its promises and potential problems, can be glimpsed in the achievements and in the mistakes of the past and in the faith and commitment of today. We should renew that faith and understand that our goals for the future can only be attained by the steps we take today.

"The United Nations will, after the Cold War, remain what it was during the Cold War—a largely irrelevant debating society. "

The United Nations Cannot Solve International Problems

Michael Lind

In the following viewpoint, Michael Lind argues that the United Nations (UN) has serious internal problems that prevent it from effectively promoting international cooperation. One of these problems, Lind contends, is the outdated organization of the UN, which gives more influence to former great powers, such as Great Britain and France, than current world powers such as Germany and Japan. The author believes that this situation weakens the ability of the UN to gain the crucial support of Japan, Germany, and other important nations. Michael Lind is a foreign policy analyst in Washington, D.C.

As you read, consider the following questions:

1. In the author's opinion, how did the nonaligned bloc in the United Nations benefit from the Cold War?
2. How does Lind believe that the UN Security Council should be reorganized?
3. What predictions for the future of the UN does the author make?

Michael Lind, "The United Nations: After the Cold War." This article appeared in the October 1990 issue and is reprinted with permission from *The World & I*, a publication of The Washington Times Corporation, copyright © 1990.

The end of the Cold War has brought hopes for a rebirth of the United Nations. After Iraq invaded Kuwait, the Soviet Union joined the United States in Security Council resolutions condemning Iraq and imposing global sanctions. The General Assembly, encouraged by the United States and the Soviet Union, has made some important concessions to Western interests, such as endorsing the importance of democracy and free markets in development. Soviet-American cooperation in the Security Council, and more moderate behavior by the Third World majority bloc in the General Assembly, suggests to some observers that the United Nations can at last undertake the mission of global crisis management and global cooperation for which it was designed.

A Disappointing History

There can be little doubt that the worst days for the organization are behind. During the Cold War, the Security Council could never function as intended, because the Soviet Union used its veto power as a permanent member of the Security Council to thwart actions opposed by its client states or by General Assembly blocs that Soviet diplomacy sought to estrange from America and the West.

Deadlock in the Security Council was not the only result of the Cold War. A "nonaligned" bloc of Asian, African, and Latin American countries sought to exploit the rivalry between the Western alliance and the Soviet bloc. As long as their defection to the Soviet camp was a credible threat, Third World countries could attempt to extort concessions from the United States and its allies. These concessions might take the form of Western economic subsidies to the Third World (such as the tax that the Law of the Sea treaty would have levied on Western business concerns) or Western acquiescence in measures promoting the interests of particular influential Third World countries (such as India, which would gain in military influence from the adoption of a General Assembly resolution calling for a "Zone of peace" without Soviet or American forces in the Indian Ocean).

The Third World bloc in the UN also sought to portray the West and the Soviet bloc as morally equivalent, distracting attention from Soviet imperialism—and the dictatorial and repressive nature of many Third World governments—by ritually denouncing Israel and South Africa and mechanically opposing U.S. military action.

For these reasons, successive U.S. administrations treated the United Nations with disdain, if not contempt. Indeed, two U.S. ambassadors to the UN, Daniel Patrick Moynihan and Jeane Kirkpatrick, became heroes to significant portions of the American population for their forthrightness in cutting through diplomatic cant and defending the interests of the United States and its friends. Nevertheless, America's objection was to the distortion of the United Nations by Soviet intransigence and Third World hypocrisy, not to reasonable international cooperation. The United States might welcome a reformed United Nations. For the United Nations to function as intended, however, the end of Cold War rivalries is not enough. Both the structure of the Security Council and the majority attitude in the General Assembly would have to be changed significantly.

Ben Sargent, *Austin American-Statesman.* Reprinted with permission.

The UN Security Council has 15 members. Each of the five permanent members of the Security Council—the United States, the Soviet Union, China, Britain, and France—possesses the power to veto any Security Council action. The Security Council was designed by the five major victors of the Second World War to ensure that the new system of collective security, unlike the League of Nations, would incorporate the major world powers into the new world body. Without a veto to protect national interests, the Soviet Union might not have joined. The United States might also have stayed out, as it stayed out of the League of Nations rather than surrender U.S. sovereign prerogatives.

No doubt the veto will be exercised by one or more permanent members of the Security Council during future conflicts among members. In the more fluid world order of the post-Cold War era, however, it seems unlikely that one power such as the Soviet Union will use the veto to systematically cripple the Security Council. A more important problem may be the composition of the Security Council.

It is absurd that the permanent members of the Security Council are the same as those in 1945. At the end of the Second World War, Britain was a global power, the U.S. and the Soviet Union were superpowers, and Germany and Japan were powerless and impoverished. Today, Germany and Japan are the most important democratic and capitalist powers after the United States, and Britain has lost its empire and joined France as a middling nuclear power. The Soviet Union seems destined to lose much of its peripheral empire and sink to the status of a regional nuclear power, a status shared not only by China but by India, a nuclear power that lacks a seat on the Security Council.

New Permanent Members

The purpose of the Security Council was to reconcile the realities of global power with the idealism inherent in a world diplomatic organization. That purpose cannot be served if minor powers are included in the permanent Security Council membership and major powers excluded. Proposals to remedy this anomaly have already been made. Japan, no longer content with being an economic giant and a political pygmy, has proposed creating six new permanent Security Council seats—for itself, the reunited Germany, India, Egypt, Nigeria, and Brazil. These new permanent members would not possess a veto. . . .

Revising the UN Charter to incorporate the new great powers in the world will be difficult, but it is essential if the UN is to have a central place in world politics in the twenty-first century. At best, Britain and France would be dropped, and Germany, Japan, and India added to China, the Soviet Union, and the United States, giving the Security Council six permanent members. As Britain and France are unlikely to agree to their demotion, the second best solution is to enlarge the Security Council to accommodate the new permanent members. If new permanent members are given the veto, however, the possibilities for deadlock over conflicts of interest would be greatly increased. The Japanese compromise—allowing the old permanent members to have a veto, but not the new permanent members—is ultimately unsatisfactory. Why should China forever have a veto but not Germany? Perhaps the absolute veto should be replaced by a qualified veto, possessed by all permanent Security Council members, Japan as well as the United States, Germany as well as the Soviet Union. If one permanent member vetoed a measure, an extraordinary majority, of two-thirds or three-fourths, would be necessary for the measure to be passed again. If this is not sufficient protection of member interests, then their objection is not to the composition of the Security Council but to its powers. In the long run, the best reform program for the Security Council may include three elements: the addition of new permanent members; the replacement of the absolute veto with a qualified veto for all permanent members; and the reduction of Security Council powers that threaten the sovereignty of its permanent members.

The Developing Nations

Making the Security Council more representative of the powerful nations may not solve the problems of the UN. Indeed, it may create a new problem—the perception that the Security Council is the instrument of world domination by the wealthy and powerful countries. Olga Pellicer, the deputy representative of Mexico at the United Nations, observed that the strengthened role of the Security Council "raises fears in the South of an hegemonic directorate."

Third World Follies

Superpower rivalry is only one source of the U.N.'s problems. A good many of the most objectionable U.N. activities originate in the radical Third World. The New World Information Order, which strengthens governments' control of media, was a Third World initiative. So are many of the anti-business, anti-growth, redistributive and regulatory schemes of the New International Economic Order.

Jeane Kirkpatrick, *Conservative Chronicle*, December 20, 1989.

With the end of the Cold War, the "nonaligned bloc" of Latin American, Asian, and African nations must find a new identity. As Mark Falcoff of the American Enterprise Institute and others have observed, there can be no "Third World" when the "Second World"—the anti-Western Soviet bloc—has largely ceased to exist. The former Third World majority in the UN may redefine itself as the poor, industrializing "South," in contrast to the rich "North" represented by the United States, Europe, and Japan. According to the ideology of the "South," the advanced industrial countries of the "North" became rich by exploiting tropical and colonial countries. In general, this is a myth; Germany, for example, never had any significant colonies. However, the new southern myth may serve its purpose—to justify the recycling of old schemes for forcing Western businesses and governments to pay the governments of backward countries for the privilege of using "global resources" such as the seabed or outer space. Other perennial proposals in the General Assembly would protect repressive governments with state-dominated economies in the developing world.

In the name of a "New World Information and Communication Order" (NWICO), for example, press controls by the governments of developing nations would be sanctioned by the United Nations. At the same time, strict standards for intellectual property rights (such as patents) would not be enforced, because these same nations see advantage in allowing their industrialists to steal Western technology. In general, most countries represented in the General Assembly are more concerned with the prerogatives of states and political elites than with the rights of individuals, as members of minority groups, as businessmen, or as journalists.

Recreating Deadlock

If a majority of the General Assembly continues to back such statist, anti-Western proposals, in the name of the "South" rather than the "Third World" or "the nonaligned nations," then the outlook for the United Nations is bleak indeed. The Security Council may find itself pitted against the General Assembly. More likely, one or more members of the Security Council—China, the Soviet Union, perhaps India in the future—may try to act as the voice of the "South" on the Security Council, recreating the combination of Security Council deadlock and General Assembly anti-Westernism that has marginalized the United Nations for decades. Should that happen, the major issues of world politics will be settled elsewhere—in disarmament talks between the great military powers; in economic summits between the industrial powers; and in negotiations under the auspices of regional organizations, such as the Conference on Security and Cooperation in Europe (CSCE). Reforms of the Security Council structure are not enough; and structural reforms in the General Assembly are difficult because of the absolute equality of all members. Without changes in the deeply rooted attitudes of the General Assembly majority, the United Nations will, after the Cold War, remain what it was during the Cold War—a largely irrelevant debating society.

"UN peacekeeping can be the central dynamic in the transition to a warless world."

The United Nations Can Prevent War

Robert C. Johansen

One of the goals of the United Nations (UN) is to prevent war. To accomplish this aim, the UN can deploy a multinational police force, known as a peacekeeping force, to intervene between hostile countries. Robert C. Johansen argues in the following viewpoint that UN peacekeeping forces could play a larger role in promoting peace between nations. If these forces were strengthened, Johansen maintains, they could enforce international law and help to create a new era of peace. The author is a scholar at the Institute for International Peace Studies at the University of Notre Dame in Indiana.

As you read, consider the following questions:

1. What does Johansen think is the problem with peacekeeping operations that are not conducted by the UN?
2. What does the author mean by "ad hoc" peacekeeping forces? What is the problem with these forces?
3. In the author's opinion, in what specific ways can UN peacekeeping forces contribute toward creating a more peaceful world?

Robert C. Johansen, "UN Peacekeeping: The Changing Utility of Military Force," *Third World Quarterly*, vol. 2, no. 2, April 1990. Reprinted with permission.

A growing number of people and governments are beginning to understand that the utility of national military force has, in many contexts, fallen clearly below the utility of multilateral peacekeeping for the purpose of maintaining peace. This recognition creates conditions in which an imaginative approach to UN [United Nations] peacekeeping can become the linchpin in developing an overall strategy for reducing the role of military power in international relations. Yet progress towards a peaceful world order is by no means inevitable. Because of its extensive influence and unrealised potential to exercise leadership, the response that the USA will make to today's more promising conditions will be of profound importance in the next diplomatic steps towards a warless world. . . .

A careful look at recent history demonstrates that multilateral peacekeeping under UN auspices, although certainly no panacea, can be more successful than unilateral and bloc-related efforts to dampen military conflicts, because unilateral acts lack legitimacy. Peacekeeping works best when it is widely perceived to be impartial, eschews violence, enjoys broad international support and implements rules established by the world community—rules interpreted by the Security Council or General Assembly which, although imperfect, do symbolically represent the human community.

Not All Peacekeeping Is Successful

Peacekeeping activities carried out by Washington or other states acting alone cannot create the legitimacy necessary for success. Even efforts to multilateralise peacekeeping, while keeping it essentially under the control of the one military bloc, have not fared well. After Israel invaded and occupied a large part of Lebanon in 1982, the USA sought to establish a multinational force to facilitate a face-saving Israeli withdrawal and to keep the peace in Lebanon. Because Israel opposed UN oversight of territory they occupied, US officials vetoed a French plan to station UN peacekeepers in Beirut, and set up its own multilateral, but not multibloc or genuinely global force, entirely outside the UN framework. The US-led force included US, British, French and Italian soldiers. In addition to seeking peace, Washington could not avoid the temptation to position itself so as to influence the internal workings of Lebanese politics better and to discourage reconsolidation of Syrian control over Lebanon.

The West defined the purposes of this force, and excluded the East and the non-aligned countries. Although Washington initially made an effort to follow UN principles of engagement for peacekeeping by remaining impartial and refraining from violence, the US-created force gradually drew itself into the Lebanese civil war. Towards the end, the USA shelled civilian residences with sixteen-inch artillery from US battleships and launched bombing strikes from aircraft carriers. Finally, the USA became a belligerent supporting the Christian Phalangist forces as they tried to retain their traditional power.

New Dimensions for UN Peacekeeping

Peacekeeping [is] an art developed and refined by successive UN secretaries-general during the cold war years to contain conflict in areas beyond the perimeters of direct superpower contention. But it is an open-ended art, capable now, with superpower cooperation in the Security Council, of much broader application. If an era of multilateralism is truly at hand, peacekeeping—with creative new dimensions—will surely mature as its primary instrument.

John Q. Blodgett, *The Washington Quarterly*, Winter 1991.

The bloc-centred peacekeeping attempt failed. After the USA withdrew with nearly 300 US marines dead, the Pentagon conducted a study which, among other findings, demonstrated the difficulty that any national military force is likely to encounter when its government favours one faction over another, but attempts to be a neutral policeman. Once US naval forces began shelling anti-government and Syrian-supported positions, US forces almost inevitably took on the role of armed partisanship. Because Washington could not claim to represent an impartial force on behalf of the world community, the US-led force quickly stimulated more conflict and eroded support for peacekeeping, rather than the opposite. Both East-West and North-South antagonisms deepened. . . .

Transition to a Warless World

The political, psychological and educational benefits of a strategy designed to enhance UN peacekeeping activity are seldom considered. Peacekeeping can become an effective central focus in the development of a global political strategy for eventually replacing the war system with a peace system.

UN peacekeeping can be the central dynamic in the transition to a warless world because it reminds us of the difference between police enforcement and military activity. It shows the possibility of global nonpartisanship in contrast to the partisanship of national uses of armed force. Even if UN peacekeepers carry arms, these soldiers have no enemies. Their function is more akin to police enforcement than to combat. UN peacekeepers seek to enforce norms established by the community, on the community, for the benefit of the community. A national army imposes the preferences of one nation or one bloc on another, against the preference of the latter. Armies seek victory; police, tranquility. Police do not seek to establish a victor's justice through unconditional surrender of one side to another, but to restore peace so that political mechanisms representing both sides can work to bring justice another day. Police seek ultimately to enforce law on individual offenders; a modern army cannot do that. In practice armies attack large segments of an entire society, well aware that those it kills are innocent recruits or civilians, not the people really responsible for making decisions in violation of community norms.

A New Peacekeeping Force

Although UN peacekeeping efforts have in several instances proved successful in preventing renewed conflict between belligerents in the Middle East, Cyprus and elsewhere, this experience also reveals several institutional weaknesses. First, some states have been reluctant to employ and respect UN forces because national governments are suspicious of *ad hoc* forces that contain contingents drawn from other national armed forces which may be viewed as serving national interests rather than the general interest in peacekeeping. Although UN forces have generally performed well in minimising this problem . . . this record has not in itself sufficiently allayed the suspicions of some governments, nor can it remove suspicions as well as an integrated, autonomous UN force could.

In addition to this problem, the secretary-general may not be able to win prompt Security Council approval to despatch a UN force. States certainly cannot be expected to rely on multilateral peacekeeping if the despatch of a force is delayed when a nation most needs one. Finally, UN forces have had trouble obtaining the financing that they need to carry out their missions effectively. These are serious problems, but they can all be addressed with reasonable reforms.

A helpful innovation could be to create a permanent UN force, individually recruited by the UN from among individuals who volunteer from many nations. Such a force could be more effectively trained, organised and employed to carry out the demanding tasks of peacekeeping and international policing than *ad hoc* forces. It would be loyal to UN authorities acting on behalf of the world community, not to the fluctuating political goals of the governments who now donate contingents to *ad hoc* forces.

A Larger Role

Such a force would, of course, enable the UN to play a role in maintaining international security that goes slightly beyond that envisioned in the UN charter. UN forces could be used in anticipation of a crisis, not just in reaction to one. Often the early use of police can prevent a border conflict from erupting into war and from arousing a felt need to employ military force later on. Early use of a standing UN force might also discourage aggression by militarily adventurous small powers and intervention by the great powers.

There are numerous examples in recent years of dangerous border conflicts where such a force might have helped. The ease with which Iraq could contemplate a cross-border attack on Iran no doubt encouraged the bloodiest war in recent times. Syrian and Israeli attacks on the Palestine Liberation Organisation in part grew out of Lebanon's failure to maintain the integrity of its own borders. UN peacekeepers could have played a vital role along the Honduras-Nicaragua border in preventing a wider war. Their presence would also have helped the US public and Congress to discern what are in fact legitimate US security interests in that region. Multilateral border patrols could also have been useful on boundaries between Libya and Chad, Libya and the Sudan, between South Africa and Angola, and in the Moroccan-Algerian dispute over the Western Sahara.

The Weak as Well as the Strong

If we are to talk seriously of a "new world order," the world's disputes and conflicts should all be a concern of the United Nations, daunting as the prospect may seem. . . . It is no longer acceptable that international action is taken only when a situation threatens the interests of the most powerful nations. . . . A system of international peace and security must be comprehensive and universal, and it must protect the interests of the weak as well as the strong.

Brian Urquhart, *The New York Review of Books*, March 7, 1991.

Disputes which remain over the creation of an interim government in Cambodia illustrate further the need to employ an international peacekeeping force in even the most difficult and delicate domestic context, providing some necessary guarantees to all factions of the dispute. The nature, composition and mandate of an international control body to monitor an agreement and keep the peace is a central issue. A permanent force, already established and experienced in dealing with such problems, would be a valuable asset.

An Educational Role

A permanent UN police or peacekeeping force could perform a worldwide educational role as vital as its coercive role. The establishment of such a force could nurture in people's minds the idea that it is indeed possible to have international enforcement of rules that must govern all people if our species is to survive.

Such a force could help all societies learn how to see self-serving tendencies more accurately. This is essential to a global learning process because nations, like individuals, hurt others not so much because they are vicious as because they do not accurately understand themselves. They do not see the unconscious reasons for their actions, or understand the way in which they are treating other nations unfairly or using a double standard to justify their own conduct. A UN police force reminds all nations that, when one acts nationally in dispute settlement, from a global point of view it is partisan.

It matters less that the proposed force cannot now solve all problems than that it be created, used where it is most able to succeed, and establish a positive reputation for standing above national partisanship in its international monitoring and enforcement.

Allowing Countries to Disarm

A standing UN force would enable UN-protected countries to become a realistic possibility—an essential stage in worldwide arms reductions. Rather than maintaining a full-scale national military, these countries could avail themselves of UN peacekeeping forces to deter encroachments upon their integrity and independence. The dishonour that would come to an aggressor in attacking a UN-protected country would help deter some aggression. With a permanent UN force, more countries could follow the example of Costa Rica, which has dismantled its armed forces. This is not a fanciful possibility, since many nations are unable to protect themselves militarily anyway: their armed forces merely drain their treasuries and often threaten democratic political processes. Rather than spending money on their own national forces, such countries could contribute more modest amounts to the cost of maintaining a standing UN police force. Moscow, Washington and Tokyo, as well as other industrialised countries, might offer substantial support to finance UN peacekeeping efforts in return for guarantees that other countries and surrogate forces would refrain from military interventions worldwide.

As the UN role in war prevention among small states was strengthened, the temptation for unilateral intervention by hegemonic powers would be reduced. By enhancing security for the less militarised states, a permanent UN force would also reduce the need such states now feel for arms purchases, military assistance and training—all of which contribute to the militarisation of their domestic and international life. It would also open the way for the eventual dismantling of foreign military bases and the establishment of an effective noninterventionist regime. . . .

Citizens can, by their own actions, do much to hold their own government accountable to international constraints which in turn enhance the security of the world community. The pressing task is to organise political support for concrete proposals that will take advantage of the underutilised potential for multilateral peacemaking and peacekeeping. Such proposals can generate educational and diplomatic programmes of political strength and moral power, and enable more and more people to see that the time has come to place peacekeeping in the hands of institutions that encompass all nations.

"Unless the United Nations reviews its own policies, it is unlikely that it can continue to serve [as] . . . a useful instrument for peacemaking."

The United Nations Cannot Prevent War

Mark A. Franz

In the late 1980s, the United Nations (UN) played a role in ending the Iran-Iraq War and negotiating a Soviet withdrawal from Afghanistan. With these and other successes, some observers have predicted that the UN will become more effective at solving world conflicts. In the following viewpoint, Mark A. Franz disagrees with this view and argues that the United Nations can play only a limited role in bringing about peace between countries. Moreover, Franz contends, fundamental flaws in the United Nations threaten its ability to carry out peacekeeping operations at all. The author is the director of the United Nations Assessment Project at the Heritage Foundation, a conservative think tank in Washington, D.C.

As you read, consider the following questions:

1. Why does Franz believe that the UN operation in Cyprus has not been a complete success?
2. What is the author's assessment of the United Nation's election monitoring activities?
3. According to Franz, why does the UN sometimes ignore problems during its peacekeeping missions?

Mark A. Franz, "UN Peace: Euphoria vs. Reality." This article appeared in the April 1990 issue and is reprinted with permission from *The World & I*, a publication of The Washington Times Corporation, copyright © 1990.

Much has been written on the purported successes of UN [United Nations] peacekeeping in the past few years. Most of it has been long on anecdotal sketches of various operations and short on critical analysis.

While this approach is understandable because the United Nations is a complex organization, it does little to enhance our ability to determine when and where a UN peacekeeping operation can actually improve the chances for the peaceful settlement of disputes—the apparent preconditions for success—and where it may do more harm than good.

The Definition of UN Peacekeeping

UN peacekeeping is not easily defined. It has evolved from no specific charter mandate and has taken on many different forms in an attempt to adapt to the requirements of the various conflicts the United Nations has addressed. Although many of the operations typically labeled peacekeeping are not, strictly speaking, traditional military observer operations, they can be categorized as part of the "good offices" missions of the secretary-general as this role has emerged over the past 44 years. The main characteristic that so-called peacekeeping activities have in common is that each was an item considered by the Security Council, which then resolved to endorse a peacekeeping mandate or a particular effort by the secretary-general.

A necessary distinction must be made between peacekeeping and peacemaking, although the former term means all special military activities, including facilitating negotiations and monitoring elections. Specifically, peace*keeping* refers to those operations of a traditional military observer force serving along a border or demarcation line to maintain a cease-fire between belligerent parties. Peace*making* refers to those efforts on the part of the United Nations, usually through the office of the secretary-general, that seek to facilitate an agreement or political settlement between hostile parties. There are as many variations on these two paradigms as there are UN peacekeeping activities, but the pair serves as a convenient framework for discussion.

Established in 1964, the United Nations Peacekeeping Force in Cyprus (UNFICYP) provides a classic example of UN peacekeeping. And since a cease-fire between Greek and Turkish Cypriots in August 1974, UNFICYP has maintained a buffer zone along the 112-mile-long demarcation line that separates the parties. In this limited, well-defined capacity, the United Nations has achieved its goal of preventing the outbreak of hostilities. It is unclear, however, whether or not this role has been useful in bringing about a permanent political solution there. The prolonged cease-fire has, to some extent, served as a disincentive for final agreement between the two parties. While the first requirement of UN peacekeeping activity—that the two parties decide to quit fighting—is present, the impetus to achieve a political settlement possibly has been diminished.

Javad © 1991 Cartoonists & Writers Syndicate. Reprinted with permission.

In this instance, the United Nations has failed to achieve its goal of a negotiated settlement despite 16 years of effort. The inherent difficulty in achieving a peaceful, permanent resolution to any conflict is painfully evident in the case of Cyprus.

The peace*making* side of the UN role in Afghanistan shows how the United Nations can serve as a facilitator or broker for an agreement between belligerent parties. No one seriously believes that the United Nations compelled the Soviet Union to withdraw from Afghanistan; however, once the decision was made in Moscow, it served as a handy forum for negotiating the framework for withdrawal. This framework, in the form of the Geneva Accords signed in April 1988, served as an international face-saving device for the Soviets and made the withdrawal policy more politically palatable at home. The importance of this kind of role should not be underestimated. The United Nations would do well to concentrate its efforts toward activities of this nature.

The peace*keeping* element of the mission in Afghanistan has been less effective. The military monitoring force of approximately 50 UN peacekeepers successfully carried out its role of verifying the withdrawal of more than 100,000 Soviet troops by February 15, 1989. This was not a particularly difficult task. The Soviet military representatives informed the United Nations Good Offices Mission in Afghanistan and Pakistan (UNGOMAP) that the withdrawal of all troops was accomplished, and UNGOMAP reported this to the secretary-general. The other half of UNGOMAP's mandate—to investigate reports of violations of the accords by participating parties—has not been as easy. Thousands of complaints have been registered, yet few have been investigated. Controversy has arisen over the status of Soviet advisors remaining in Afghanistan. UNGOMAP has no mandate with regard to the internal conflict between the mujahideen and the Kabul regime. It is doubtful if it could do anything toward fulfilling that kind of mandate even if one existed.

The cease-fire in the war between Iran and Iraq provides another example of the United Nations' facilitating a cessation of hostilities between warring parties once those parties decided it was in their respective interests to stop killing one another. The United Nations Iran-Iraq Military Observer Group (UNIIMOG) is a traditional peacekeeping operation in the mold of UNFICYP; it has an established border to patrol and the task of monitoring a cease-fire. Though UNIIMOG has done a remarkable job in maintaining peace in an extremely volatile situation, peace is only possible for as long as both Iran and Iraq perceive that it is not in their interests to pursue their political objectives by military means. If either party decides to attack the other, UNIIMOG can do nothing but dodge the bullets.

The UN Election Watch

Election monitoring is a relatively new and different kind of UN activity, but it is subject to many of the same determinants as peacekeeping and peacemaking.

The United Nations Angola Verification Mission (UNAVEM) has the mandate of monitoring Cuban troop withdrawal from Angola. The United Nations Transition Assistance Group (UNTAG) was established by the Security Council in 1978 to carry out a mandate of independence for Namibia through free and fair elections to be monitored by UNTAG. Both UNAVEM and UNTAG were instituted after a 1988 tripartite agreement between Angola, Cuba, and South Africa and a bilateral agreement between Angola and Cuba, part of a comprehensive settlement brokered by the United States with the Soviet Union's tacit approval.

The United Nations eliminated itself as a potential broker in southern Africa when, in 1977, the General Assembly declared the Marxist South-West Africa People's Organization (SWAPO) the "sole authentic representative" of the Namibian people. In addition, from 1975 until 1989, SWAPO received millions in UN financial support, including $420,000 per year to operate its observer mission to UN headquarters in New York. Despite this bias, UNTAG set about the task of monitoring the November 1989 elections in Namibia. Hence, a new brand of UN peacekeeping emerged.

Limited Power

However improved the superpower relationship and the consequent functioning of the Security Council may be, the UN's powers will remain those of persuasion, of setting the scene for peaceful negotiation. Intractable disputes will give way to negotiated settlements only when all the parties, albeit for different reasons, need a settlement simultaneously.

Anthony Parsons, *World Press Review*, October 1988.

The day the independence process began under UN supervision, April 1, 1989, 1,200 armed SWAPO guerrillas crossed the border into Namibia from Angola in violation of the agreements. UNTAG did nothing, and South African forces repelled the invasion, which resulted in 142 casualties. Documented reports of the torture of SWAPO opponents were ignored by UNTAG, as were those of continuing SWAPO detention of Namibian dissidents in camps throughout the frontline states.

Other Problems

Meanwhile, the commander of the UNAVEM forces stated that the number of Cuban troops in Angola was unimportant. The Cubans have since suspended their withdrawal, while the government, which they support, has launched a massive offensive under Soviet military direction against Jonas Savimbi's forces in southern Angola. UNAVEM has been conspicuously silent.

That the United Nations did manage to observe an election in Namibia—run by South Africa, it is important to note—that appears to have been free and fair does not necessarily indicate a causal relationship between UN presence and electoral success.

Events in Nicaragua, where ONUVEN (United Nations Observer Mission to Verify the Elections in Nicaragua) monitors the election process, have shown that the mere presence of a UN force does not automatically provide the conditions necessary for a free and fair election.

Sandinista violence against opposition supporters has been widespread. On December 11, 1989, at an opposition rally in the town of Masatepe, about 30 miles south of Managua, the Sandinistas conducted a brutal attack on opposition supporters. Victims were stoned, stabbed, and beaten. ONUVEN not only failed to investigate the incident but later announced with certainty that the February 25, 1990 elections would be carried out fairly.

Peace at Some Time?

Some argue that a large UN presence in and of itself can make a difference in the conduct of free and fair elections. Yet, regardless of the size of the contingent, the observers need to know what to look for. A blind presence will serve as no deterrent to fraud, intimidation, and ballot rigging. Due to UN requirements of regional representation in any and all of its incarnations, this is a fundamental problem, since any true understanding of representative democracy (a prerequisite to effective monitoring) requires experience with the institutions of democracy.

Most visible in the case of UN peacekeeping is its institutional tendency to avoid addressing problems with regard to its mission. Consequently, rather than make an issue of the irregularities in the voter registration process, or atrocities committed during the final phases of troop withdrawal, and attempt to deal with them (which runs the inherent risk of leading to a "failed mission"), it is easier to ignore those problems or to try to diminish their importance and declare that the process is moving along as planned. The United Nations Interim Force in Lebanon (UNIFIL) may provide the sharpest illustration of this "ostrich in the sand" syndrome. From 1978 to 1982, relatively unbiased observers watched UNIFIL pretend not to notice the widespread incursions that its mandate specifically called on it to monitor and dissuade.

The notion that peace is breaking out all over thanks to the United Nations is belied by the facts. Where hostilities have been quelled, it has played a limited role at best. In many instances, the evidence suggests that the United Nations may be doing more harm than good by providing the false impression that all is well, when in fact, much still remains ill. International pleasure over the apparent winding down of some long-running regional conflicts should not be transmuted into euphoria over UN peacekeeping.

Where the United Nations has managed to maintain a relatively impartial position in a conflict, there is the possibility that it can serve as a facilitator to an agreement once the parties have concluded that they would rather talk than fight. Beyond this limited role, the influence of an institutional predisposition to avoid appearing to fail at a given mission becomes very strong and is likely to result in an inability to carry out the mission fairly and effectively. Unless the United Nations reviews its own policies, it is unlikely that it can continue to serve even in the limited capacity of a useful instrument for peacemaking.

"If NATO's original mission of protecting Western Europe from the USSR has been fulfilled, then the alliance . . . is no longer needed."

NATO Is Obsolete

Doug Bandow and Ted Galen Carpenter

The North Atlantic Treaty Organization (NATO) is a military alliance of twelve Western European nations and Turkey, Canada, and the United States. One of the primary goals of NATO since its establishment in 1949 has been to deter Soviet bloc aggression. In the following viewpoint, Doug Bandow and Ted Galen Carpenter argue that the end of the Cold War eliminates the need for NATO. With the dramatic lessening of the Soviet threat, Bandow and Carpenter assert, NATO no longer has a meaningful task. Although NATO supporters have devised a number of alternative missions that the organization could take, the authors contend that none of them withstand serious scrutiny. Bandow is a senior fellow at the Cato Institute, a public policy think tank in Washington, D.C. Carpenter is the foreign policy director at Cato.

As you read, consider the following questions:

1. What do the authors think is wrong with the "nothing's permanent" argument to preserve NATO?
2. What alternative missions for NATO have been proposed, according to Bandow and Carpenter?

Doug Bandow and Ted Galen Carpenter, "Preserving an Obsolete NATO," *Cato Policy Report*, September/October 1990. Reprinted with permission.

The stunning events of 1989 and 1990 have transformed the political landscape of Europe, but they have had little discernible impact on proponents of the NATO [North Atlantic Treaty Organization] alliance and America's military presence on the Continent. Many NATO partisans are so determined to preserve the cold war status quo that they embrace an assortment of obsolete, implausible, and frequently contradictory policies. If they succeed, they will continue to saddle American taxpayers with an expensive military commitment despite the waning Soviet threat and the rush by Washington's West European allies to cut their own defense forces and cash in on the "peace dividend." Why NATO partisans seem willing to sacrifice America's well-being in that fashion is a study in the politics of institutional self-preservation.

Preserving the Obsolete

Die-hard Atlanticists believe that, despite the political transformation of Eastern Europe, NATO and the U.S. military presence on the Continent should be permanent geopolitical fixtures. That is a curious assumption. Why should such arrangements be perpetuated if the Soviets relinquish their political grip on Eastern Europe—and especially if Moscow demonstrates a willingness to end its military occupation of the region? After all, the purpose of an alliance is not simply to have an alliance. Nor should the United States retain its troop presence out of a sense of tradition—especially when that commitment costs American taxpayers $130 billion a year.

NATO advocates, including President George Bush, either do not realize or do not care that the alliance's original reason for existence is rapidly becoming irrelevant. NATO was created four decades ago to protect a weak, war-devastated Western Europe from a rapacious Soviet Union that had already extinguished liberty in Eastern Europe. The subsequent U.S. troop commitment that began in 1950 has continued to the present day, even though Western Europe long ago ceased to be a war-ravaged waif incapable of providing for its own defense. As long as the Soviet threat remained, however, enabling the Pentagon to periodically trot out its tables and charts showing overwhelming Warsaw Pact military superiority, American participation in NATO's security arrangements was viewed as indispensable.

But the Soviet threat is hardly what it was in Stalin's—or even Brezhnev's—day. Moscow's new tolerance of political pluralism in Eastern Europe, the de facto dismantling of the Warsaw Pact, and the accelerating pace of Soviet troop withdrawals are erasing the principal Western grievances that led to the cold war. As the raison d'etre for NATO becomes obsolete, it would seem logical to begin planning for the day when the alliance—along with the

Warsaw Pact, if it long survives the proliferation of noncommunist governments in Eastern Europe—can go into a well-earned retirement. That . . . should be easily attainable before the end of the century. . . .

A Public Choice View

NATO partisans, in a practical demonstration of the public choice economic theories that won James Buchanan the Nobel Prize in 1986, have circled the wagons in a desperate attempt to preserve their beleaguered institution. They have also been astonishingly creative in coming up with new reasons not only to maintain NATO but to keep U.S. troops in Europe.

The first rationale is based on outright denial of changes in the Eastern bloc. Gorbachev's internal reforms and Moscow's repeal of the Brezhnev Doctrine are said to be simply a sophisticated Leninist ruse to lull the West into a false sense of security. Soviet expansionist objectives remain fundamentally unaltered, so naturally NATO must be maintained or even strengthened. That school of thought was more prominent before the breathtaking developments in the last half of 1989. Now it seems confined to the political fringe and a few unreconstructed cold warriors, primarily in the armed services leadership.

One must give such defenders of the status quo credit for tenacity. It is difficult for them to keep the faith in the face of mounting evidence that threatens to make them look as quaint as their ideological forbears who still argued in the late 1960s that the Sino-Soviet split was a sham. Probably for that reason most NATO defenders have moved on to a more sophisticated and plausible response: "nothing's permanent."

A Deceptive Argument

Members of the "nothing's permanent" faction concede that the changes in Soviet foreign and domestic policies are genuine and significant, but they doubt their durability. Mikhail Gorbachev might be overwhelmed by the ethnic turmoil and economic problems in his country and revert to Stalinist tactics to restore order, or his conservative adversaries might stage a palace coup. Consequently, the West must keep up its guard, which naturally requires maintaining NATO with only minor alterations, until it is certain that the changes in the Eastern bloc are permanent.

That view has a number of advocates, including former secretary of defense Caspar Weinberger, who contends that "even if Mr. Gorbachev should be completely honest and sincere in all that he has said, we have no indications whatever of how long he may remain in office, and we do not know who or what his successor would be. Under those circumstances, it would be folly for us to reduce the strength of our military." . . .

Their argument is more plausible because it does contain an element of truth: a reversal of trends in the Soviet Union and Eastern Europe could take place. But even Central Intelligence Agency director William Webster does not believe that such a reversal is likely. Even if it did occur, it would not mean a complete resurgence of the Soviet military threat. Objective economic and political conditions in the Soviet Union will create serious constraints on external adventurism for the foreseeable future. And even an expansionist Soviet regime would find it exceedingly difficult to put the fragmented Warsaw Pact back together as a military organization capable of offensive operations.

Jeff MacNelly. Reprinted with permission: Tribune Media Services.

Furthermore, the whole argument is insidiously deceptive. Proponents never bother to answer the question of how the permanence of Eastern bloc reforms is to be measured. Will five years of uninterrupted progress be enough? Ten? Twenty? Nor do they acknowledge the ability of the prosperous and populous West European nations to defend themselves should a Soviet military threat reemerge. . . .

Alternative Missions for NATO

As the magnitude of the changes in Eastern Europe and the Soviet Union has undermined the lack-of-permanence ploy, NATO supporters have fallen back to the final Atlanticist redoubt—finding an "alternative mission" for the alliance. Robert Zoellick, Secretary of State James Baker's counselor, cheerfully acknowledges that the department's policy planning staff is working with the European Affairs Bureau "to look at how you transform established institutions, such as NATO, to serve new missions that will fit the new era." That is not an easy task, however, for NATO has been the quintessential anti-Soviet security arrangement. NATO was established to defend Western Europe against either Soviet blackmail or an all-out Warsaw Pact invasion. The latter danger has receded into the realm of paranoid fantasy; even such cold war hard-liners as Richard Perle and James Schlesinger concede that the Warsaw Pact is an empty shell with no military significance. And the prospect of Soviet blackmail seems increasingly improbable as Moscow gropes toward a market economy and a multiparty political system. If NATO is no longer needed to counter such threats, one must ask what on earth its purpose should be. . . .

In the frantic search for new tasks, . . . three have emerged as the most prominent candidates. The first, propounds the *Economist*, is to respond to security threats in other regions. But NATO has never been an effective instrument for power projection outside Europe; in fact, the United States has consistently met resistance from its NATO allies to its policies toward Central America, Libya, and the Mideast. The lack of a looming Soviet threat will undoubtedly make such cooperation more rather than less difficult. . . .

The second alternative role, mentioned prominently by high-level NATO officials, is to "manage" the political transition in Eastern Europe. How a predominantly military association would be able to make a productive contribution to what is a political and economic process has been left, shall we say, a trifle vague. The notion of NATO as an effective political vehicle is especially dubious when one considers the debilitating disagreements that have plagued the alliance over the years. In the late 1980s the members did not even agree on the seriousness of the Soviet threat, let alone the proper response. The acrimonious U.S.-West German controversy over nuclear modernization in the spring of 1989 was only the most visible manifestation of such discord.

Policing Europe

A third possible task for a "new NATO" is to promote stability in Europe. Put bluntly, Europeans have spent centuries killing each other. Only when the United States (and some would argue the USSR as well, though that point is disputed) deigned to occupy the continent did peace reign. Therefore our troops should stay. (A more subtle version was the *New Republic*'s formulation: "There simply is enough change going on in Europe now without introducing new and unpredictable forces.") President Bush has stressed that theme, asserting that NATO and the U.S. military presence will be needed in the future not to deter a Warsaw Pact invasion (which he concedes is now highly improbable) but to guard against "instability and unpredictability."

But the prospect of greater instability, especially in Eastern Europe, is an argument for a lower U.S. military profile on the Continent. It is difficult to argue that the United States should be unduly concerned about disputes between small European states, since such quarrels would rarely impinge on vital American interests. Indeed, it would be better to insulate the United States from a conflict between, say, Hungary and Romania over the status of Transylvania than to preserve security arrangements that might entangle American troops in it.

Many Americans as well as Europeans have narrowed the stability argument to apply to just one country: Germany. The United States, it is argued, must maintain troops in Europe (namely West Germany) to contain German power. The *New York Times* reports that members of the State Department's policy planning staff assume that NATO will be needed "more than ever" as a mechanism for "alleviating friction among the allies, and, in its bluntest form, to help constrain German influence and keep Germany under a Western umbrella.". . .

No Reason for NATO

I see no earthly reason for NATO, a military alliance. Talking about converting it into a political structure is simply whistling in the graveyard. They're trying to prevent the demise of an institution which is now irrelevant, and I just can't see throwing away hundreds of millions of dollars in attempting to perpetuate this gargantuan bureaucracy which is trying to have a life of its own, quite apart from the fact that its purpose is no longer relevant.

Eugene J. Carroll Jr., *People's Daily World*, August 11, 1990.

The cynicism of the convenient reemergence of a "German threat" is astonishing. Not long ago the Federal Republic was being hailed as NATO's brave front-line state and the West Germans as dedicated allies in the struggle to contain the Soviet menace. Now those prosperous, freedom-loving burghers have apparently reverted to being the rapacious Hun; avuncular Helmut Kohl is projected to become the new Kaiser Wilhelm; and the 495,000-member Bundeswehr, facing cuts of one-fifth by the mid-1990s, is deemed capable of threatening a Soviet military nearly 10 times its size backed by thousands of nuclear warheads.

Atlanticists have really entered the conceptual Twilight Zone when they think it reasonable for NATO's primary mission in the 1990s to be the containment of the alliance's most vibrant European member. While history can never be forgotten, it also cannot justify obsolete alliances. (Else we would need a mechanism to constrain a potential Napoleonic revival in France.) The German containment thesis seems more the product of a desperate search for a "necessary enemy" to justify NATO's continued existence than of any reasonable geopolitical analysis. . . .

The Future of NATO

If NATO's original mission of protecting Western Europe from the USSR has been fulfilled, then the alliance—in contrast to American political, economic, and cultural engagement in Europe—is no longer needed. We should celebrate its success and enjoy the financial benefits of reduced military obligations. But the tenacious efforts of NATO partisans to preserve the alliance suggest that obsolete institutions are even more durable than old soldiers, who, intoned Gen. Douglas MacArthur, "never die, they just fade away." NATO is not fading away; it is trying to achieve organizational immortality.

6

"All of the objective factors certainly argue in favor of retaining . . . the Atlantic Alliance system."

NATO Is Not Obsolete

William E. Odom

During the Cold War, one of the primary purposes of the North Atlantic Treaty Organization (NATO) was to deter Soviet bloc aggression. Consequently, the improvement of Soviet-American relations and the collapse of most of the Eastern European communist regimes has led some experts to conclude that NATO is no longer needed. In the following viewpoint, William E. Odom argues for the continuing importance of NATO. NATO and the American presence in Europe, Odom reasons, have provided a source of stability for Europe. Without NATO, the author concludes, tensions among European nations could develop. Odom is the director of National Security Studies at the Hudson Institute, a public policy research center in Indianapolis, Indiana.

As you read, consider the following questions:

1. Why does the author believe that cutting military spending will not help the economies of Europe and the United States?
2. According to Odom, how could the United States be hurt by European problems?
3. What impact might instability in Eastern Europe have on Western Europe, in the author's opinion?

William E. Odom, "Is the Guns-Butter Curve Valid for NATO in the 1990s?" speech delivered to the Hudson Policy Forum, New York, NY, March 29, 1990.

The dramatic events in the Soviet Union and East Europe during late 1989 and early 1990 mark the end of the Cold War. At least that is the conventional wisdom. Soviet power appears to be inexorably in decline. All of the communist regimes in the East European Warsaw Pact states have collapsed. . . .

Time to Celebrate?

The jubilant mood surrounding this historical turning point is understandable. Events are vindicating America's containment policy. Germany is winning Konrad Adenauer's gamble in the early 1950s that the best route to reunification with liberty was through Washington. The East European states, to be sure, led by Poland, precipitated this collapse of Soviet hegemony. All of this is very well. We have much to cheer about. Our team seems to have won. Why not go home and celebrate?

I may sound like a spoilsport at the post-game party, but I believe there are several reasons not to celebrate. The first and most obvious is that international relations are not a ball game. They do not end on an agreed schedule. They go on and on with no referee and very weak rules. States which appear to have lost soon reassert their power. States which appear to have won find victory like a spring rose. The bloom is beautiful, but it fades rapidly.

I sound this note of caution because I testified before the Joint Economic Committee with Congressman Stephen Solarz in the chair. He was calling for a redefinition of national security. He made the Cold War seem like a ball game we have won, giving us the opportunity to come home, to shift our resources from military to domestic social programs. Some witnesses before his committee agreed. They believe that we can now beat our swords into plowshares. Education and highway repair are better investments for our national security than military forces.

It is not easy to disagree. For the past couple of years, it has become fashionable to insist that we are militarily overextended. Our share of the world economy has declined. The way to gain it back is to cut our military commitments and to rebuild our economy. Let the Europeans tend to their own security. Admittedly, this line of reasoning is attractive. But is it valid?

The Guns-Butter Curve Is Invalid

I am highly skeptical. Pursuing such a course is more likely to bring a general economic decline in the West. Let me explain why. In the first postwar decade, the United States built an international security order in Europe and East Asia. Within that structure we have witnessed unparalleled economic development. Our military security and our economy are interdependent. The security order has made the economic order possible.

Can we dismantle the security order without a deleterious impact on the world's economy?

To state the proposition another way, we do not face the choices indicated by economists' concept of a guns-butter curve. We cannot have more butter by reducing what we spend for security. Paying for guns has made it possible to have unprecedented amounts of butter. Our military outlays are essential overhead cost for economic success. If this is true, then a rapid reduction of our military commitments will adversely affect the economies of the tri-lateral regions.

Can we demonstrate convincingly the truth of this proposition? Perhaps not to everyone, but a strong case can be made. The easiest way to grasp the relationship is to think about why European economic integration has proceeded as far as it has. In the first place, the very idea was the product of a search for a new and stable security order in Europe. Economic integration did not proceed smoothly at first. Mistrust among former adversaries —primarily Britain, France, and Germany—was not conducive to it. The very idea, advanced by the French visionary, Jean Monnet, was conceivable only because the United States was willing to maintain large military forces in Germany and to take the lead in NATO [North Atlantic Treaty Organization]. At the same time, the United States provided unprecedented economic aid through the Marshall Plan. This coupling of security and economics soon showed dramatic results. . . .

A United Europe

By the late 1960s, there were doubts about ever achieving a united Europe. Yet economic integration continued to make progress. Why was that possible? Most European leaders knew the answer, but they did not like to admit it. The overarching American military presence created a climate in which former adversaries could trust one another. NATO became a de facto surrogate for a supranational political authority in Europe. It was the sine qua non for continued progress in the European Community. In a sense, the United States made the political decision for Europe.

In the 1980s economic integration gained new momentum. The German Bundesbank has effectively become the reserve bank for all members of the European Community. In other words, German bankers now have the task of controlling inflation in Italy, France, and other member states. Why will these countries allow their monetary policy to be dictated by foreign bankers? . . .

There are many reasons they do so in Europe, but one rather critical factor is the security climate created by NATO. Will a common monetary system, the kind the European Community [E.C.] seeks, come about if we withdraw our forces from Europe?

The answer, I believe, is surely no. Some would disagree and argue that the E.C. is leading to a new political order which can become a substitute for NATO. That is not convincing. The E.C. will do well to make progress in economic affairs. It certainly is not ready to shoulder the NATO role. It does not even include all NATO states.

A European Power

The United States should remain a European power in the broadest sense—politically, militarily, and economically. And, as part of our global responsibilities, the foundation for America's peaceful engagement in Europe has been—and will continue to be—NATO.

George Bush, address at Oklahoma State University, Stillwater, May 4, 1990.

American leaders have always been ambivalent toward the E.C. Will it become a new tariff wall? We have our occasional "chicken war" or "beef war" with Europe. Feelings become highly emotional on these occasions, but we have managed them without lasting damage in our trade relations. What is the probability that we will continue to manage them successfully if our forces are withdrawn? It is bound to be smaller. And damage to our trade is almost certain. . . .

Transatlantic Trade

Let us now consider some other dynamics within Europe that are likely to accompany the withdrawal of U.S. forces.

A number of observers are awakening to the impact that German reunification may have on EC-92. The demands for capital to rebuild the East German economy promise to have an inflationary impact on Germany's economy and perhaps the whole of the E.C. At the same time, nervous attitudes are emerging in France and Britain about the political ramifications of German unity. What impact will they have on the EC-92 schedule? Political confidence about stability in Europe based on an enduring NATO would probably allow the proponents of economic integration to convince the skeptics. Yet what Congressman Solarz proposes would remove the military pillar on which such political confidence has traditionally rested.

These points, I believe, are sufficient to suggest that the traditional guns-butter curve is not the paradigm that governs the security-economic relationship within the Atlantic Alliance. If we proceed on the assumption that it does, then we are likely to discover that we must pay for reducing our military commitments with a reduction in our economic benefits from transatlantic trade.

The issue, however, does not stop with Germany. It also concerns developments in Eastern Europe. Those who anticipate a peace dividend take an optimistic view of the future of Poland, Czechoslovakia, Hungary, and Romania.

Enthusiasm for liberal democracy and market economics in these countries is indisputably great. The speed with which they have begun dramatic political and economic reforms is indeed impressive. What are their prospects for success? We cannot say with confidence, but we can judge their chances by reflecting on the structural conditions these states must overcome.

Today's East European states are fairly young. Since the Third Partition of Poland in 1795, none of them knew independence until after 1919. During the brief interwar period they experienced great political turbulence. Three factors dominated their politics. First, border disputes; second, ethnic minority problems; and third, large land-hungry peasant populations struggled to survive on petty acreages. . . .

The postwar era under Soviet hegemony has brought enormous changes in these states. Their borders have changed in major ways. Accordingly, the politics are likely to be different. Poland and Hungary are almost ethnically homogeneous, but the other states are not. Ethnic minority problems are still serious. . . .

Instability Is Likely

The changed economic structure is also dramatic. Large capital investments have been made, particularly in heavy industry. Sadly, however, those investments were not determined by market forces. Thus the inefficiencies in the industrial structure are enormous. Market forces will prove most industrial firms unviable. They will be forced into bankruptcy unless state funds subsidize them.

Let us assume the best of conditions. Let us anticipate that adequate capital will be made available to reconstruct these economies. That will take more than a few years. In the interim, unemployment will abound. Economic growth will be small. Incomes will likely decline for a time. Political stability in this period of transition will not be easy.

How will the governments respond to the demands of large working classes and unemployed bureaucrats? If economic progress is fairly rapid, such demands may be adequately met. If it is slow, they could prove beyond the control of democratic institutions. The predictable public cry for the governments to do something about the unhappy situation will likely bring a return to authoritarianism. At the same time, national and ethnic sentiments will sharpen. Old border disputes and nationalism will become major factors in the politics of the region, just as they were before World War II. Moreover, we could see a resurgence of fascism in some places.

Will adverse developments in East Europe have no impact on the politics and economics of Western Europe? While it is difficult to specify precisely what the impact would be, it certainly cannot be favorable. And it is hardly going to inspire a common West European policy if there is no Atlantic Community involving a continuing U.S. presence in Central Europe. One possible scenario would be a split between Germany and the other major Western states over how to deal with Eastern Europe. That in turn could lead to France and Britain trying to cultivate support among East European states against Germany. Even today, as German businessmen seize the initiatives in Poland, Czechoslovakia, and Hungary, France is struggling for a leading position in Romania.

The lack of a NATO structure to coordinate Western policy, even moderately, is almost bound to encourage competition among Western policies. That, in turn, will permit the East Europeans to strike diplomatic arrangements with West European states that help reinforce mistrust and disputes within Europe as a whole. . . .

A Home for Germany

NATO is still needed as a home for Germany. Nobody has an interest in a neutralized and united Germany, unattached and tempted again to be a freewheeling major player or subject to fits of insecurity because of real or imagined threats from the East or West.

Stanley Hoffmann, *The New York Times*, May 27, 1990.

I cannot argue that the retention of a strong NATO with a significant U.S. presence in Europe would change the economic scenarios in East Europe in any significant way. It would seem, however, to provide a forum within which multilateral Western policies could be made to reduce the adverse impact on the West. Equally important, it would provide a guarantee against the uncertainties of border disputes and anti-democratic political developments in East Europe causing serious tensions among West European states. . . .

Retain NATO

Given the enormous vicissitudes facing both political and economic development in Europe, can we comfortably conclude that it is time to reduce our military commitments to NATO? Can we prudently go along with those who call for a post-Cold War celebration and beat our NATO swords into the plowshares of domestic programs?. . .

All of the objective factors certainly argue in favor of retaining, although in a reduced and modified form, the Atlantic Alliance system. Yet we can see many forces that can undermine it in the near future.

My message is simply that we should not view the outcome with economic equanimity. To lose the security order will also be to lose something of the economic order. The two are more interdependent than conventional wisdom suggests.

Power and Liberty

To put it more generally, let me cite Professor Samuel Huntington who observed in a major treatise on American politics a few years ago that there is a strong correlation between American power and the expansion of liberty abroad. When we have been weak and passive, it has declined. To the extent that liberty and economic prosperity are related, and I believe they are inextricably intertwined, we can also say that when we have been militarily strong, there has been greater economic prosperity in the world. I leave it to you to ponder whether the global economy will prosper if we are militarily weak.

a critical thinking activity

Understanding Words in Context

Readers occasionally come across words they do not recognize. And frequently, because they do not know a word or words, they will not fully understand the passage being read. Obviously, the reader can look up an unfamiliar word in a dictionary. By carefully examining the word in the context in which it is used, however, the word's meaning can often be determined. A careful reader may find clues to the meaning of the word in surrounding words, ideas, and attitudes.

Below are statements based on viewpoints in this chapter. In each excerpt, one of the words is printed in italics. Try to determine the meaning of each word by reading the excerpt. Under each excerpt you will find four definitions for the italicized word. Choose the one that is closest to your understanding of the word.

Finally, use a dictionary to see how well you have understood the words in context. It will be helpful to discuss with others the clues that helped you decide on each word's meaning.

1. The international *SANCTIONS* imposed on Iraq effectively isolated the country from the rest of the world.

   SANCTIONS means:

   a) penalties   c) benefits
   b) revenge   d) programs

2. Because the majority of United Nations members are from the Third World, this *BLOC* of nations often determines UN policies.

   BLOC means:

   a) pressure   c) series
   b) group   d) government

3. Two U.S. ambassadors to the United Nations cut through diplomatic *CANT* and explained the interests of the United States in clear, simple language.

   CANT means:

   a) efforts
   b) immunity
   c) jargon
   d) limits

4. With the fall of many of the communist governments of Eastern Europe, the Soviet Union lost much of its *PERIPHERAL* empire.

   PERIPHERAL means:

   a) aligned
   b) ready
   c) recent
   d) outermost

5. As we look toward the twenty-first century, *MULTILATERAL* diplomacy will be of growing importance as nations realize they must work together to solve global problems.

   MULTILATERAL means:

   a) many-sided
   b) self-interested
   c) pointless
   d) conditional

6. The profound global changes now occurring affect not just one nation or region, but *TRANSCEND* all borders.

   TRANSCEND means:

   a) perpetuate
   b) surpass
   c) close
   d) elevate

7. The United Nations was formed to speak with the voice of moral authority, *SUBJUGATING* the individual interests of member states to the greater good of the world community.

   SUBJUGATING means:

   a) authorizing
   b) contemplating
   c) subduing
   d) fortifying

8. Human rights are matters of international concern. A state that abuses human rights may not hide behind the shield of national *SOVEREIGNTY.*

   SOVEREIGNTY means:

   a) hypocrisy
   b) patriotism
   c) conspiracy
   d) autonomy

Periodical Bibliography

The following articles have been selected to supplement the diverse views presented in this chapter.

Harry Anderson with Margaret Garrand Warner and Ann McDaniel
"A New Role for NATO," *Newsweek*, July 16, 1990.

Mona Charen
"What New World Order?" *Conservative Chronicle*, March 31, 1991. Available from Hampton Publishing Co., 9 Second St. NW, Hampton, IA 50441.

Brian Crozier
"Handling the United Nations," *National Review*, April 1, 1991.

Rosemary Fiscarelli
"NATO Confronts the 1990s," *USA Today*, January 1991.

Stanley Hoffmann
"Today's NATO—and Tomorrow's," *The New York Times*, May 27, 1990.

Jeane Kirkpatrick
"The UN's Record Has Been Disappointing," *Conservative Chronicle*, December 20, 1989.

Eckhard Lubkemeier
"NATO's Identity Crisis," *The Bulletin of the Atomic Scientists*, October 1990.

Bhaskar P. Menon
"The United Nations and Its Critics," *Social Education*, September 1989. Available from the National Council for Social Studies, 3501 Newark St. NW, Washington, DC 20016.

Connor Cruise O'Brien
"A Majority of Two," *World Press Review*, October 1988.

Torsten Orn
"Soldiers of Peace," *World Monitor*, October 1989.

David Popper
"Gateway of Opportunity," *The Humanist*, January/February 1990.

Eduard Shevardnadze
"The Rebirth of the UN," *Vital Speeches of the Day*, December 15, 1990.

Brian Urquhart
"Learning from the Gulf," *The New York Review of Books*, March 7, 1991.

Ernest van den Haag
"Is the United Nations Useful?" *Social Education*, September 1989.

Richard S. Williamson
"Rethinking the UN: Agencies of Change," *The American Enterprise*, November/December 1990.

Organizations to Contact

The editors have compiled the following list of organizations that are concerned with the issues debated in this book. All of them have publications or information available for interested readers. The descriptions are derived from materials provided by the organizations. This list was compiled upon the date of publication. Names and phone numbers of organizations are subject to change.

American Enterprise Institute for Public Policy Research (AEI)
1150 17th St. NW
Washington, DC 20036
(202) 862-5800

The American Enterprise Institute is a research and educational organization supported by grants from foundations and contributions from corporations and individuals. Its goals are to assist policymakers, scholars, businesspersons, the press, and the public by providing a free-market, pro-American analysis of national and international issues. Publications include the bimonthly *American Enterprise*.

American Friends Service Committee (AFSC)
1501 Cherry St.
Philadelphia, PA 19102
(215) 241-7000

AFSC, founded by Quakers, seeks to relieve human suffering and promote nonviolent approaches to world peace and social justice. The committee's work in twenty-two countries includes refugee relief, education, and community organization. Publications include the books *Beyond Detente: Soviet Foreign Policy and U.S. Options, The Global Factory*, and the monthly periodical *Friends Journal*.

The Asia Society (AS)
725 Park Ave.
New York, NY 10021-5088
(212) 288-6400

The Asia Society is a nonprofit public education organization dedicated to increasing American understanding of Asia and its growing importance to the United States and world relations. Publications include briefings on Korea, India, China, Burma, Taiwan, and other Asian countries. Contact the society for a list of available publications.

The Brookings Institution
1775 Massachusetts Ave. NW
Washington, DC 20036
(202) 797-6000

The institution is a public policy research organization that publishes materials on economics, government, and foreign policy. Publications include the quarterly *Brookings Review*, the biannual *Brookings Papers on Economic Activity*, and books such as *An American Trade Strategy: Options for the 1990s* and *Europe 1992: An American Perspective*.

Cato Institute
224 Second St. SE
Washington, DC 20003
(202) 546-0200

The Cato Institute is a public policy research foundation dedicated to promoting limited government, individual liberty, and free-market economics. It contends that the end of the Cold War allows the United States to drastically reduce military spending. Publications include the *Cato Journal* and the bimonthly *Cato Policy Report*.

Citizens Against Foreign Control of America (CAFCA)
PO Box 3528
Montgomery, AL 36109
(205) 279-0531

CAFCA advocates the free-enterprise system and supports trade policies restricting foreign investments, imports, and foreign ownership of U.S. corporations. Publications include the periodic *CAFCA Newsletter* and the brochure *Guess Who's Coming to Dinner?*

Communist Party of the United States of America (CPUSA)
235 W. 23rd St., 7th Fl.
New York, NY 10001
(212) 989-4994

CPUSA is a revolutionary organization dedicated to replacing capitalism with socialism. The party analyzes world affairs in terms of the conflict between capitalists and workers. Publications include the monthly *Political Affairs*, the bimonthly *Jewish Affairs*, and the newspaper *People's Weekly World*.

Conservative Alliance
1315 Duke St., No. 200
Alexandria, VA 22314
(703) 683-4329

The alliance is comprised of individuals and corporations interested in a strong national defense, private enterprise, and limited government regulation and spending. Publications include the monthly magazine *Call for Action*, the annual *Congressional Scorecard*, and periodic newsletters.

Council on Foreign Relations (CFR)
58 E. 68th St.
New York, NY 10021
(212) 734-0400

CFR is comprised of individuals with specialized knowledge of and interest in international affairs. The council's purpose is to study the international aspects of American political, economic, and strategic problems. Publications include the monthly magazine *Critical Issues* and the quarterly *Foreign Affairs*.

Delegation of the Commission of the European Communities
2100 M St. NW, 7th Fl.
Washington, DC 20037
(202) 862-9500

The delegation is concerned with explaining to Americans the nature and goals of Europe's 1992 integration. It offers various scholarly analyses on the topic and publishes the monthly magazine *Europe* and booklets such as *European Unification: The Origins and Growth of the European Community, The European Community and its Eastern Neighbours,* and *Europe—A Fresh Start.*

Economic Policy Institute (EPI)
1730 Rhode Island Ave. NW, Suite 812
Washington, DC 20036
1-800-541-6563

The goal of EPI is to encourage the study of economic issues and to broaden the public debate about strategies to achieve a prosperous and fair economy. It advocates trade policies that protect U.S. jobs and develop U.S. industries. EPI publishes position papers, the bimonthly *Challenge* magazine, the quarterly *International Journal of Political Economy,* and reports, including *Beyond Free Trade and Protectionism* and *Getting Rid of the Trade Deficit.*

Economic Strategy Institute (ESI)
1100 Connecticut Ave. NW, Suite 1300
Washington, DC 20036
(202) 728-0993

ESI is dedicated to developing a strategy for American economic success. ESI believes that the United States can remain militarily strong and politically independent only if it has a national strategy for maintaining a strong and vital economy. Publications include the book *Powernomics: Economics and Strategy After the Cold War* and conference reports on U.S. trade law, Third World manufacturing, and other topics.

Essential Information
PO Box 19405
Washington, DC 20036
(202) 387-8030

The goal of Essential Information is to promote investigative journalism and public education regarding social, environmental, corporate, political, and global affairs. Publications include the monthly magazine *Multinational Monitor* and other periodicals.

The Foundation for Economic Education Inc. (FEE)
30 S. Broadway
Irvington-on-Hudson, NY 10533
(914) 591-7230

FEE is a tax-exempt foundation devoted to promoting the principles of the free market, limited government, and private property. FEE publishes a monthly journal, *The Freeman,* and occasional books and pamphlets.

Global Interdependence Center (GIC)
3814 Walnut St.
Philadelphia, PA 19104-6197
(215) 898-9453

GIC is concerned with increasing public awareness about the increasing economic interdependence among nations. It is dedicated to exploring ways countries can cooperate in dealing with global economic problems. Publications include the booklets *Changing Capital Markets and the Global Economy, Shaping the Tariff and Trade Regimes for the Next Decades,* and *International Economic Policy: A Proposal for Reform.*

The Heritage Foundation
214 Massachusetts Ave. NE
Washington, DC 20002
(202) 546-4400

The Heritage Foundation is a public policy research institute dedicated to the principles of free competitive enterprise, limited government, individual liberty, and a strong national defense. Publications include the weekly *Backgrounder,* the quarterly *Heritage Members' News,* and other research papers, studies, books, and monographs.

Hudson Institute
PO Box 26-919
Indianapolis, IN 46226
(317) 545-1000

The institute studies the public policy issues of national security and national and international economics. It contends that the United States must continue to play a leading role in international affairs. Publications include the periodic *Hudson Institute Briefing* and *Hudson Institute Opinion,* the quarterly *Hudson Institute Report,* and research papers and books.

Institute for Defense and Disarmament Studies
675 Massachusetts Ave., 8th Fl.
Cambridge, MA 02139
(617) 354-4337

The institute conducts research and education in an attempt to minimize the risk of nuclear and conventional war, reduce military spending, and promote the growth of democratic institutions. It publishes the biweekly *ViennaFax* report, which provides news, analysis, and commentary, the monthly *Defense & Disarmament Alternatives,* and various books and pamphlets.

Institute for Democratic Socialism
15 Dutch St., Suite 500
New York, NY 10038-3705
(212) 962-0390

The institute is an educational foundation dedicated to the ideals and values of democratic socialism, including economic democracy and equality. Publications include the bimonthly *Democratic Left* and the quarterly *Activist.*

Liberty Lobby
300 Independence Ave. SE
Washington, DC 20003
(202) 544-1794

Liberty Lobby is a populist political organization. It opposes American entanglement in international affairs and supports a protectionist trade policy to preserve American jobs and industry. Publications include the weekly *Spotlight* newspaper and books and pamphlets.

National Committee on American Foreign Policy (NCAFP)
232 Madison Ave.
New York, NY 10016
(212) 685-3411

NCAFP is comprised of individuals from all areas of American life who are interested in foreign affairs. Its purpose is to stimulate citizen interest in the immediate and long-range national security concerns of the United States. Publications include a monthly newsletter, books, monographs, and pamphlets.

Reason Foundation
2716 Ocean Park Blvd., Suite 1062
Santa Monica, CA 90405
(213) 392-0443

The foundation promotes individual freedoms and free-market principles. It supports free-trade policies and contends that the United States should avoid the extremes of isolationism and interventionism in its foreign policy. Publications include the monthly *Reason* magazine, newsletters, research reports, and books.

Revolutionary Communist Party/USA
3449 N. Sheffield Ave.
Chicago, IL 60654
(312) 528-5353

The Revolutionary Communist Party advocates the overthrow of capitalism in favor of a communist economic system that it believes would not exploit workers. It believes that the revolutions in Eastern Europe mark an end to Stalinism, not communism. Publications include the quarterly magazine *Revolution*, the weekly newspaper *Revolutionary Worker*, and various books and pamphlets.

Trilateral Commission
345 E. 46th St., Suite 711
New York, NY 10017
(212) 661-1180

The commission encourages closer cooperation among North America, Western Europe, and Japan. It works to develop proposals for joint action among the three regions. Publications include the annual magazine *Trialogue*, the semiannual *Triangle Papers*, and books and brochures.

United Nations Association of the United States of America (UNA-USA)
485 Fifth Ave., 2nd Fl.
New York, NY 10017
(212) 697-3232

UNA-USA is a nonpartisan, nonprofit membership and research organization dedicated to strengthening the United Nations and U.S. participation in it. Publications include the bimonthly newspaper *The Interdependent* and reports such as *Pulling Together: A Program for America in the United Nations* and *Washington and the World: Organizing Economic Cooperation in an Age of Global Competition*.

United States Business and Industrial Council (USBIC)
220 National Press Bldg.
Washington, DC 20045
(202) 662-8744

USBIC is a national organization representing fifteen hundred American business leaders committed to preserving American economic preeminence. Publications include the book *American Economic Preeminence: Goals for the 1990s* and numerous position papers.

United States Institute of Peace (USIP)
1550 M St. NW, Suite 700
Washington, DC 20005-1708
(202) 457-1700

The institute is an independent, nonpartisan organization established by Congress to support and promote the peaceful resolution of international conflict. Publications include the monthly *In Brief . . .* and *Journal* newsletters.

World Federalist Association (WFA)
418 7th St. SE
Washington, DC 20003-2796
(202) 546-3950

WFA works to transform the United Nations into a democratic world federation capable of ensuring peace, economic progress, and worldwide environmental protection. Publications include the quarterly *World Federalist*, the periodic *New Federalist Papers*, and various books and pamphlets.

World Policy Institute (WPI)
777 United Nations Plaza
New York, NY 10017
(212) 490-0010

The World Policy Institute formulates and promotes policy recommendations for international political and economic issues. Its goal is to create policies that benefit all nations. Publications include the quarterly *World Policy Journal*, books, monographs, and pamphlets.

Bibliography of Books

James Adams — *Engines of War: Merchants of Death and the New Arms Race.* New York: Atlantic Monthly Press, 1990.

Samir Amin et al. — *Transforming the Revolution: Social Movements and the World-System.* New York: Monthly Review Press, 1990.

Alfred Balk — *The Myth of American Eclipse: The New Global Age.* New Brunswick, NJ: Transaction Publishers, 1990.

Jagdish Bhagwati — *The World Trading System at Risk.* Princeton, NJ: Princeton University Press, 1991.

Zbigniew Brzezinski — *The Grand Failure: The Birth and Death of Communism in the Twentieth Century.* New York: Charles Scribner's Sons, 1989.

Bogdan Denitch — *The End of the Cold War: European Unity, Socialism, and the Shift in Global Power.* Minneapolis: University of Minnesota Press, 1990.

Jean-Claude Derian — *America's Struggle for Leadership in Technology.* Cambridge, MA: MIT Press, 1990.

William Kinkade Domke — *War and the Changing Global System.* New Haven, CT: Yale University Press, 1988.

Peter F. Drucker — *The New Realities.* New York: Harper & Row, 1989.

Gregory A. Fossedal — *The Democratic Imperative: Exporting the American Revolution.* New York: Basic Books, 1989.

Benjamin M. Friedman — *A Day of Reckoning: The Consequences of American Economic Policy Under Reagan and After.* New York: Random House, 1988.

Norman J. Glickman and Douglas P. Woodward — *The New Competitors: How Foreign Investors Are Changing the U.S. Economy.* New York: Basic Books, 1989.

Joseph M. Grieco — *Cooperation Among Nations: Europe, America, and Non-Tariff Barriers to Trade.* Ithaca, NY: Cornell University Press, 1990.

Michael Harrington — *Socialism: Past and Future.* New York: Arcade Publishing, 1989.

Gary Clyde Hufbauer, ed. — *Europe 1992: An American Perspective.* Washington, DC: The Brookings Institution, 1990.

Shintaro Ishihara — *The Japan That Can Say No: Why Japan Will Be First Among Equals.* New York: Simon & Schuster, 1989.

DeAnne Julius — *Global Companies and Public Policy: The Growing Challenge of Foreign Direct Investment.* New York: Council on Foreign Relations Press, 1990.

Robert L. Kahn and Mayer N. Zald, eds. — *Organizations and Nation-States: New Perspectives on Conflict and Cooperation.* San Francisco: Jossey-Bass Publishers, 1990.

Paul Kennedy — *The Rise and Fall of the Great Powers.* New York: Random House, 1987.

Janos Kornai — *The Road to a Free Economy: Shifting from a Socialist System: The Example of Hungary.* New York: W.W. Norton and Co., 1990.

Joel Kotkin and Yoriko Kishimoto	*The Third Century: America's Resurgence in the Asian Era.* New York: Crown Publishers Inc., 1988.
Anne O. Krueger	*Perspectives on Trade and Development.* Chicago: University of Chicago Press, 1990.
Paul R. Krugman	*The Age of Diminished Expectations.* Washington, DC: Washington Post Co., 1990.
Paul R. Krugman	*Rethinking International Trade.* Cambridge, MA: MIT Press, 1990.
Robert Kuttner	*The End of Laissez-Faire: National Purpose and the Global Economy After the Cold War.* New York: Alfred A. Knopf, 1991.
Christopher Lasch	*The True and Only Heaven: Progress and Its Critics.* New York: W.W. Norton and Co., 1991.
Robert Emmet Long, ed.	*Japan and the U.S.* New York: The H.W. Wilson Co., 1990.
John H. Makin and Donald C. Hellman, eds.	*Sharing World Leadership? A New Era for America and Japan.* Washington, DC: AEI Press, 1989.
Joshua Muravchik	*Exporting Democracy: Fulfilling America's Destiny.* Washington, DC: AEI Press, 1991.
John Naisbitt and Patricia Aburdene	*Megatrends 2000.* New York: William Morrow, 1990.
Henry R. Nau	*The Myth of America's Decline: Leading the World's Economy into the 1990s.* New York: Oxford University Press, 1990.
Joseph S. Nye Jr.	*Bound to Lead: The Changing Nature of American Power.* New York: Basic Books, 1990.
Kenichi Ohmae	*Fact and Friction: Kenichi Ohmae on U.S.-Japan Relations.* Tokyo: Japan Times, 1990.
John Charles Pool and Stephen C. Stamnos Jr.	*International Economic Policy: Beyond the Trade and Debt Crisis.* Lexington, MA: Lexington Books, 1989.
Michael E. Porter	*The Competitive Advantage of Nations.* New York: Free Press, 1990.
Clyde V. Prestowitz Jr., Ronald A. Morse, Alan Tonelson, eds.	*Powernomics: Economics and Strategy After the Cold War.* Lanham, MD: Madison Books, 1991.
Robert B. Reich	*The Work of Nations.* New York: Alfred A. Knopf, 1991.
Nicholas X. Rizopoulos, ed.	*Sea-Changes: American Foreign Policy in a World Transformed.* New York: Council on Foreign Relations Press, 1990.
Adam Roberts and Benedict Kingsbury	*United Nations, Divided World: The UN's Roles in International Relations.* New York: Oxford University Press, 1990.
Elizabeth D. Sherwood	*Allies in Crisis: Meeting Global Challenges to Western Security.* New Haven, CT: Yale University Press, 1990.
Thomas W. Simons Jr.	*The End of the Cold War?* New York: St. Martin's Press, 1990.
Joan Edelman Spero	*The Politics of International Economic Relations.* New York: St. Martin's Press, 1990.
Paul Taylor and A.J.R. Groom	*Global Issues in the United Nations' Framework.* New York: St. Martin's Press, 1989.

Raymond Vernon and Debra L. Spar
Beyond Globalism: Remaking American Foreign Economic Policy. New York: The Free Press, 1989.

William Wallace
The Transformation of Western Europe. New York: Council on Foreign Relations Press, 1990.

Howard M. Watchel
The Money Mandarins: The Making of a Supranational Economic Order. London: Pluto Press, 1990.

Ben Wattenberg
The First Universal Nation: Leading Indicators and Ideas About the Surge of America in the 1990s. New York: Free Press, 1991.

Burns H. Weston, ed.
Alternative Security: Living Without Nuclear Deterrence. Boulder, CO: Westview Press, 1990.

Richard S. Williamson
The United Nations: A Place of Promise and of Mischief. Lanham, MD: University Press of America, 1991.

Index

Aburdene, Patricia, 96
Adler, Selig, 85
Alfonsin, Raul, 165
Angell, Norman, 122
Attali, Jacques, 24, 93, 95

Baird, Vanessa, 185
Balk, Alfred, 17
Bandow, Doug, 232
Bissell, Richard E., 192
Blodgett, John, 220
Blustein, Paul, 41
Boron, Atilio, 166
Buchanan, Patrick J., 71
Bush, George, 242

Carpenter, Ted Galen, 86, 232
Carroll, Eugene, 237
Cheney, Richard, 87
Cohen, Eliot, 118, 166
corporations
  are increasingly multinational, 139-
    140
  as harmful, 132-137
  causes
    technology, 133-134
    U.S. government support, 136
  European
    European Currency Unit (ECU)
      will help, 57
    rely on government aid, 56-57, 95
  evade taxes, 136

Delors, Jacques, 47
De Michelis, Gianni, 48
democracy
  Argentina and, 165-166
    economic hardship, 163, 164-166
    extremist political groups, 167-168
    fascism, 168
    traditional values, 163
  growth of, 153-160, 174-176
    America's role in, 156-157
  Islam and, 166-167
  is possible in any country, 155-157
  Latin America and, 165-166, 175
  peace is fostered by, 171-174
    con, 183-184
  Poland and, 165

U.S.S.R. and, 162
Dhungane, Daman, 164
Dole, Robert, 187
Drozdiak, William, 53

Edelmann, Mark, 187
European Bank for Reconstruction
  and Development (EBRD), 51
European Community (EC)
  corporations
    European Currency Unit (ECU)
      will help, 57
    rely on government aid, 56-57, 95
  defense and
    is weak, 55
    should defend themselves, 90
    see also North Atlantic Treaty
      Organization (NATO)
  Eastern Europe and
    investment by West will be costly,
      56, 95
    trade will increase, 50
  economies
    are changing, 48
    depend too much on Middle
      Eastern oil, 54-55
    growth rate, 48
    inefficiencies, 55-57
    political problems, 55, 58
    U.S. competition with, 51-52
    will be a leading world power, 46-52
      con, 52-64
  European Currency Unit (ECU)
    corporations will be helped by, 57
    represents growing strength of
      European Community, 51
Eyskens, Mark, 55
Ezell, Edward, 84

Falcoff, Mark, 216
Franz, Mark, 225

Gamble, Ed, 73
global economy. See world economy
Gorbachev, Mikhail, 25
Greenspan, Alan, 101
Grew, Joseph, 158

Hawkins, William, 79

Hoffmann, Stanley, 244
Hunter, Robert, 58, 116
Huntington, Samuel P., 20, 21, 22, 23

Iklé, Fred Charles, 36
Ishihara, Shintaro, 32

Japan
  aid to foreign countries
    is crucial to modernizing developing
      world, 36-37
  banks are largest in the world, 104
  can defend itself, 35
  culture, 29-30
  defense
    military spending, 35-36
    U.S. Security Treaty is unfair, 33-34
  democracy in, 156-157, 158
  economy
    aging population will affect, 40, 42
    budget deficit, 39-40
    power will be limited, 38-45
    productivity is not as high as in
      U.S., 39
      con, 103
    role in Asia, 100-101
    trade deficit is lessening, 42-43
  investment capital
    is decreasing, 42
    will structure industries of future,
      29
  wages are competitive disadvantage,
    43
  world market share, 29
Joffe, Josef, 64
Johansen, Robert, 218

Katz, Mark, 66, 197
Kennedy, Paul, 18, 126
Kirkpatrick, Jeanne, 76, 216
Kishimoto, Yoriko, 57
Kotkin, Joel, 57, 92
Krauthammer, Charles, 72
Kristol, Irving, 65, 154
Kwan, Ronald, 131

Luckovich, Mike, 88
Latin America
  democracy in 165-166, 175
  role in world economy, 146
Legro, Jeffrey, 83
Lind, Michael, 212
Lippit, Victor, 128
Lippmann, Walter, 78
Luttwak, Edward, 111, 123

Major, John, 188
Makin, John H., 19
Malabre, Alfred, 126
McManus, Doyle, 161, 187
Mead, Walter, 93, 143
Mearsheimer, John J., 123, 177
Menem, Carlos, 166
Meyer-Larsen, Werner, 103
Michnik, Adam, 165
Moisi, Dominique, 57
Morris, Charles, 94
Moss, David, 125
Muravchik, Joshua, 153

Nacht, Michael, 81
Nakanishi, Terumasa, 36
New Wave Economics, 126
North Atlantic Treaty Organization
  (NATO)
  alternatives for, 235-237
  German threat as argument for
    maintaining, 242, 244
    con, 237-238
  is obsolete, 232-238
    con, 239-245
  maintains stability in Europe, 241,
    243-245
    con, 236-237
  U.S. role in, 89, 233, 241-242
Nye, Joseph S., 21

O'Cléireacáin, Séamus, 46
Odom, William E., 239
Ohmae, Kenichi, 138

Pacific Rim,
  Japan will control, 31
  organizing as rival to Europe, 30
  trade imbalance reveals U.S. decline,
    26-28
  see also Japan
Packenham, Robert, 155
Parsons, Anthony, 229
peacekeeping forces. See United
  Nations
Pellicer, Olga, 216
Perez de Cuellar, Javier, 207
Popper, David 210
Powell, Colin, 81, 83
Prestowitz, Clyde, 30

Ravenhill, John, 190
Reich, Robert, 136
Rich, Robert, 141
Rise and Fall of the Great Powers,
  The, 18

Rusher, William, 69
Russett, Bruce, 169
Rustow, Dankwart, 159

Samuelson, Paul, 104
Schmidt, Helmut, 23
Scowcroft, Brent, 167
Selimuddin, Abu, 98
Shchekochikhin, Yuri, 162
Shiva, Vandana, 189
Shubeilat, Laith, 167
Simpson, Carol, 135
Singer, J. David, 172
Sked, Alan, 55
Small, Melvin, 172
Snow, Donald, 83
Solarz, Stephen, 240
Strange, Susan, 21, 22

Thiele, Rudiger, 95
Third World
  aid from developed nations
    does not permanently cure poverty,
      195
  Cold War's end will harm, 185-191
    con, 192-204
  dictatorships are being challenged,
    189-190
  economic reform, 196-198
  ideology, erosion of, 194-196
  member countries, 193
  toxic waste is being dumped in, 188-
    189, 191
  trade with West
    must be pursued, 199
    will be difficult, 188
  United Nations and, 194, 216-217
  weapons trade may increase in, 190
Thurmond, Strom, 159
Todd, Emmanuel, 168
Triad economy, 139-140

Ullman, Richard, 175
United Nations
  Afghanistan, peacemaking in, 228
  Angola, election monitoring in, 228-
    229
  Cyprus, peacekeeping forces in,
    226-227
  functions of, 207
    conflict resolution, 209
    diplomacy, 210-211
    election monitoring, 228-230
    problem solving, 209-210
    refugees, 208

history, 206-207
international problems can be
  solved by, 205-211
  con, 212-217
peacekeeping forces
  benefits of, 220-221
  Cyprus, failure in, 226-227
  definition of, 226
  ignore problems, 230-231
  permanent force
    could be educational, 222-223
    protection would allow
      disarmament, 223-224
    would be more effective, 221-222
  Security Council
    permanent members should
      change, 215-216
    Third World countries' demands
      affect, 214-215
  war
    U.N. can prevent, 218-224
      con, 225-231
    world's disputes should all be of
      concern, 222
United States
  as superpower, 67-68
    con 24-31
  debt, 104
  economy
    decline of, 98-105
    trade deficit, 103
    Europe compared to, 94-97
    grew in 1980s, 21, 94
    post-World War II growth was
      exceptional 19-20, 94
    productivity, 39, 95, 103, 129
    savings rate, 102
    statistics, 20-21, 28
    world leadership, 20
      is threatened, 98-105
      will continue, 92-97
    in decline, 26-29
      con 17-23
  involvement in Third World, 66, 81-
    82
    is necessary, 64-70
      con, 71-78
  military
    expenditures must be cut, 77, 90-
      91
    international role, should maintain,
      79-85
      con, 86-91
    troops should be withdrawn from
      abroad, 74-76

con, 83-85
trade deficit
  Asia and, 28, 100, 101
  consumers, corporations, and, 103
  Japan and Germany compared to,
    102
workforce
  is highest paid, 104
  is inferior, 103
    con, 39, 95, 96-97
world market share, 20-21
  decrease in, 28, 101-103
  may be restricted to weak trading
    bloc, 146-147
  remains consistent, 94
  statistics, 101-102
Urquhart, Brian, 222
U.S.S.R.
  is no longer serious threat, 90
  military
    improvement, 84
    potential for conflict with U.S.
      remains, 66-67, 82
    troops should be withdrawn from
      Europe, 74-75

Vernon, Raymond, 113

war
  Cold War's end will lessen chances
    of, 169-176
    con, 177-184
  deterrence
    democracy as, 170-176
      con, 122, 177-184
    in Europe, 178-179, 181-183
    NATO can prevent, 243-244
  United Nations. *See* United Nations
  world economy
    will replace military conflict, 111-
      117
      con, 118-124, 177-184
Wealth of Nations, The, 126
Weeks, Albert, 84
Weinberger, Caspar, 234
Williamson, Richard, 205
Wina, Arthur, 189
world economy
  causes of, 133-134
  corporations in
    are increasingly multinational,
      139-140
    as harmful, 132, 134-137
    evade taxes, 136
  Europe and Japan will compete for

  dominance in, 25-26
  history of, 144-145
  is beneficial, 125-130
  is endangered, 143-147
  is unified, 138-142
  nations will benefit, 125-130
    only wealthy will benefit, 131-137
  opposition to, 144-145
  trading blocs will emerge in place
    of, 145-146
  U.S. conceived, 144
  U.S. role in
    lessening importance of, 104-105
    maintaining importance of, 94, 96
Wright, Robin, 161, 187

Yardeni, Edward, 125

Zinsmeister, Karl, 38
Zoellick, Robert, 235